John Jefferson Bray

John Jefferson Bray

A Vigilant Life

John Emerson

Foreword by The Hon. Michael Kirby AC CMG

MONASH University Publishing

Monash University Publishing
Matheson Library and Information Services Building
40 Exhibition Walk
Monash University
Clayton, Victoria 3800, Australia
www.publishing.monash.edu

Monash University Publishing brings to the world publications which
advance the best traditions of humane and enlightened thought.

Monash University Publishing titles pass through a rigorous process of
independent peer review.

www.publishing.monash.edu/books/jjb-9781922235619.html

Series: Biography

Design: Les Thomas

Cover image: Erika Clarke

National Library of Australia Cataloguing-in-Publication entry:

Creator:	Emerson, John, author.
Title:	John Jefferson Bray : a vigilant life / John Emerson.
ISBN:	9781922235619 (paperback)
Notes:	Includes bibliographical references and index.
Subjects:	Bray, J. J. (John Jefferson), 1912–1995.
	South Australia Supreme Court.
	Judges--South Australia--Biography.
	Justice, Administration of--South Australia--History.
Dewey Number:	347.94035092

Printed in Australia by Griffin Press an Accredited ISO AS/NZS
14001:2004 Environmental Management System printer.

CONTENTS

ACKNOWLEDGEMENTS

The publisher would like to thank *The Advertiser* and individual photographers for permission to reproduce photographs of John Bray.

FOREWORD

The Hon. Michael Kirby AC CMG*

John Jefferson Bray served with distinction as Chief Justice of the Supreme Court of South Australia from 1967 to 1978 and as Chancellor of the University of Adelaide from 1968 to 1983. He derived from a distinguished colonial family. He was educated in expensive boarding schools. He won a rare doctorate of laws degree for research on aspects of insolvency and private international law. He took silk at an appropriate age. He appeared in lots of important cases, including in the High Court of Australia. For a time he served as deputy to the Lieutenant Governor of his State. On the face of things, the reader might think that someone who had followed this golden path to high judicial office and public service would be worthy – but unlikely to have lived a life that would set the pulse racing.

However, as John Emerson's new biography shows, Bray, whilst being an outstanding lawyer and judge, was anything but a stereotype. Especially for his time and place, South Australia in the second half of the twentieth century, Bray was unique: a one off. The central interest of this biography lies in unravelling the puzzle of how such a gifted legal scholar, advocate and judge could, at the same time, live a life that so outraged the orthodox expectations that descended upon him. And how he managed to remain steadfastly himself, despite the pressures imposed to conform to the contemporary standards of his class, profession and high offices.

Let there be no doubt that Bray was an exceptionally gifted lawyer and jurist. His LLD, like that of H.V. Evatt earlier in Sydney, was not honorary. It

---

*   Justice of the High Court of Australia (1996–2009); Chair of the United Nations Commission of Inquiry on North Korea (2013–14).

was earned by an outstanding, highly technical, thesis that, ironically, he was never once to utilise in his professional work. He had performed extremely well at school, particularly in studies that suggested that he was destined for the law: top in Scripture, and third in English and in history. Although never a florid advocate or colourful courtroom personality, his sheer intellectual brilliance soon won him the top accolades at the Bar. He was appointed Queen's Counsel in 1957. He appeared in dramatic circumstances for the young Rupert Murdoch. This book gives examples of the ingenious legal arguments that he advanced for his clients, often with success.

It was when the soon-to-be Premier of South Australia, Don Dunstan, unexpectedly appointed Bray as Chief Justice of the State that his mastery of the principles of the common law and his gifts of expression came to be recognised not only at home, but in judicial decisions in other states and eventually in the High Court of Australia and courts overseas. In 1997, after Bray's death in June 1995, I wrote a chapter for a book honouring him. I collected, and illustrated with many decisions, cases in which resort was made to his reasoning, simply because he was recognised as a great judge.[1]

Our legal system celebrates and utilises the writings of fine judicial minds. Bray was respected, I also suggested then, because of 'the catholicity of his knowledge of the law'; because of the presence of a 'powerful grasp of basic common law principles' and because of his utilisation of 'legal history, the wide spectrum of his learning and the power of his inquisitive intellect'. Yet I suggested, then, that a second quality helped to explain the influence of Bray's judicial writings, both in the High Court of Australia and elsewhere. This was his love of words. 'Some people', I concluded, 'have the power to express themselves in vivid word pictures... Only a small proportion of them are lawyers. But when to discontent with verbal formulae alone is added a very considerable power in the use of language, you have a judicial writer of rare talent. Such was Bray'.

---

1   M.D. Kirby, 'Bray's Impact on Australia's Jurisprudence', in Wilfrid Prest (ed), *Portrait of John Bray*, 1997, pp. 96–97.

Now, with this biography, there is evidence, far beyond the instances I deployed, to support my assessment written nearly 20 years ago. Bray delighted in language. He would probably have preferred to have been remembered as a poet and playwright rather than as a judge. In his judicial reasoning (sometimes in dissent) he could put things vividly and with unusual style. A lot of judicial writing is dense and impenetrable. This biography celebrates the life of a legal writer who did not think judicial writing had to be boring and unintelligible in order to be orthodox.

In my earlier reflection on Bray's life, I recalled the last time I had seen him. It was in March 1993. A federal election was underway. Unexpectedly, it delivered the treasury benches of the Commonwealth once again to the outgoing government of Paul Keating, whom the pundits had predicted would lose. Bray and I had been invited to an event in Adelaide, attended mostly by lawyers, examining Mr Keating's proposal that Australia should become a republic.[2]

Neither Bray nor I was a fervent tabloid monarchist. Neither of us was attracted much to the hereditary principle, primogeniture or social rank as destiny. Yet we both saw certain advantages in retention of the Crown in the Australian Constitution. We felt that it should certainly have a voice before any final decision was made. As in many things, we saw eye to eye. In the event, in 1999, four years after Bray's death, a majority of the Australian electors, voting at referendum, thought likewise. The total vote in favour of the referendum proposal was 44.74% and that against was 54.40%. The republic was not carried nationally or in any state. The vote in South Australia against change was 55.92%.[3]

So far, I have indicated the features of this biography that would appear to promise a worthy but not especially exciting read. Yet the great advantage of Dr Emerson's work is that it reveals how, under the raiments of lecturer,

2   The paper read on that occasion was M.D. Kirby, 'Australia's Monarchy' in G. Grainger and J. Jones (eds), *The Australian Constitutional Monarchy*, ACM, Sydney, 1994, p. 87.

3   M.D. Kirby, 'The Australian Referendum on a Republic – Ten Lessons', *Australian Journal of Politics and History*, 2000, 46, pp. 510–528.

Queen's Counsel, Chief Justice and University Chancellor, the person that was John Bray challenged elements in his society in a way that almost resulted in his destruction. Certainly, he was nearly passed over for the high offices that he so brilliantly fulfilled. He had many powerful enemies.

Bray had attributes that stopped conventional power-brokers in Adelaide and South Australia in their tracks. He was a lifelong bachelor. This station in life was repeatedly raised against him. Later it was revealed that he had acknowledged the paternity of a child of a suggested youthful sexual indiscretion. But he rebuffed at least two serious approaches by women whom he had attracted, proposing marriage to him. And his unmarried status compounded rumours that came to circulate as to his sexuality. These rumours led to his close surveillance by police, continuing even when he was chief justice.

Then there was his unseemly 'lifestyle'. He distained official cars. He walked to work or caught public transport. This would never do. He refused to abandon visits to familiar pubs and drinking spots, where he had long mixed with friends, poets and people of the arts. Shocking. His 'over-exalted view of bohemianism'. Outrageous. He made no bones about his opposition to the prudish culture of censorship in his day that permeated Australian society. He questioned the enforcement of morals by the courts of law, particularly in things sexual. Stubbornly, unlike other judges, he would not even wear a hat. Little wonder that he was blackballed by the Adelaide Club and denounced by a drunken guest there, when he made one of his rare visits to that hallowed place.

Future generations will look with astonishment at the long-standing, prurient interest displayed in the minor question of whether Chief Justice Bray, in his private moments, was homosexual or had engaged in homosexual acts. Certainly, many of his friends were homosexual. Several of them tried to defend Bray, their friend, from scandal. One at least (Christopher Pearson) later claimed to have been his lover. Others accompanied him overseas, including to well-known gay venues. Many acquaintances assumed that he was gay and wrote to him on that assumption but were set aback by his discouraging replies.

It will be hard for future generations of Australians to recapture the hatred and animosity targeted at homosexuals at the time that Bray and his friends were living and working in Playford's South Australia. At that time, it would have been unsurprising that a person, of even modest talent and ambition, would deny their own sexual reality, if they were homosexual. People had been doing this for millennia; and still do so in many parts of our world. So Bray's reticence would be no surprise, whatever his orientation might be.

In one letter quoted in this book, Bray admits to enjoying the company of a male correspondent 'in and out of bed'. But he declares that 'romantic sexual attachments are no part of my plan of life'.

Bray may have been homosexual, bisexual, omnisexual or heterosexual in his orientation. His actual sexual life appears to have been very limited indeed: especially by today's standards. All of which would be uninteresting and immaterial to his talents but for the gross abuse of public power that the rumours called forth from police, legal and other authorities. It finally took an inquiry by Acting Justice White and a Royal Commission by Justice Roma Mitchell (both of the Supreme Court of South Australia) to demonstrate the monstrous lack of balance and proportion that subjected citizens high and low to police surveillance and intrusions into their adult, consensual, private lives. Bray suffered such wrongs with astonishing forbearance. Today's generation would be likely to be less forgiving.

This, then, is the ultimate fascination of the dichotomy at the heart of the life of John Jefferson Bray. It gives us a glimpse into the character of Australia's society and institutions, a mere 50 years ago. It illustrates the serious over-reach of official power and its resistance, to the last, to dignity-respecting control over that power. The abuse of power, recorded in those pages, stands as a warning to us. It shows that no one is immune from such outrageous wrongs. Not even a gifted chief justice. Still less a fine poet. Even less the idiosyncratic and singular friend of liberty who was John Bray.

Michael Kirby
Sydney, 7 February 2015

PROLOGUE

King: *Then I must wear a false face all my life?*

Oropastes: *My son, all men do that: the wise ones know it.*
              The fools mistake their false face for the true.

King: *And never know my own identity?*

Oropastes: *My son, no man knows that: fools think they do.*
              The wise man knows he does not know himself
              The wisest know no one can ever know.

John Bray, from 'A Word in Your Ear' (Unpublished play)

In 2002, I began work on two books, *History of the Independent Bar in South Australia*, and a book on the five South Australian Chief Justices of the 20th century, eventually published as *First Among Equals* in 2006. One of the members of the University of Adelaide's John Bray Law Network advised me to interview Brian Medlin, one of John Bray's last surviving close friends. He also warned me that Brian was seriously ill and that I best do it quickly.

At the time I still knew very little about John Bray, only what I had read in *Portrait of John Bray*, published five years earlier.[1] Brian agreed to an interview and on 19 October 2002, I drove out to his home in rural Victoria.

We spoke from 4 pm until the early hours of the following morning. The transcript of the interview reached over 20,000 words. I realised immediately that John Bray deserved far more than the mere chapter in *First Among Equals*. I was also fascinated by his unrepentant individuality, while at the same time insisting on the same right of other people to their own individual nature. Brian summed up John as 'tolerant to an intolerable degree'.

---

1   *Portrait of John Bray*, ed., Wilfrid Prest. Adelaide: Wakefield Press, 1997.

Brian had been the foundation Professor of Philosophy at Flinders University, and aside from the series of recordings, we also discussed books and ideas. One of those books was John Ralston Saul's bleak over-arching history of social and economic structures in Western societies, *Voltaire's Bastards*.[2] Ralston Saul deplored the rise of form over content, which broadly meant that hierarchy, power and status were considered of more value than human qualities such as wisdom, experience and individualism. For me, John stood out as an example of how human qualities could still eventually triumph.

So germinated the seed of a biography of John Bray. After the interview with Brian, I wrote to the two other of John's closest surviving friends, Peter Ward and Christopher Pearson. Peter replied, politely telling me that he was writing his own book featuring John Bray and could not help me. Christopher Pearson did not reply, and only eight years or so later with the help of a friend would he assent to talking to me.

Brian proved puzzlingly critical of my subsequent draft chapter on John for *First Among Equals*, even to the point of being counter-productive. I began to gain a small insight into John's legendary tolerant nature. Brian's criticism was savage, inconsistent and confusing.

In 2006, I published *History of the Independent Bar* and *First Among Equals* and began work on the full biography of John Bray. My main concern was that without Peter Ward's support I would be left with only the papers the literary executors made available to the State Library of South Australia. Close surviving friends were reluctant to talk frankly after seeing Susan Mitchell's edited selections of their words in her account of crime in Adelaide published in 2004.[3]

In late 2008, Peter had a change of heart and lent me two boxes of John's most private papers. They included folders of papers on John's estate and finances, personal correspondence, and correspondence after his death between surviving friends and relatives.

---

2   John Ralston Saul. *Voltaire's Bastards*. New York: Vintage, 1993.

3   Susan Mitchell, *All Things Bright and Beautiful: murder in the city of Light*. Sydney: Pan Macmillan, 2004.

What follows is strictly *a* biography of John Bray, not exhaustive, not definitive. John left no diaries, the Bray papers in the State Library of South Australia consists mainly of letters John received, and a few drafts of those he sent in later life; speeches, poems and plays, of which only one was performed, and miscellaneous material often as modest as hotel receipts. Almost all of the material can be freely accessed in the State Library of South Australia, and many Australian libraries would hold copies of John's published works. A select bibliography is included at the end of the book. Literary readers keen to read all of John's poetry should pester the University of Queensland Press to reprint his *Collected Poems 1962–1991*, and legal readers can now easily find his full-text judgments online.

Mostly this book was written on my own resources. Additional funding was gratefully received from the Law Foundation, the University of Adelaide, and a number of anonymous donors through the John Bray Law Network. The University of Adelaide's Law School was exceptionally supportive. I particularly thank for their moral support: Rob Cameron, Anthony Crocker, Astrid Macleod, James McWha, Peter Norman, Rosemary Owens, Wilfrid Prest, John Timlin, Peter Ward, Alex Wawryk, John Williams, and the late Brian Medlin.

Chapter 1

ATHENS, 1974

But I left with high steps, for the moment convinced of two propositions,
Propositions I had always hoped and sometimes believed to be true,
One concerning the power of the arts, one concerning the nature of man.

John Bray, from 'Epidaurus 1974'

The sun seemed to beat down on Athens even hotter and harder that late July afternoon. The temperature was rising, and so were the Athenians. The colonels' military dictatorship had outstayed its welcome.

It was late July 1974. A week earlier in Cyprus, the colonels had sponsored a *coup d'état*, replacing President Makarios with a newspaper photographer, Nikos Sampson. Five days later the Turks invaded Cyprus, removed the freshly appointed President Sampson, and now it looked like they would also invade Greece.

The colonels were panicking. They called up all available men to fight and imposed a dusk-to-dawn curfew. Tourists were abandoning the Greek capital as fast as they could, but the airport was closed and many were stranded.

In the old Plaka district, the Electra Palace Hotel sat at the foot of the northern slope of the Acropolis under the gaze of the Parthenon. The males among the hotel staff were among those called up, so guests were filling in as amateur cooks and waiters.

One of the guests, not taking on a service role, was defying the blistering heat and climbing up to the Parthenon. This was his first trip to Greece and his first trip outside of far-off Australia in 37 years. It might be his last chance to see the aging architectural triumph of the classical period.

He was leaving Athens that night; his fellow traveller Peter Ward had bought some tickets on the black market for a boat leaving for Italy from Piraeus.

They had arrived in Greece a month earlier and had witnessed an amazing event in the theatre at Epidaurus. The colonels unwittingly turned up to the classic play about resisting tyranny: *Prometheus Bound*. The 14,000-strong audience jeered them relentlessly and they left.

Under the suspicious eyes of the junta police, the two Australian visitors had also reunited with actress Miranda Murat, whom they had met at the Adelaide's Writers' Festival a few years before. The colonels had imprisoned her along with other Greek artists who contested their claim to govern. She had been liberated thanks in part to their efforts, her health broken, but not her Promethean defiance.

The climber held his large head a little to one side, as if his thoughts were heavy. With a long flowing beard he might have been Socrates, Sophocles or Euripides, all of whom were living when the Parthenon was being built.

The ascent was as hot as Orpheus's from Hades. The temperature was around 40 degrees Celsius. Today the cradle of Western civilisation was abandoned and the climber seemed to have it to himself. His shirt was soaking in sweat and he was out of breath, when he saw a tap.

He sat down, pulled off his shirt and turned it on. He rinsed his shirt in the cool water and splashed himself. He put the wet shirt back on and got up to march on to the time-worn marble steps at the base of the Parthenon. He suddenly heard a step echo and looked up. Two well-dressed women, complete with hats and parasols, were looking down at him from the columns. Having been spotted, they came down the steps hesitantly, not sure of their reception.

'Excuse me', said one of them, 'aren't you Dr John Bray, the Chief Justice of South Australia?'

The climber nearly fell down the Acropolis hill. He was indeed John Bray. He was astonished to be recognised so far from home, by the only two people in sight, in the place that had so deeply influenced his life. He nodded and shyly mumbled what might have been a 'yes', then continued up the steps.

John Bray and Peter Ward escaped Athens safely that night by sea. After a few days in Italy they flew home to Australia, on the other side of the world, to a city that some then were comparing to classical Athens.

Colonised in 1836, around the time Athens became capital of modern Greece, the city of Adelaide in 1974 was enjoying a golden age. Echoing a little of Pericles, Premier Don Dunstan was also a skilful orator who challenged conservative factions of government and put a lot of money into new infrastructure and reforming laws. There was a general sentiment of change, of moving forward. The policy development from 1970 to 1975 in South Australia has been described as 'probably without emulation in this country'.[1] In a few years Dunstan had transformed its small capital into the leading social and cultural city of Australia. The Festival Centre opening the previous year was the most visible sign of this cultural ebullience, attracting 20,000 visitors. The smaller Playhouse was opened in November 1974, and Premier Don Dunstan read a poem written for the occasion by the Chief Justice, John Bray.

John had also written a poem about his extraordinary experience seeing the Greek colonels booed out of the arena during the performance of 'Prometheus'. 'Epidaurus 1974' was later published in his *Poems 1972–79*. In a review of the collection, Kevin Pearson wrote that the poem 'carried the full weight of a man's whole life and belief'.[2] It was John Bray to the core, expressing his most cherished principle, that people had the right to live their own lives, and to resist attempts to curtail that right. More than that, it was also an expression of a fundamental optimism: that the Arts could move people to act.

---

1   Andrew Parkin, 'Transition, Innovation, Consolidation, Readjustment,' in Flinders History of South Australia (Political), 292–338. Adelaide: Wakefield Press, 1986), p. 302.
2   Friendly Street Poetry Reader, 1980. Adelaide: Adelaide University Union Press.

Rare if not unique for an Australian judge of his time, John had published on themes of resisting oppression, censorship and class values. Even his judgments were becoming known for their defence of human rights: including privacy, individuality and the right to a fair trial. Living in Australia, he had been protected against the extreme forms of political rule. His only brushes against dictatorships were during his first overseas trip in 1937 when he had watched Mussolini's black shirts in Rome with alarm, and in 1974 in Greece during the colonels' *junta*.

Nevertheless, hard-line conservative governments had dominated post-war Australia; and South Australia in particular. Premier Sir Thomas Playford had attracted industry to South Australia and invested in fundamental infrastructure that the State benefits from to this day. But his record 27-year rule got uncomfortably close to unofficial dictatorship over his citizens' private lives, and John unintentionally fell foul of the Playford vision of justice.[3] In 1960, the Playford government sued the editor of Rupert Murdoch's *News* for seditious libel. John was his lawyer and successfully defended him. The government was furious, but John had no other motive than his professional obligation to defend his client against injustice. There would be reprisals, however, hidden from sight until later.

The two respectable ladies watching their Chief Justice rinse his shirt out in the scorching heat on the Acropolis did not know about Police Commissioner John McKinna's attempt to prevent John Bray's appointment to the Supreme Court of South Australia, nor of the preceding seven years of police surveillance, nor of the politically motivated reasons behind why he was watched. They would never have imagined that the file kept on their Chief Justice would directly motivate a sequence of events leading to the sacking of John McKinna's successor as Police Commissioner, Harold Salisbury, in 1978.

Brigadier John McKinna was undoubtedly one of the State's most historically significant Police Commissioners. In early 1967, he learnt that his

---

3   Even Stewart Cockburn's biography written with Sir Thomas Playford's son John was entitled
     Playford: benevolent despot. Published by Axiom: Kent Town, 1991.

good friend and fellow churchgoer at Pilgrim's Church, Mr Justice Roderic Chamberlain, would not be Sir Mellis Napier's replacement as Chief Justice. The new Labor Premier Don Dunstan's choice was John Bray, the defence barrister from the *News* case. The Police had been unofficially keeping patrol reports on John since the *News* case, which suggested a lifestyle that did not conform to the Playford ideals. John was not married, he stayed out late on weeknights, he associated with literary and artistic people, and he did not wear a hat. Most seriously from their point of view, however, was that their patrol reports implied John was possibly homosexual. In those days, there could be legal implications.

A later chapter discusses John's reaction to those patrol reports. His eleven years as Chief Justice more than justified Don Dunstan's choice; in more than 600 judgments written over that time, on no matter what area of law, one detects overwhelmingly a sense of fairness and respect for not just the basic rights of the common law citizen, but of all human beings. His succinct articulations of often profound principles have been cited across Commonwealth jurisdictions since.

The man behind the lawyer, the poet, the playwright and the judge was as complex as any human being might be. As we see in the lines quoted at the head of the Prologue, from his unpublished play 'A Word in your Ear', he did not necessarily attempt to understand himself, nor others. Rather, he accepted the essential difference in people, tolerated it, respected it, and hoped only to be given the same respect in return.

Chapter 2

POCAHONTAS

The air serene, yet sombre
Where sun and shadow join
The bank of summer failing
Pays out in copper coin.
The mood is introspective.
The ghost walks in the groin.

John Bray, from 'Indian Summer'

At the beginning of the 17th century, a 'soldier of fortune' arrived on the Virginian coast with two other adventurers hoping to establish a colony there. The soldier, Captain John Smith, seemed to have the good fortune of being saved by beautiful women whenever he was caught and on the point of execution, or at least he told people that. According to his own word, he had been saved at the last moment by a Greek slave imprisoned in Turkey, and at another timely moment, by the wife of a Russian nobleman. On the 26 April 1607, he was again miraculously saved seconds from death. As he knelt down waiting for the Indian chief Wahunsunacock to ritually kill him with a stone, the 12-year-old chief's daughter Pocahontas threw herself over the very vulnerable Captain Smith, pleading for his life.

This is the story the Captain told in a letter sent ten years later to Queen Anne, asking for her to treat the Indian princess with dignity. Diplomatic relations with her father's tribe had collapsed since Captain Smith's near death with the realisation that they were not being courted but conquered. Wahunsunacock had taken some prisoners and in response, in 1614, the

English took Pocahontas. She was held hostage for a year, feeling betrayed by her father's refusal to compromise, and during that time she met John Rolfe, the original pioneer tobacco grower. They fell in love and married on 5 April 1614. She gave birth to a son, Thomas, on 30 January 1615.

Probably if not for these extraordinary events, the unique genealogical web that produced John Bray would not have existed, and hence, neither would he. Pocahontas died at age 22 in 1617 leaving only the one son Thomas, who in turn only had one daughter. But over the decades and centuries that followed, some of the most influential families of Virginia – like the Randolphs and the Jeffersons – and later of other parts of the world, could trace their ancestry back to the precociously fearless Indian princess. John Bray was Pocahontas's distant descendant, though he knew up to two million people could make the claim.[1] Among them are President Woodrow Wilson's wife Edith; Admiral Richard Byrd; socialite Pauline de Rothschild; Nancy Reagan; first Chief Justice of the United States John Marshall, President Thomas Jefferson and first Australian Commonwealth Solicitor-General Sir Robert Garran.

John used to mockingly refer to himself as 'John Jefferson Pocahontas'. He is related to her through his mother Gertrude, who was the great-granddaughter of Thomas Quinton Stow, a founder of one of South Australia's first churches. Thomas's wife Elizabeth was in turn the granddaughter of Captain William Randolph, and from the Randolphs the family traces back to Pocahontas. John was named after his distant ancestor third United States President Thomas Jefferson, as are a number of the Stows and Randolphs.

Thomas Quinton Stow arrived in Adelaide with his wife and four young sons in October 1837 on the *Hartley*. The family had come from Suffolk where Thomas's family had been farmers over generations around Stow-market and Hadleigh. He was one of the pioneer religious dissenters who left Anglican England seeking to found a society that supported religious freedom. A month after arriving, he was part of the group who built a hut

---

1   J J Bray Papers, State Library of South Australia, PRG 1098/66.

on North Terrace out of eucalyptus posts, pine rafters, walls of old sail cloth and a reed-thatched roof. This was the Congregational Church in South Australia.

It is tempting to see in him a trace of John. Douglas Pike wrote: 'Stow was proud of the Independent tradition, and in the pulpit and in private was assiduous in expounding the case for Dissent. [...] He would not join in political movements nor tolerate radicalism in politics.'[2] Thomas nevertheless managed to exert sufficient influence in the volatile politics of the late 1840s. He was emphatic that States should not fund churches. The South Australian government was proposing grants, and he succeeded in the idea being abandoned in 1851. He suffered financially for this, and had to lease a farm next to the River Torrens to augment the meagre takings from congregations. The suburb of Felixstowe is named after his farm.

Thomas also taught classics in a daily academy he began in the same reed and sail-cloth hut, and can therefore be credited with effectively founding tertiary education in South Australia. By November 1840 that reed and sail-cloth hut had evolved into a stone chapel in Freeman Street. The chapel in its turn was the predecessor to the Stow Memorial Church in Pirie Street, opened in 1867, five years after Thomas's death.

His eldest son, Randolph, John's great-great-uncle, became one of South Australia's first three Queen's Counsel in 1865, and a judge of the Supreme Court from 1875 until his sudden death from liver disease in 1878. As well as being a successful lawyer, he was a member of South Australia's upper house of government, the Legislative Council, from 1861 to 1875.

Thomas's second son Jefferson, born in 1830, was John's great-grandfather. After his first wife died he went off to the Victorian gold rush, returning in 1854 to marry again and father 12 children. One of his five daughters was named Jourdiana Claire Pocahontas. The oldest child, John Wycliffe Stow, was Gertrude's father. Wycliffe, as he was known, became a lawyer, but

---

2   Douglas Pike. *Paradise of Dissent: South Australia 1829–1857.*/ Melbourne: Melbourne University Press, 1967, p. 257.

died in July 1892 at 35 years of age. Gertrude Eleanor Stow (born 16 May 1886) was only six years old and hardly knew her father. She married Harry Midwinter Bray on Saturday, 12 June 1909, two days after Harry's thirtieth birthday, at St Michael's Church in Mitcham. She was 23 years old. There is no record of their early relationship and, in fact, little survives about them at all.

Harry was at the time recorded as earning his living as a share-broker. He had attempted to study medicine after leaving school, but failed, at two separate institutions. Much later, his second son, Bill, admitted knowing little about his father's education: 'He certainly studied medicine at Trinity College, Dublin for, I think, one year but failed his exams. My memory is that he also studied some course other than medicine at some Australian university (Melbourne) and also failed the first year but it remains vague in my mind.'[3]

It certainly would not have helped that, at the time he was ready to enter medical school, Adelaide was the victim of an ongoing strike. From March 1896 to March 1900, there were no courses in medicine at the University of Adelaide because of Premier Charles Kingston's hot-headed intervention in the Royal Adelaide Hospital board. The entire medical fraternity of South Australia were on strike, most audibly the 17 members of the hospital's honorary medical staff who were also the lecturers in medicine.

Harry's surviving results from 1894 at St Peter's College when he was 15 are not promising. In the third and fourth terms terms he passed with average marks and when placed against the rest of the class he was third from bottom each term. But he had only started at St Peter's in the middle of that year after returning from two and a half years in England. His father had died in June on the voyage back.

Harry's grandparents, Tom Cox Bray (1815–1881) and Sarah Pink (1813–1877), were two of the first wave of immigrants to South Australia. They came from Portsmouth to the tent and mud hut camp that was Adelaide in

---

3   Letter to Peter Ward, 5 October 1996. Private Correspondence.

1838, where Tom set up shop as a humble cordwainer – shoe-maker. Sarah's father, William (died 1853), also migrated to South Australia and worked as a labourer with the survey team.

At this point, no one would have predicted that one of their sons would one day become Premier and build a large mansion on Hutt Street. Even less would they have suspected that the shoe-maker, himself the son of a shoe-maker, would shortly inherit a fortune, and go and spend the rest of his days in England as a wealthy gentleman. But this is exactly what happened.

Tom Cox Bray's father William had been estranged by his own father, Charles, for marrying Ann Cox (1789–1840), the daughter of a farmer, before dying at age 26 in 1816. But William's father, Charles, was no shoe-maker. He was a wealthy merchant who had made a lot of money from shipping between England and Australia, and when he died he left all his fortune to Tom. Exact details and dates are mysteriously absent from the records and biographical accounts, but it must have been around 1860. The shipping records show a Mr and Mrs Bray departing Adelaide 11 March 1862 on the *Harwick*.[4] At the time, Tom and Sarah had two sons and two daughters, born in Adelaide around the 1840s. They moved back to England with three of their Australian-born children, and left one behind to continue his law studies. This was John Bray's grandfather, John Cox Bray, named in honour of his maternal grandmother.

Also absent from the records for Tom and Sarah was a marriage certificate. John Jefferson Bray obtained an extract of the birth certificate of his grandfather's sister Sarah after a request from a cousin:

This shows that she was the daughter of Thomas Cox Bray, described as of Hindley St., bootmaker, and Sarah Pink.

It also discloses that these two were not married. John was older than Sarah, so if the parents were not married when she was born, it follows

4   Horner index [microform] to shipping departures 1836–1887, State Library of South Australia.

that they could not have been married when he was born. This does not upset me but I wait curiously to see if Nancy [his grand-aunt] wants me to pursue these enquiries any further.[5]

There has been little kept about this John Cox Bray's early life. He was born in Adelaide on 31 May 1842. Most of his biographical material concentrates on the period after he entered State Parliament as MP for East Adelaide in 1871. St Peter's College records for that period are not complete, but John Cox Bray is recorded as being enrolled in 1853, when he was eleven. His last year there was probably 1856. He was admitted as a lawyer in 1870, but only practised briefly. What he did in the ten or more years between leaving school and being admitted has been lost. But his family did return to visit him in 1864, when he was 22 years old. Tom and Sarah, with two daughters, Sarah, who was 20, and Blanche, who was 16, travelled in a first class saloon on the *City of Adelaide* on its maiden voyage. They were living in splendid style in Harrogate, Yorkshire.

John Cox Bray married Alice Hornabrook in January 1870 at St Michael's Church in Mitcham. There are five of Alice's dance cards remaining from the late 1860s. They list between 16 and 24 different dances, such as polka, galop, quadrille, waltz, with a blank line next to each to write the name of the respective dance partner. Three are undated but Alice's first dance on each is with John Cox Bray, and on a fourth card he is her second partner of the night. One of these is at the Town Hall, which was only finished in 1866, except for the clock, which had to wait until 1935. On three of the dances one other name also appears – a possible rival suitor – C W Draper. One dated card is for the Bachelor's Ball in 1866 and the other of a dance on Friday, 4 December 1868 on the ship *South Australian*. There were 20 dances, and John Cox Bray was the only partner Alice danced with twice – for the second, a quadrille 'Gorilla', and the tenth, a polka mazurka. C W Draper was again testing his instep – he was her partner for the 18th dance, a valse.

---

5   Letter from John to Bill, 5 April 1986. Private collection.

Over the course of the 1870s, John and Alice founded their family while John built his successful political career. Cecil was born in 1874, Arthur in 1875, Harry in 1879 and Blanche in 1881. Arthur died two months short of his fourth birthday in 1879 – one story says he was killed in a carriage accident and another that he was scalded to death. Their father in the meantime became Minister of Justice and Education in 1875, Attorney-General from 1876 to 1877, and Leader of the Opposition to the Jordan ministry from 1877 to 1881. In 1883 and 1891 he attended the Federation conventions in Sydney.

In 1881, two events lifted John Cox Bray's life into a new level. First, his father Tom died and left him a significant part of the shipping fortune, and second, he became Premier of South Australia, and governed for a record three years. In the 24 previous years of South Australia's self-government there had been 32 premiers, some lasting as little as ten days.

In 1884 and 1885 he left South Australia to visit England and America, and returned to serve over the next seven years at various times as Chief Secretary, Treasurer and Speaker. Around 1886 he began turning the house he had bought on Hutt Street into a mansion. His income for that year was £1,358 – £630 from 'exertion' and £728 from property – a total income a little more than a Supreme Court judge's salary at that time. The property income made it possible to leap up the ranks.[6] Sir George Strickland Kingston designed the house, and it was built in 1847. The original dwelling on the site – that had previously served as a temporary residence for Captain Grey in 1840 until he replaced Governor Gawler in Government House – became the laundry. Sir George also designed Ayer's House on North Terrace. John commissioned architect Rowland Rees to add a large, ornate front wing, complete with Italianate columns on the full verandah facing Hutt Street. Visitors could be shown into either of the two enormous front rooms through towering panelled doors.

---

6   Just as a point of interest, taxation then was considerably less. Sir John's income was around 13 times the average, yet his tax bill for the year was just over £26, or 5 per cent.

Sir John Cox Bray, around 1885. Courtesy State Library of South Australia.

Bray House, around 1885. Courtesy State Library of South Australia.

In 1890, John Cox Bray was awarded a Knight Commander of the Order of St Michael and St George, and his grandson kept the 53 congratulatory letters and telegrams that followed. The writers included *Advertiser* proprietor, J Langdon Bonython; future long-time premier, Charles Kingston; former premier, Sir Henry Ayers and Chief Justice Samuel Way. With the combination of Sir John's successful political career, inherited capital and the knighthood, the Bray family's status in Adelaide was unbroachable.

On one day of that year, Sir John was walking with a friend down Rundle Street past the recently opened Adelaide Arcade. He told his friend that he had been offered some shares in it and was still deciding to accept or not. His friend advised him that although he would see little return himself, future generations of Brays would. The Adelaide Arcade had been built five years earlier in 1885. It stretched over almost a hectare from Rundle Street to Grenfell Street and included 50 shops with a second-storey workroom and Turkish baths. Sir John bought the shares and the Bray family have remained shareholders since.

In January 1892 he was appointed Agent-General for South Australia in London and he resigned after more than 20 years of politics. A farewell was held at the Adelaide Town Hall on 19 January. The menu included oysters, oxtail soup, suckling pig, Bavarian pudding, strawberry ice-cream and 'wines of South Australia': riesling, chablis, hock, claret and frontignac. The family moved to England, but Sir John's mental health began to fail him after just two years and he was recalled home, with symptoms that suggest a brain tumour or encephalitis. His oldest son, Cecil, was 18 and the letters he wrote on that voyage home reveal the tragic circumstances of his father's illness.

On 6 June 1894, the ship reached Port Said and he started having paranoid delusions that his London doctor had plotted against him and his cashbox was going to be robbed. Two days later he was much better and playing whist and euchre with Harry, Alice and Cecil. His health began to worsen again and the letters die out after 10 June, Harry's 15th birthday. Sir John died on 19 June between Aden and Colombo, and was buried at sea. The Adelaide newspapers over the two days following reported his death, and the Adelaide Town Hall flag was flown at half-mast. Two weeks later, the family arrived back in Adelaide, and moved back into the mansion on Hutt Street.

In the intervening 18 years before John was born, tragedy would again strike the family. Blanche, who was 13 when the family returned to Adelaide, married John Lavington Bonython (1875–1960), son of John Langdon Bonython (1848–1939) owner of the *Advertiser* daily paper, in 1904. They had two daughters and one son, John Langdon, named after his grandfather. Then, in 1908, Blanche died in childbirth with the third child. She was just 27. John Lavington Bonython would marry again, to Constance Warren (1891–1977), whose mother was a Downer.[7] Among their children was Kym Bonython, John's cousin by marriage, who later would be known for his art and jazz collections. By Adelaide standards in the early 20th century, John Jefferson Bray would be virtually born into the aristocracy.

---

7   Joyce Gibberd, *Australian Dictionary of Biography*. Online adb.anu.edu.au.

Chapter 3

ADELAIDE, 1912

Staid Goddess in thy padded seat
And bombazine,
What millions worshipped at thy feet
With Vicky Queen.

Now flying from thy shrine they go,
All else thy loss,
Save where thy altars blaze below
The Southern Cross.

Fair Adelaide! Thy latest seat,
Sealed with thy kiss!
Dearer to thee King William Street
Than Styx to Dis.

John Bray, from 'Hymn to Respectability'

The South Australian capital Adelaide was not normally the centre of Australian politics, but on Monday, 16 September 1912, both the Prime Minister, Andrew Fisher, and the Governor-General, Lord Denman, were in town. They had come to celebrate the turning of the first sod of the 1,063-mile railway from Port Augusta to Kalgoorlie.

Also on that day, John Jefferson Bray was born, into the Adelaide respectability that he would spend his life both respecting and mocking. He was born at home, as was customary at the time, in a villa called 'Trecarrel', on Davenport Terrace, Wayville.

John was the first child of Harry and Gertrude Bray, who had married in 1909. From the little that is recorded of these earliest childhood years, it seems it was happy for the most part. After his mother's death, one of her friends told John that Gertrude loved her children and 'had so much fun with you'.[1] Like all the middle and upper classes then, a live-in maid did the housework and prepared and served meals. The presence of a servant in the house structured daily life. John wrote: 'The baby-sitting problem to a large extent solved itself. Meals were served with almost pedantic punctuality, the midday meal at 1, the evening meal at 6, 6.15, or in advanced households, 6.30. Displays of exhibitionism or bad temper were inhibited. A greater decorum prevailed. Contentious topics were not discussed before the servants.'[2] The maid was most often a young uneducated working-class girl who was filling in time before she married, and domestic service was easier work than long, hard shifts in factories before safety laws.

Because meals were prepared by the maid, most of them were eaten at home: 'Cooking was solid unadventurous Anglo-Saxon', John reported. 'Roast lamb, roast beef, hot on Sunday, cold on Monday, rissoles on Tuesday, hash on Wednesday, and so on. Occasionally the monotony was relieved by pork or poultry. Then milk pudding or tart. All sorts of strange stodgy objects which have almost disappeared from the modern kitchen used to follow the main course; like tapioca or sago.' The maid cooked with a wood-stoked stove and oven. The ingredients were fresh, as there were no refrigerators. In the summer ice-chests were used to preserve perishables as long as possible. Each morning milk and cream straight from the cow appeared on the verandah, followed a little later in the morning by bread and meat deliveries from the baker and the butcher in horse-drawn carts. The maid herself collected the eggs each day from hens kept in the back yard. The children were allowed an occasional between-meals treat of a slice of bread crust with butter or dripping. John preferred dripping and, according to his friends, he kept a

---

1   PRG 1098/5/2 letter from Lindsay (no surname).
2   *Satura*, p. 163.

dripping tray into his old age despite it long having disappeared from most people's homes. The maid also kept the fires going in each room in the winter, and did the family's washing by boiling the clothes in a wood-fuelled copper and running them through a hand-wringer before hanging them to dry, and finally ironing them.

John would have barely remembered 'Trecarrel', as the family moved to Moseley Street, Glenelg, when he was around three or four. This was where his sister, Nancy Rowena, was born, in 1917. John attended Mrs Hill's School for the next two years. Harry was earning a living as a stockbroker around this time, but in 1922, he moved the family to a fruit block at Penwortham, in the heart of South Australia's Clare Valley. In 1923 another boy was born, Robert Stow Bray, but always called Bill. John was enrolled in Sevenhill State primary school, which he attended from 1922 to the end of 1924: 'At one stage I rode a pony to school about four miles each way by road. Before then I walked through the bush about three miles each way. There were perils on these journeys from snakes or accidents but not from human molestation.'[3]

John also remembered summers in Penwortham as being infested with mosquitos, and everyone sleeping under nets. There was also the problem that ice was not delivered in country areas, and people used to store food in cellars, and cool drinks and beer in buckets of cold water at the bottom of wells. The wells were often four or five storeys deep. John remembered 'one occasion in a Penwortham summer when the rope broke and the beer and cool drinks had to be rescued by an intrepid descent of the well shaft.'

The happy days in the Clare Valley came to an abrupt end at the beginning of 1925 when his father decided John was ready to be sent to boarding school. It had become tradition in Adelaide since 1847 for well-heeled families to send their sons to St Peters College, which was closely modelled on the Rugby School after Thomas Arnold's reforms in Britain. Harry had gone to St Peter's in the 1890s; and his father before him, Sir

---

3   *Satura*, p. 164, and p. 163 for the following quote about the descent of the well shaft.

John Cox Bray, had been one of its first generation of students during the 1850s.

John was very shy and introverted. At 12, just on the cusp of puberty, the last thing he wanted was to be sent away to live with strangers. Sixty years later the trauma still haunted him in a poem he wrote in empathy with a pet pigeon he had rescued in Hurtle Square:

> But the day came when he had to be sent to board with the vet for
>   three weeks,
> Seized by dear and familiar hands suddenly turned alien and menacing,
> Plunged in a carrying box, in panic, traumatized, his safe world
>   shredded.
> I know of course that all innocence has to be violated in the end,
> That to prolong it too far into adolescence is unhealthy and unbracing.
> That it will do him good to mix with other avians and rub off his angles,
> That the experience, if he survives it, will make a bird of him.
> But I remember being driven for the first time to boarding school,
> Still in blue serge, prickled by strange underwear, neck yoked in
>   celluloid,
> Praying that God would crash my father's car.[4]

John would never really fit in:

> I was recalcitrant to the ethos of the college. I resisted the pressures to conformity. My time at the primary school had made me insufficiently sensitive to social and class distinctions and the minutiae of dress and manners. I thought then, and still think, that the attainments of the body were absurdly overvalued at the expense of the attainments of the mind. I resented what seemed to me the whipping up of spurious loyalties over contests on the football field and the cricket pitch which meant no more to me than the fight between Tweedledum and Tweedledee.[5]

---

4   'The Crested Pigeon', *Collected Poems*, p. 225.
5   *Satura*, p. 162, and for the following quote.

But it was the the first two terms of 1925, living at the boarding house, that were the worst. The general comment in his first school report for the Lent term of 1925 recorded: 'He has ability and has made very satisfactory progress. With more experience he should do very well.' John was placed eleventh in a class of three dozen when he was still 12 years old and the average age of the other boys was 14. But the second term report was revealing: 'He shows considerable promise, especially in literary subjects. Unfortunately he has been greatly handicapped by absence.' His placing plummeted to 32nd, almost bottom.

Harry wrote to the headmaster on 17 March 1925 requesting him to drop John to the form below, but the head advised keeping him there. Harry wrote back a week later, accepting the head's advice, but adding: 'John seemed a bit disheartened and bewildered when I was last down.' Two months later, after John came to stay during the school holidays at Penwortham, Harry could no longer let his son suffer. He wrote again to the head master, firstly requesting that John could stay with him over the weekend during a visit to Adelaide:

> Also, I must tell you that I propose to withdraw him from Brooks at the end of this term, and let him become a day boy. He is troubled by a cold which has been with him practically all the time he has been at College and I believe that his health will be benefited.[6]

The cold may have been a result of a drafty dormitory but it might also have been the result of a run-down immune system from not adapting to boarding. The head did not allow John to spend the weekend with his father so soon after his return from holidays, and was sorry to note Harry's request for John to be a day student: 'I am quite sure that it is far better for him that he should be among boarders at the School.'

John was a day student at St Peters from the middle of 1925 until the end of 1928 when he matriculated, not long 16 years old. It was not all bad:

---

6   Letter dated 26 May 1925, St Peter's College Archives. The letter dated 17 March that same
     year is also held at St Peter's College Archives.

I did receive an excellent education in the humanities. I acquired a framework of history, linguistics and literature which has stood me in good stead ever since. At the time I was insufficiently appreciative of this. I was a moody, introspective youth whose real life was in the world of books and the imagination. I carried this too far but on the whole I do not regret it.

For the remainder of his time at St Peter's College John's marks were consistently good, but although he was always close to top, he rarely was the best student in a subject. In the Lent term of 1926, which finished in April, John achieved a final place in his class for all subjects of third out of 35. The headmaster's comment: 'A good trier, a satisfactory place.'[7] John was top in Scripture, with 91 per cent, third in English with 78 per cent, fourth in Latin with 80 per cent, eleventh in French, with 66 per cent, third in history with 64 per cent, second in Maths with 79 per cent and 13th in Chemistry, with 47 per cent. He was a full 12-months younger than his classmates – the average for the class was 14 years and seven-twelfths. Later that year he was placed fourth at the end of the middle term of Trinity. He had dropped to twelfth place in Latin with just 44 per cent, but had topped Maths with a perfect score. On 11 August of that year, John Bray was also confirmed into the Anglican Church at St Peter's Collegiate Chapel.

Given John's life-long passion for reading the Latin and Greek writers in the original, his poor marks at school at first could seem unexpected. In his final matriculation marks for 1928, he topped Scripture, English and Ancient History. He also was House Prefect for Short House. In Latin he was just eighth out of a class of eleven with 45 per cent – a fail. He was placed overall second for the whole school and his headmaster commented sadly: 'But for his Latin, he would have been head of the school.'

Yet John's poor Latin result was not because he was struggling or lazy. He was in fact pursuing his own extra-curricular education in Latin, having discovered it had been carefully censored:

---

7   Bray papers, PRG 1098/67, for all references to his results at St Peter's College.

In Latin I discovered Catullus, an author unrepresented in the school curriculum. I was also indebted to the editions of the Loeb classics in the State Library for an education in the bypaths of erotica. That excellent series has the Latin on the left page; the English on the right. When a particularly embarassing passage occurred in the seamier authors, like Martial or Suetonius, the prudent editors either left the English blank or inserted a version in Italian. When you saw a blank or slab of Italian on the right you simply looked across to the left, got out the Latin dictionary and improved your knowledge of the language and the world.[8]

The Loeb classics showed John the dangers of relying on an intermediary, revealing to what degree original works could be distorted. He saw the limits imposed by the ideological apparatus of the education system. John's intellectual curiosity was too great to skip over the untranslated parts, and though he may have been shy socially, he was far from shy intellectually. Of course, he was not interested in Latin texts specifically just because they were in Latin, but for the quality of their content, their bolder, deeper and broader explorations of human behaviour, transporting him far and beyond the narrow horizons dictated by an Adelaide he considered 'blanketed in unctuous Puritanism'.

This discovery made it impossible for John to conform automatically. Half a century into his own future, at St Peter's Speech Day in 1978, he reflected on the era and its pressures:

In 1928 the sun was still refusing to set on the Union Jack and no one thought that it would ever fail in its duty. Empire had not yet been replaced by Commonwealth, Australia basked in fancied security under the protection of the British Navy. Attitudes of the kind now deprecatingly described as colonial, attitudes which in the light of hind-sight we can see were anachronistic even then, reigned unquestioned

---

8   *Satura*, p. 167.

in the higher echelons of the South Australian establishment, and not least in this College which its rulers at that time conscientiously strove to model in the image of the nineteenth-century Arnoldian English public school.[9]

John added with caution:

> The pressures to conformity were great. I resisted them as silently and unobtrusively as I could and the lessons I learnt in so doing have enabled me to resist them with much less trouble ever since. I hasten to add that I am not recommending nonconformity for its own sake. If you can conform happily no doubt you would be foolish not to do so. Some people can't.

At a speech around the same time given to the Prince Alfred College Annual Dinner in 1978, John also justified his nonconformity, saying 'he felt that, in a free society, independent judgment and choice were greater values than tractability.'[10]

During most of his College days John lived with his grandmother Alice, Lady Bray, in the mansion on Hutt Street. Alice by now was in her seventies. Bill remembered her later: 'Lady Bray was a fairly fearsome old lady, consciously modelling herself on Victoria Regina. I believe you can find the source of "Staid goddess in this padded seat and bombazine" there as well as in portraits of Queen Victoria.'[11] St Peter's College was a pleasant walk through the east parklands. Around 1928, Harry, Gertrude, Rowena and Bill moved back to Adelaide, initially in the suburb of Payneham, before settling in to a bungalow at 18 Baliol Avenue, College Park, where John joined them.

---

9   Speech Day 1978, St Peter's College. Published in the St Peter's College *Magazine*, December 1978, pp. 12–14, for both indented extracts.

10   *PAC College Magazine*, 1978, p. 78.

11   Bill Bray. Letter to Peter Ward, 5 October 1996.

Outside Bray House, around 1928. Standing: Harry Bray, John Bray. Seated: Robert (Bill) Bray, Nance (Rowena) Bray, Gertrude Bray. Courtesy State Library of South Australia.

That final year of school, Harry gave John a motorbike for his 16th birthday. He no doubt hoped his son would be thrilled, but it showed how little Harry understood John. Many years later, he 'continued to recall the moment of the gift with bewilderment. His son had looked at the gleaming machine for a bare 30 seconds and then, without saying a word, had turned and gone back into the house, never again to express interest in it or driving.'[12] A few years earlier Harry had given John a set of wood-working tools, which were never used. Neither did he ever understand John's complete distaste for all games. He expressed his regrets about this to Bill, but Bill did understand, he knew that John's lack of sport sense 'was completely inherent to [his] character.'

But John survived. At the end of the year, he won a scholarship to go to the University of Adelaide. His schooldays were over, and except for the odd visit as an old boy, he could say farewell to St Peter's.

---

12   Peter Ward, *Portrait of John Bray*, pp. 2–3.

Chapter 4

BACCHUS

Zeus streams down the rain. A great storm approaches out of Heaven.
The flowing rivers have been stiffened into floors of ice.
Throw down the storm, pile up the fire.
Let us drink large quantities of very sweet wine
And put on funny hats.

John Bray, adaptation from Alcaeus: 'Drinking in Winter'

John wanted to study arts at university, but his parents advised him to do law as it held more promise of a career. So in 1929, still only 16 years old, he began his first year as a law student, studying some arts subjects such as European History.

Four of his university essays survive, in handwriting that is neat and readable. One is entitled 'Elements of Law', and it begins: 'More than any other system of law past or present, the English system relies on precedent or case law. It is the second source of English law and while it lacks the final clear-cut and arbitrary force of legislation, it is far more extensive and detailed.'[1] A few pages later John broaches the continuing debate of whether judges create law:

> But are we then to admit that English law is made by judges? Here we are confronted by two conflicting opinions. One, the older theory, declares that judicial decision is only a declaration and exposition of what was already the Common Law which has existed from time immemorial.

---

1   Bray Papers, SLSA, PRG 1098/68.

The law was there all the time though not clearly discerned. On the other hand another school, headed by Austin and Bentham, boldly declares that we must throw aside the 'childish fiction' that judges are merely expounding a certain miraculous and intangible something which has existed from time immemorial and recognise that judges in fact do make new law and occupy almost if not quite the same function as the legislator. Somewhere between the two points of view the truth exists. There are a number of cases where the judge has to lay down a rule for the first time without any assistance from statute or previous decision.

This may be a draft as it has no teacher's comments or mark on it, unlike the one on 'The Reign of Lady Jane Grey'. John opens the essay: 'The unfortunate heroine of that famous nine days drama, the most attractive figure of an unattractive age and a selfish and blood-stained line, was born in 1537.' The marker's comment in the margin disagrees: 'This rather too personal. Most people find the age attractive.' At the end of the paper John is given a mark of 84/105 with the comment: 'You have used your material well and your narrative is accurate and readable. I should have liked you to foot-note your authorities.'[2]

Life at home was not perfect. Bill recalled the two brothers' relationship with their father:

> Much of his thoughts, facts, sentiments and philosophy were literally drawn from the Readers' Digest of the 1920s and 1930s which he quoted frequently with approval. ... It is in my mind that he laboured under a sense of scholastic under-achievement and added to that he may have suffered among his peers from an absence of participation in World War 1.[3]

On the other hand Bill noted that John was very close to his mother:

---

2   Bray Papers, PRG 1098/68.
3   Letter to Peter Ward, 5 October 1996.

JJB and Gertrude were wholly entwined. She loved him unstintingly with all of her usual uncritical loving nature. He, I believe, returned this love fully. She was the key to much of his lack of necessity to socialise, and womanise ... One of the sights of my earlier manhood was of my wholly contented mother, darning a pair of JJB's sox and listening to 'Information Please'. She was completely happy. Harry's shortcomings also fed this relationship. When Dunstan made JJB Chief Justice, Gertrude, a life-long conservative, voted Labor.[4]

At 17, John made a discovery: 'At the end of 1929 I went to the University Concert and to a party afterwards. I drank several glasses of wine and beer and got home at dawn. A new world was opening before me.'[5] Around the end of that year Harry went to see his lawyer Keith Wilson, a partner at Genders Wilson & Pellew, who agreed to take on John's articles – the old on-the-job training that was replaced by the Graduate Diploma in Legal Practice in 1977. He began in early 1930 on the initial salary of 10 shillings per week – one dollar – which at that time was roughly a quarter of the average weekly income, and continued his studies at the University.

That year was also the beginning of the Great Depression, which hit South Australia hard with her reliance at the time on agricultural exports. Hundreds of families in Adelaide were forced to live in tents on the banks of the river Torrens, and the unemployment rate hit a peak of over 30 per cent. John's scholarship and family support protected him from the worst effects:

I was fed, clothed and sheltered by my parents. But I had very little spending money. As a result I acquired habits of frugality which have now become engrained to the distress of my friends. I have still a reluctance about taking taxis where it is not unavoidably necessary. I still walk or use public transport wherever I can. I don't mind drinking

---

4   Same. 'Information Please' was a radio program John participated in regularly during the 1940s.

5   *Satura*, p. 164.

flagon wine. Though I enjoy food, I still like bacon and eggs about as much as anything.[6]

Harry and Gertrude were not feeling the pinch too much as they left their children in the care of Lady Bray at the beginning of March 1930 and went on a holiday to England and Europe for five months. John was 17, Rowena 13 and Bill seven. Gertrude's diary of the voyage is not very illuminating, she only recorded bare details of events, rarely her feelings or opinions, except that she was often tired from the travelling around. In London Harry and she went out to the theatre regularly and saw Edgar Wallace's 'The Calendar', and met up with some of the Bray relations, which included Sir Denys and Lady Bray. They went to the Folies Bergère in Paris, through Lausanne and Interlaken in Switzerland to Austria and the Oberammergau passion play, and back to London to see Harry Hopman at the Davis Cup before a trip up to Edinburgh Castle. The only interesting thing historically about her diary is that all the pages from 19 August to 1 November have been brutally torn out.

John took up smoking around this time and tried to develop his social skills:

> In 1930 I took dancing lessons and eventually managed to shuffle around the floor without being too conspicuously disgraced. I acquired a dinner suit, and later tails, which I wore on appropriate occasions with uneasy self-consciousness mitigated by the weary flourish of a cigarette.[7]

Bill remembered John's dancing: 'JJB was one of the world's most disastrous dancers. Ladies were firmly grasped and walked the full length of one side of the dance floor. At the end they were inexpertly turned left and the march proceeded. Ladies asked to dance accepted with the enthusiasm of St Stephen advancing into the square of Pharises.'[8]

---

6   *Satura*, p. 165, and also cited by Peter Ward in *Portrait of John Bray*.
7   *Satura*, p. 166.
8   Bill Bray to Peter Ward, 5 October 1996.

John did well in his studies and became increasingly interested in the law as he discovered its intellectual side. He won a Stow Prize in 1930, and the David Murray prize in both 1931 and 1932. He took his Bachelor of Laws at the end of 1932, and his Honours Laws at the end of 1933. John was noticed by one of the leading lawyers of the day, Frank Villeneuve Smith, who was appointed a King's Counsel in 1919 at the age of 35. By the 1930s, Frank Villeneuve Smith KC was celebrated as much for his theatrical behaviour in court as for his ability. Jack Elliott introduces him in the first pages of his *Memoirs of a Barrister*: 'Entertainment rather than instruction led me to sit in on criminal trials. It was much better than going to the pictures. The star was Villeneuve Smith. Dark, handsome, arrogant and witty, he sought to dominate proceedings from the moment he swept into court followed by juniors and solicitors.'[9]

In October 1933 the star sent John a book with the accompanying comment:

> I really and genuinely mean it when I repeat that I expect very big things of you. I am sure you are a conqueror but of course it means and it requires effort. But this effort – when rewarded – means satisfaction. You only have to persevere in order to succeed.[10]

Just after graduating, John met one of his life-long friends, John Davey. Peter McCusker writes of the moment of their meeting in 'Bray and Davey', an article he published in *The Adelaide Review*:

> A group of young men had organised a fishing trip of some days in the Gulf. A respectable sized vessel was chartered together with its Master. Apart from the enjoyments one might expect, the main purpose was to engage in drinking. Bray would later recall being woken on the first morning of the voyage with the image of a tall muscular red headed figure standing at the top of the stairs leading into the cabin where the

---

9   Jack Elliott, *Memoirs of a Barrister*, p. 2.
10 Bray Papers, SLSA, PRG 1098/1/1. Date 25 October 1933.

rest were still in their bunks, holding what appeared to be a very large and lively shark. This was Davey.[11]

Davey, born the year before Bray, was studying law at the University of Adelaide and was in the South Australian State cricket team in 1933 and 1934. As Peter McCusker pointed out, given Bray's contempt for all sport, it did not seem likely the two men would become close friends. But Peter also recalled in the article that Bray had found in Davey 'a little of Prometheus'. It was Davey's spirit of independence and fearless defiance of unjustified authority that appealed to John. The two would meet almost each weekend for the next 40 years at the Amateur Sports Club each Friday and Saturday night and, in a cloud of tobacco smoke between drinks, would try to outdo each other's wit.

John was reading a random assortment of literature, extending past the school list that stopped at Tennyson. He preferred Sir Walter Scott to any 19th-century English author. He taught himself Greek to be able to read the original, which were probably also translated censoriously like the Latin texts. It would be years still before he encountered any Australian literature, even the idea of it. Patrick White at this time was beginning to write, but he had moved to London to do so.

One of John's Latin discoveries in this period was an obscure but colourful Roman emperor called Gallienus, who lived from around 218 to 268. The study of this emperor was to become John's most enduring interest over the course of the rest of his life. He decided early to write a biography of him, though it would take 60 years for it to be finished, and it was only published after he died. The choice of Gallienus is of particular interest, as the emperor was as flamboyant as John was introspective. He described Gallienus as 'a vivid and many-sided personality':

He was addicted to freakish and exhibitionistic behaviour which went far beyond, although it also included, the traditional forms of

---

11   Peter McCusker, 'Bray and Davey' in *The Adelaide Review*, September 1995, p. 34.

libertarianism. Two examples may be cited. In the procession at his decennalia, the celebration of the tenth anniversary of his reign, there marched 1200 gladiators in women's gold-embroidered dresses. He issued a series of coins on which his bearded image appeared with the head-dress and attributes of a goddess, either Demeter or Persephone, and the legend 'Gallienae Augustae'.[12]

Did Gallienus live his life with a boldness that John could never show? Or was he merely fascinated by someone who freely exhibited his eccentricities in public? John's recorded reason for the choice is: 'I can only say something about him and his situation made a strong appeal to me.'[13]

On 23 February 1934 John Bray received a letter from the secretary of the XX Club, Chas. H Jocelyne, inviting him to join. The club had been formed in June 1927 and membership was restricted to 20. Members at the time included John's cousin John Langdon Bonython (son of Harry's late sister Blanche), Eustace Genders, Lance Pellew and Keith Wilson. The latter three were the partners of the law firm where John was now a junior practitioner.

The main object of the XX Club was declared as 'Beer', and its capital, 'one million gallons'. On the form proposing membership were questions such as:

Can you hold your liquor?

If so, how much and for how long?

Have you ever been sober?

If 'yes', why?[14]

The club was registered at the Oriental Hotel, on the corner of Pulteney and Wakefield Streets (at the time of writing, a backpacker's) and being a club 'duly licenced and registered at the Police Court, Adelaide, and thus above the law until 11 pm.

---

12   *Satura*, p. 4.
13   *Satura*, p. 3.
14   Bray Papers, PRG 1098/85.

A dress-up party from one of John's clubs, around 1933. John is seated, second on the left.
Courtesy State Library of South Australia.

The law referred to was the six o'clock closing for all hotels in Adelaide: 'Bars and bottle departments closed at 6 pm on six days of the week and entirely on the seventh. A lowering Sabbatarianism prohibited public and inhibited private entertainment on Sunday. These laws were bitterly resented and contemptuously violated.'[15] The law had been in force since a referendum of March 1915. It would take until 1967 to relax it, after a Royal Commission set up by Attorney-General Don Dunstan. Ironically, John Bray would represent the hotels who, even more ironically, resisted the proposed extensions to the hours.

The XX Club was one of the many private clubs established to legally bypass the early closing laws that applied only to hotels; restaurants were

---

15   *Satura*, p. 166.

only allowed two more hours before removing customers' wine and beer from the table. Apart from meeting at the Oriental Hotel, each month one of the members of the XX Club would host a satirical debate. On one occasion they dressed up in silly hats. In April 1936 they held a dinner on a motor car theme. Eustace Genders became 'Gas O Lean Genders' and Keith Wilson 'Krankcase Wilson'. The menu included 'hornets and wasps on toast' – presumably in response to the problems encountered in open-top motoring – 'throttle soup', 'piston poisson' and 'nuts and bolts' to finish. In the first debate of August 1936 at Mr Reid's home, the topic was 'Should provision be made to enable cars to park nearer the South Australian Hotel?'[16] Given their charter, the members were inevitably very keen to take the positive side.

On 17 August 1936 they met at John Bray's home to debate that the best form of government was democracy. Present according to the minutes were 'Moore, Goodhart, Bruce, Tulloch, Facey, Boykett, Oldham, Russell, McGregor, Reid, Treloar, Knapman, Jocelyne, McKirdy. Genders and Pellew ill. Wilson late.' The minutes also summarise the development of the debate:

> Mr Russell shared in the imperfect historical knowledge, which was characteristic of most of the speakers. … Mr Bonython stated that people were just as free under a dictatorship as under a democracy. He also said that no true democracy existed today because infants and lunatics were not allowed a vote. Having stunned his audience by these outstanding statements he developed his argument with great force and eloquence.[17]

The negative side won.

John was already a foundation member of the Amateur Sports Club, which had begun in 1932. For the next 44 years on Friday and Saturday nights, this is where he would be found with exceptions. Initially on the top floor of the old LCL building on 175 North Terrace, from 1936 until its closure 40 years

---

16 One of the State's grand old hotels, the South Australian was demolished around 1970 to make way for what is now the Stamford Plaza Hotel, opposite Parliament House on North Terrace.

17 Bray papers, SLSA, PRG 1098/36.

later, it was located in the basement. John celebrated his 21st birthday at the Amateur Sports Club on 16 November 1933. The dinner included oxtail soup and fillets of whiting. On the back of John's copy of the menu are signatures of those who helped him celebrate. The readable ones include D A Thomas, Ian Boucaut, Reg Kearnan, Jack Quayle and K G Walsh.[18]

John was admitted to the South Australian bar in 1933 and was working each day as a fully qualified lawyer while pursuing his studies for his Honours degree. The decision he made now would distinguish him in the legal profession. He decided to prepare a thesis for the Doctor of Laws degree. He would be one of the rare people to complete one and be awarded the degree. Among distinguished lawyers who tried and could not were Albert Hannan, Crown Solicitor and biographer of Samuel Way, and future Supreme Court judge, Herbert Mayo. In fact, John would be the last to be awarded the LLD for a thesis – future theses would be considered for the PhD and the LLD would be reserved for a body of published work that had had a substantial impact on its area.

The topic of the thesis as originally accepted in 1934 by the Faculty of Law was 'Assets in private international law'. On 12 August that same year, the Faculty granted him permission to change the topic to 'Bankruptcy and the winding up of companies in private international law'. He had finished and explained what he had modified:

> This means that the subject of the administration of a deceased person's estate will not be included except in so far as it incidentally affects the law with regard to bankruptcy and winding-up, which it does to some extent.
>
> On the other hand, I have included a chapter on the effect of bankruptcy as a discharge in private international law which would come within the scope of the original subject.[19]

---

18 Bray Papers, PRG 1098/85.
19 Bray Papers, PRG 1098/67.

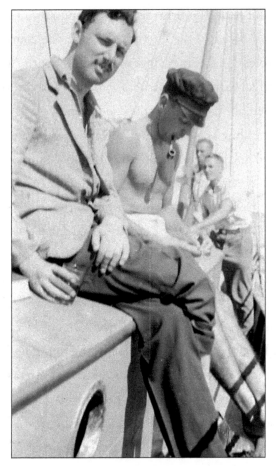

John Bray and a friend around 1936.
Private collection

John was successful and in July 1937 he would be awarded the doctorate. Two or three years earlier, another practiner, Ralph Hague, submitted his thesis on the history of the first 30 years of law in Adelaide, which was rejected. It was no easy task.

The legal profession in the mid-1930s in Adelaide was quite small, around 250. The Chief Justice was Sir George Murray, who also was Chancellor and Lieutenant-Governor, and there were four puisne judges. The only State courts were the Police, Local and Supreme Courts, who dealt with a very much wider spectrum of cases than they would after the mid-1970s when the State District Courts and the Commonwealth Federal Courts and Family

Courts were established. The firms usually had no more than three or four partners, and were based in the city not far from the courts. There was no division of the profession like in Sydney or London. South Australian lawyers were all admitted as barristers, solicitors, proctors and attorneys, and could practise where their abilities and clientele led them.

The two outstanding leaders of the Adelaide bar in the 1930s were Ted (Edward Erskine) Cleland KC (1869–1943) and Frank Villeneuve Smith KC (1883–1956). Both had a celebrity status due to the fact that members of the public in the pre-television days would often fill court-rooms when high profile cases or lawyers were listed. Ted Cleland was fearless and was known for his ability to isolate the core point of a given case. This reputation was cemented in 1929 when he appeared in the High Court. After a long address from Counsel for the other side, he spoke from 12.30 to 12.35 pm, and answered one question from Justice Owen Dixon. His client won.[20]

Ted Cleland KC was appointed a judge of the Supreme Court in 1936, a day that must have greatly disturbed Justice Herbert Angas Parsons. Barely a year earlier, according to Jack Elliott, then in his second year of articles, Ted Cleland had defied the imperious then Acting Chief Justice Herbert Angas Parsons who refused to allow him to reply to Frank Villeneuve Smith's address one afternoon:

'Then I shall reply to the wall', said Cleland and turning to the wall nearest to him began his speech.

Angas Parsons and his fellow judges sat silently. Never did I see judges looking more sheepish.

After about twenty minutes distinguishing three or four of Villeneuve Smith's cases, Cleland announced, 'And that concludes my reply'.[21]

---

20   From Howard Zelling's entry on E. E. Cleland in the *Australian Dictionary of Biography*, volume 8, pp. 22–23. The case was *Sinclair Scott v Naughton* (1929). adb.anu.edu.au/biography/cleland-edward-erskine-5678.

21   Jack Elliott, *Memoirs of a Barrister*, p. 9.

Frank Villeneuve Smith KC was not so known for his grasp of the law in the same way as Ted Cleland, but for his oratorial skills:

> Villeneuve Smith possessed formidable gifts as an advocate. His forceful personality was enhanced by an extraordinary command of language and a ready wit. Tall, dark and handsome, he exploited his imposing bearing. Large pince-nez, attached to a long black silk ribbon worn around his neck, were used to devastating effect. Indeed, his effect on juries was almost the trigger that brought about their abolition.[22]

Frank Villeneuve Smith identified John's abilities early in his career, as we saw earlier in his letter of 1933, and also knew of the young lawyer's passion for classics. At the end of 1935, he wrote a brief note to John asking him if he knew the origin of the term 'When Greek meets Greek'.[23]

John also was acquainted with the other silk who appeared in a large number of cases then, the Crown Solicitor, Albert Hannan KC (1887–1965). There is a letter from Mr Hannan dated 3 September 1935, expressing his appreciation at John writing to him. It is not known about what subject John had written but Hannan had ended with: 'For my part I was more irritable than usual that morning.' Albert Hannan had always worked for the Crown since his admission to the bar, and was also interested in the academic side of law. He did not complete the doctoral thesis he started in 1916, but in 1960 he published a biography of former South Australian chief justice, Sir Samuel Way. John would criticise this biography for not including Way's illegitimate family of five children. Although John did not know it, Albert Hannan had originally written of the family, but had to remove all references, even to Tasmania at all, before it was published.

John would eventually become the first silk of the Genders firm since it opened its doors in the 1880s. He did not follow the personal style of either Cleland or Villeneuve Smith, but showed equal courage. He began appearing

---

22   John Playford's entry on Villeneuve Smith in *Australian Dictionary of Biography*, Volume 11, pp. 642–643. Juries for civil trials were abolished in South Australia in 1927.

23   Bray Papers, PRG 1098/1/1. Same for the letter from Albert (A J) Hannan.

as a junior barrister in the Supreme Court with his firm partners in his early 20s, and his name first appears in the 1935 State Reports when he was 22 years old. The Adelaide legal profession in the 1930s was no bigger than 200 in total – the size of the current independent bar that takes most of the superior courts matters – and so it may have been easier. It is also more difficult for a lawyer of this age to become a partner in a modern firm, but John bought a share of Genders in March 1935 for £100 entitling him to 1/22 of the net profits. The name of the firm would remain at this point Genders Wilson & Pellew.

Most of the work at the firm was the day-to-day work of solicitors, but occasionally a client was in one of the courts, most commonly for divorce. John's first published case in the Supreme Court of South Australia was assisting Eustace Genders in defending a client against a personal injury claim in front of Acting Justice Geoffrey Reed – *Deed v Liddle*.[24] Their client was found to be liable for an accident at a dangerous intersection between Port Elliott and Victor Harbor.

Later that year John appeared alone in the Supreme Court before Justice Richards representing a Mrs Hopkins, who was seeking a divorce from her husband. They had both been involved in affairs outside the marriage, but the judge found in her favour due to her husband's cruelty. The *Matrimonial Causes Act 1929* allowed for adultery condoned, and this is why John's client was successful in obtaining her divorce – had her husband not consented to her affairs she would have been doomed to stay married to him.

John was in the State Reports again in 1936 representing clients seeking divorces. In *Tonkin v Tonkin* Justice Richards, who was a strict Methodist, did not accept John's argument that his client was entitled to a divorce on the grounds of desertion because his wife, though living under the same roof, had refused him any sexual relations for over five years. Desertion by law required actual separation for five years, and Mrs Tonkin had returned in 1931 after a year's absence as a paid house-keeper.

---

24   SASR [1935], p. 188, and for the second case, p. 295.

Later that year John was appealing a divorce before the Full Court, comprising Chief Justice Sir George Murray, and the two old adversaries, Justices Herbert Angas Parsons and Ted Cleland. Ted Cleland had been appointed a judge in March 1936, and maintaining his independence, he wrote his own judgment separately from the joint one prepared by Sir George Murray and Herbert Angas Parsons. Both judgments referred the case back to the trial judge, Acting Justice Geoffrey Reed, but Ted Cleland was more favourable to John's argument than the other two judges. Geoffrey Reed had hoped that the Full Court would resolve some of the seeming inconsistencies in the cases John had found to back up his argument that his client should be allowed a divorce.

The problem was that although the wife of John's client was living in an adulterous relationship, he had admitted to adultery himself during that period. In such a case, the *Matrimonial Causes Act 1929* gave unfettered discretion to the judge as to whether he would grant the necessary order to dissolve the marriage. Although Justice Cleland found the cases John referred to less problematic than did his learned colleagues, he ultimately agreed that none of these cases could prevent Acting Justice Reed from exercising his judicial discretion. Because only he had heard the matter in its entirety, then he remained the best-qualified judge to do this.

Later that year John presented his thesis to the Faculty of Law and it was accepted on 2 March 1937. In June the Chancellor, Sir George Murray, also the Chief Justice, formally awarded him the degree of Doctor of Laws. This was a rare degree in a profession where even the Bachelor of Laws was not a requirement for admission. Some silks, Frank Villeneuve Smith KC, for example, did not hold a law degree.

Alice Bray died in 1935 and the family moved from College Park to the 15-room mansion on Hutt Street. It had been John's home on and off for almost ten years, but now it became his permanent home, and he would not move until it was sold 36 years later. Harry became an approximately one-third share-holder of the Adelaide Arcade, and John was left a 3/99 share.

Gertrude bought the house from Harry and his surviving siblings in March 1936 and would remain the sole proprietor until she died.

The family was flush with funds, and in July 1937, gave both John and sister Rowena, barely 20 years old, a five-month trip to Europe. The price of the first class fares alone was £142 each, at a time when the average wage was just touching £4 a week. The two new world adventurers set sail on the 20,000 ton *RMS Orama* First Class from Port Adelaide on 22 July 1937, first stop Fremantle, bound for Southampton.

Chapter 5

VOYAGE

I saw the plum tree blossom prematurely in late winter.
And the rain beat on it and the hail slashed it and the wind
wrenched the pale pink stars off the branches and hurled
them into the streaming gutters.
And the tree was helpless before them,
Like a virgin martyr stripped for the lions in the arena ...

John Bray, from 'The Plum Tree'

John's passport issued in July 1937 describes him as six feet tall, with black hair and hazel eyes. He found quite quickly that his role as chaperone to his 20-year-old attractive sister, Rowena, was to be a full-time job. She was very keen to meet men. The voyage to England would take around a month, calling at established British ports on the way: Colombo, Aden, Cairo, and Gibraltar.

John kept some of the menus and receipts. First class dinner on board for the 28 July 1937 offered a menu in a blend of French and English: consommé tortue claire, fillet of sole meunière, spinach en branches and cream, roast chicken with ham croquettes, salad and soufflé for dessert. Rowena and John based themselves in London after arriving in late August and travelled around England and Scotland, staying at the Glen Aber Hotel on 21 September 1937, at a cost of £2 2/-.

John liked Edinburgh more than London, but discovered he was not the most organised of travellers. He wrote to his mother:

I have acquired a distressing habit of leaving articles of personal use behind me and a trail of my belongings stretches through Scotland. I have lost in this way a cigarette case I got in Colombo, a bottle of hair oil, the razor strap Dad got before I left and a shilling worth of stamps.[1]

Back in London, John went shopping for what were probably gifts: he bought a painting by Mrs Stanley Turner at a shop in Hanover Square for around £4 and a certified Queen Anne silver ladle. He bought some legal paraphernalia. In November he went to Ede Ravenscroft and spent a total of £21 6d on a bar wig, circuit case and a gown. At Hardy Brothers in Pall Mall he made some more serious purchases on behalf of two brothers who were among his best friends. He bought a fishing line for David Thomas and a rod for David's brother Stuart, known as Mac from his middle name, Macdonnell.

David Thomas was one of John's regular correspondents while he was away discovering another world. He and his brother Mac were dairy farmers in the Adelaide Hills. David began writing very soon after John left, and his letters reveal the cryptic language of friends that means little to outsiders, for example from the letter of 26 July 1937: 'I have just passed a very quiet weekend. Lindley was our guest and beyond a Sunday afternoon call at Longwood we "kept house" in a most convincing manner.' David also revealed his blokey, light-hearted humour and affection for John in a letter in October to report on a fishing trip: 'His wife, his brother's wife and his brother, his dog and his cockatoos join with him in wishing you the best of good fortune and a safe speedy return.'

Another regular correspondent during this period was Paddy, who had moved to Geraldton in Western Australia, to discover that his old friend from Adelaide's writing was difficult to read:

---

1   Letter from John to Gertrude, 10 October 1937. Bray Papers, SLSA, PRG 1098/2/3.

Geraldton, 16 September 1937

Dear John,

I have had two of your indecipherable scripts but not knowing your address could not answer them. (Answer is hardly the right word since I cannot read your writing and so do not profess to know what the letters were about.)[2]

While he was in Europe, the University of Adelaide awarded John the Bonython Prize for his LLD thesis. It was announced in *The Advertiser* on 27 August, and friend Neste Gwynne sent John the cutting. The prize was £200. After John returned, he wrote to his old school, St Peter's College, asking them if he could donate the scholarship to a student who was in financial hardship. The Depression was still having its effect and the headmaster was grateful. The lucky beneficiary was a 12-year-old son of a bankrupt accountant who had ended up working at John Martin's department store in Rundle Street for £4 a week. The donor of the Bonython Prize, Sir Langdon Bonython, was curious about how John was going to use his new title as 'Doctor'. Gertrude wrote to John in London: 'Sir Langdon tackled me again at Warren's dance about you calling yourself Dr Jefferson Bray, are you going to, if you are, you had better come back as Jefferson.'[3]

John also received a letter in England, which is of great interest in tracing the origins of his poetic and literary career. Charles Jury wrote to John from the Mistra Hotel in Athens, Greece:

Is there any chance of your coming down here? It's an amazing place in some ways, and it has some excellent things in it, but it's a very long way out of the way. I wish sometimes that I was in Paris. But we could have a bit of tender veal together if you did. Anyway, I hope we shall meet next year in Adelaide.[4]

---

2   Bray Papers, SLSA, PRG 1098/1.
3   PRG 1098/2/4. Gertrude to John, 17/9/1937.
4   Bray Papers, PRG 1098/1/36. Letter dated 31 October 1937.

Jury's letter writing was obviously not his strong point. He was a poet most strongly influenced by the classic period who had been born in Adelaide in 1893. With the help of his parents, he published his first work of poetry, *Spring is Coming*, in 1906 at the age of 13. While he was studying at Oxford for an arts degree, war broke out with Germany. He joined the Oxfordshire and Buckinghamshire Light Infantry and went to fight in France until he was severely wounded. After the war a private income allowed him to devote all his time to writing poetry. He lived much of the next 20 years in Greece and Sicily, living in Adelaide briefly in the early 1930s to lecture in English at the University of Adelaide, before again returning to Greece.

John did not take up the invitation to go to Athens; even a long way from home he was already a creature of habit and not given to making plans spontaneously. By this time he seems to have even given up leaving the hotel. Friend Colin Kerr wrote to him in November inquiring as to whether the rumour was true that he 'has refused to budge from [his] hotel to see the sights of London, while Rowe was fraternising with titled speed merchants.'[5]

John left London on Sunday, 5 December 1937. He spent a week travelling by train over the continent, first spending two days in Paris. John preferred Paris 'infinitely' to London and saw Josephine Baker and Maurice Chevalier.[6] According to Bill, writing much later, one of John's duties in Paris was to 'extricate Rowena who had swiftly married a Frenchman, later killed on the Maginot Line'.[7] The rest of the family, including Bill, would not learn of Rowena's marriage for almost 40 years. But if extricating had been one of John's duties in Paris he failed, as she would stay on in Europe, extending her holiday well after the original return date.

John broadened the knowledge of the world he had first learned of in the original Latin texts. John appeared to have boasted about his experiences to 'Paddy' – Denis Glynn. Though John's letter is not available, Paddy's response reveals a little of what it may have contained:

---

5   Bray Papers, PRG 1098/1/35. Letter dated 30 November 1937.
6   John Bray to Bill Bray 11 November 1937. Bray Papers SLSA, PRG 1098/2.
7   Bill Bray to Peter Ward, 5 October 1996.

Still, with your Parisian experience behind you, no doubt you will be endeavouring to show off, and I expect to derive considerable pleasure and profit out of the viewing of your manoeuvres. I expect some of your newer, subtler 'demi-mondain' leads will puzzle the wily Lucifer, and drive him frantic with chagrin.[8]

Europe at this time was simmering with Fascist governments, Hitler in Germany, Franco in Spain and Mussolini in Italy. After a few days in Paris, John took the train to Lucerne, then for two more days in Milan, one in Florence and two days in Rome. There he saw the Italian dictator's black-shirts marching through the streets of Rome, and he was happy to leave and get away as far as possible. A week after leaving London, he caught the *SS Ormonde* at Naples to sail back to Adelaide. He arrived back in Adelaide in January 1938 and just as he was settling back down to the routine of legal practice at Genders Wilson & Pellew and long nights each weekend at the Amateur Sports Club, one of his closest friends John Davey was struck with a life-threatening disease.

Davey was now 25, and was still known for his State cricket success. He had just been admitted to legal practice when he was bowled down by what Peter McCusker understood was a neurological disease and Russel Ward, another Amateur Sports Club friend of Davey, understood was 'disseminated sclerosis'.[9] Davey ended up on the verge of death in St Andrew's Hospital on South Terrace, weakened even more from not having eaten or drunk for several days:

Bray begged him to take something or he would die. The feeble Davey requested a half glass of Cooper's Sparkling Ale. The Matron said it was not possible given the hospital rules. An outraged Bray threatened the most dire consequences if the dying man was not given his wish. The now over-borne Matron gave way. Davey had the half glass of

---

8   Paddy (Denis Glynn) to John Bray, 6 December 1937. Bray Papers SLSA, PRG 1098/1/1.
9   Russel Ward, *A Radical Life*, p. 80.

Coopers. Half an hour later the now apparently less feeble Davey had another request. Could he have the rest of the bottle.[10]

John Davey would recover but the disease destroyed his optic nerve and he was blind. He would nevertheless build up a legal practice, eventually becoming a partner in Gun & Davey, the firm still bearing his name at the time of writing. Friends would call each lunchtime and keep him up to date with reported judgments, and his secretary would read him the documents of daily practice.

John was now heading towards his 26th birthday, and reflecting on the path his life was following. A literary career seemed out of reach, particularly in Australia, especially in Adelaide. At that time there would have been no professional literary writers (even now it is rare), while the law was obviously far more reliable financially. Overseas, Patrick White, who was born the same year as John, was able to write thanks to a private income provided by his family. But even if John's family were relatively well off, they were not sympathetic to a life in the arts. Even more, John knew little about Australian writing, even about more recent English work:

> The English course at school stopped to all intents and purposes at Tennyson. I never encountered any Australian literature till long after I left school. I don't think I even read *Robbery Under Arms* till the forties or fifties. In fact, I had hardly known there was any Australian literature.[11]

And John was not sympathetic to the writings of modernist English authors such as T S Eliot, Ezra Pound, James or D H Lawrence:

> When I did read *The Waste Land* – I think about 1939 – I was scandalised by what seemed to me to be outrageous violations of the laws of prosody. I had learned all about scansion at school and to me the laws of metre were like the laws of the Medes and the Persians.

---

10   Peter McCusker, 'Bray and Davey', *The Adelaide Review*, September 1995, p. 34.
11   *Satura*, p. 167, and for the second quote.

There are two or three undated play scripts in his papers that show that he was toying with the idea of writing during the 1930s. One rough way of dating John Bray's early handwriting is its readability, which diminishes to requiring specialist study by about the 1940s. Even the library archivist, normally not given to making personal or humorous comments, has recorded in the index: 'Handwriting is legible so must be by a young J J Bray.'

The most readable play, and therefore most likely to be the first one written is untitled, and around 14 pages. It is set in pre-Norman Anglo-Saxon England, with three characters, King Edgar, Ealdorman Athelwold and Edmund. The simple plot is not very original and follows an arranged marriage with an unseen girl from faraway Devon. The character names hint that John may have been inspired to create something with this medieval setting after reading or seeing Shakespeare's *King Lear*. The second play, slightly less legible, is entitled *Loyalties*, and appears to be influenced by the upper-class Edwardian parlour antics of P G Wodehouse. The play has a theme much deeper than its plot and a striking one for the period: anti-semitism. The setting is a country mansion and the main character is Charles Winsor. Some money won in cards is stolen from under a pillow, and the character called De Levis is suspected automatically because he is Jewish. The money turns out not to be stolen at all, but the prejudice has been revealed. One of the last lines in the play – only about 15 pages long – is: 'It's becoming a sort of Dreyfus case – people taking sides quite outside the evidence.'[12] The theme is a sign though of John's sense of justice.

Meanwhile John's younger brother Bill, 15 in 1938, was dabbling in acting. The University of Adelaide's Theatre Guild was founded that year and one of the plays proposed was Stephen Spender's *Trial of a Judge*. Bill was selected to play the role of 'A Communist', but there is no record of the performance.

---

12   Bray papers, PRG 1098/52/4. Caution: these two plays are misfiled. *Loyalties* is actually under 1098/52/5 and the untitled play under 1098/52/4 – not as catalogued.

That year was also the one when Charles Jury moved to Adelaide permanently after almost 30 years of living in England and Greece. Jury's move would have a profound effect on the course of John Bray's life. Jury, still with family-endowed private means, was living as a full-time writer. This made him a very exceptional person in 1930s Adelaide. Like John, he lived and breathed the classical authors. He was also conscious of the need to stir up some literary activity in Australia.

Even after 150 years of British settlement, Australia was not seen as a place in which a serious literary work could be set, least of all South Australia. Jury himself gave his poetry and plays classical settings, even though they were often allegories of contemporary themes. Australia's only Nobel Prize winner, Patrick White had to begin his career in London to have any hope of credibility. For decades to come, Australians hoping to begin a career in the arts of any kind would still need to go to England or the United States, with notable examples including Errol Flynn, Judith Anderson Barry Humphries, Clive James and Charles Tingwell. In fact, to this day Australian literature, cinema and theatre remains peripheral to the world stage when compared to, for example, the relatively large impact of a small country such as Ireland.

There was nevertheless in Melbourne a small group of people determined to do what they could to maintain an Australian arts movement: the Heide circle founded by John Reed at Bulleen. Sidney Nolan painted his iconic Ned Kelly series there. In Adelaide, the Jindyworobak movement was founded in 1938 by Rex Ingamells with a concentration on myths of Aboriginal Australia. Although the Jindys are virtually unknown today, they fired up aesthetically minded Australians as to what would constitute Australian art.

Max Harris would become one of John Bray's closest friends. Max was just beginning his arts degree at the University of Adelaide, but he had already made a mark on the local scene and could not see why the Jindyworobaks could justify disconnecting themselves from the modernist movements in Europe. He was very inspired by the surrealists and was either publishing poetry where he could, or organising public readings. He was the editor of the university's student magazine *On dit*, but he and Donald Kerr wanted to start a cutting-edge art and poetry publication that would go where no publication had dared go before.

Around 1941, Charles Jury turned up and listened to Max – now 19 years old – reading a poem he written about drunken youths in evening suits:

> We know of no mithridatum of despair
> as drunks, the angry penguins of the night,
> straddling the cobbles of the square,
> tying a shoelace by fogged lamplight.[13]

Jury spoke up from the audience: 'That's exactly what you young iconoclasts are – angry penguins!' Donald Kerr and Max Harris realised immediately that 'Angry Penguins' would make a perfect title for a magazine they were planning to publish. Charles Jury helped fund the early issues of *Angry Penguins* and, given the incredible and enduring legacy of its publication of Ern Malley – which we will come back to later – Max Harris put Australian poetry on the map in a way no one else could.

Little remains in the records about the friendship between Charles and John until the early 50s. Unfortunately, after Charles's sudden death in 1958, members of his family hastily, and without care for posterity, filled a trunk with letters and papers for burning. Until 1953, Charles lived in one of the Frome House apartments at 273 North Terrace, opposite the Royal Adelaide Hospital. His apartment became increasingly a place where artists and writers could meet. On Friday nights he hosted poetry readings to invited guests, but John did not join this till the late 1950s. According to one of Charles's surviving friends, Charles did not think John would be enthusiastic due to his dislike of many of the English poets that they favoured such as Wordsworth.

But there are surviving traces of their friendship in the columns Charles began writing in the 1940s for *The Advertiser*. Called 'Answers' by C R Jury,

---

13   Alan Brissenden, 'Max Harris: A Life and its Legacy', in *The Age*, 4 February 1995, Books, p. 8.

each column featured two or three questions by correspondents known only by their initials. These varied from week to week but over a month each one seemed to reappear regularly – one of these was 'J J B'. One of his questions was: 'Is it better to succeed in doing a small thing or to come short of doing a great thing?' Charles Jury's response was that it was by far better to be an imperfect Shakespeare than be a perfect Meleager (a minor figure of Greek mythology). Another question of 'J J B' was: 'Is it fair to attribute to an author the views he puts into his character's mouth?' Jury's response was that it was not.[14] The questions seemed very much to have come from evenings of protracted but relaxed discussion. The topics were always disconnected from current affairs, the articles were purely for distraction.

But John and his friends did not entirely ignore what was happening around them:

> My contemporaries and I in the thirties were a fairly careless and self-indulgent lot outside our jobs but we did not entirely neglect pubic affairs. In 1930, as I have said, the Great Depression was at its peak. There was much talk about theories of money and recipes for the escape from the paradox of the deliberate restriction of production in a starving world, the burning of wheat, for example, and the paying of farmers not to raise pigs, in order to keep up the price.[15]

They discussed Keynes's theories and meanwhile could not help what was happening in Germany. John wrote:

> In January 1933 Adolf Hitler became Chancellor of Germany. Gradually the focus of interest changed from economics to international affairs. With fascinated horror we watched the victors of 1918, like fuddled topers at the racecourse, muddle away the fruits of victory for the benefit of an autocracy far more malevolent and evil than any

---

14   Jury Papers, PRG 20/53, Newspaper clippings.
15   *Satura*, p. 168, for both the quotes.

of its predecessors in the lamentable roll-call of human tyranny. In September 1939 Hitler invaded Poland and the whole world changed.

In the changing world, John was considering life as a solicitor at Genders Wilson & Pellew. With the support of Keith Wilson, now a federal Senator, he began applying for academic posts. One of his first attempts was for a part-time lectureship in jurisprudence and Roman Law at the University of Adelaide in September 1938. It was given to assistant Crown Solicitor Ralph Hague. In 1939 John applied for the chair, although it sounds more of a sofa, in 'Roman Law, Jurisprudence, Constitutional Law, International Law and Conflict of Laws' at Victoria University College in New Zealand. With all his prizes and qualifications, and with his referees including two Supreme Court judges – Angas Parsons and Napier – the Dean of Law at the University of Adelaide Law School, Professor Arthur Campbell (who did not hold a law degree) and his employer, Keith Wilson, he was not successful.

The following year, 1940, John applied for two positions. One was as a senior lecturer in law at the University of Melbourne, offering a salary of £550 a year. The second was the Chair of Jurisprudence and International Law at the University of Sydney. Once again, his referees were impeccable: his partner at Genders, Senator Wilson; Professor Campbell; George Ligertwood KC; and Justices Angas Parsons and Napier. But John's application letter reveals how little was his ability to sell himself. He drew attention to the fact that he had been rejected by the AIF (Australian Imperial Force – the volunteer personnel of the Australian Army of the two world wars) for 'defective eyesight', and also to his previous unsuccessful application to the chair at Victoria University College.

Again unsuccessful, at least John was appointed for the year 1941 to replace Ralph Hague as the lecturer in Jurisprudence and Roman Law while Ralph went off to the war. This was really a poor second as Ralph had won that position over John three years earlier. Over the next ten years, John kept copies of his occasional attempts to enter academic life. The last one is dated 1949, to the University of Adelaide itself, for the Bonython Professor of Law. In

The Registrar,
        University of Sydney,
        SYDNEY,   N.S.W.

Dear Sir,

        I hereby make application for appointment to the
Chair of Jurisprudence and International Law in the
University of Sydney.

        My name is John Jefferson Bray.   I am 28 years of
age being born on the 12th September 1912.   I am unmarried.
I received the ordinary degree of Bachelor of Laws in the
University of Adelaide in 1932, the Honours degree in 1933
and the degree of Doctor of Laws in 1937.   This degree
was awarded for a thesis on "Bankruptcy & the Winding up
of Companies in Private International Law".   I received
the Stow Prize in 1930 and the David Murray Prize in 1931
and 1932.   In October 1933 I was admitted as a barrister
and solicitor of the Supreme Court of South Australia.
In March 1935 I became a partner in the firm of Genders,
Wilson & Pellew of Selborne Chambers, Pirie Street, Adelaide
and I have practised as a barrister and solicitor and a
partner of that firm ever since.   I am the lecturer in
Jurisprudence (including Roman Law) in the University of
Adelaide for the year 1941.

        I might add that I was rejected from the A. I. F. in
June 1940 on the ground of defective eyesight.   I was
rejected as medically unfit for the militia on the same
ground in March of this year.

        I enclose herewith testimonials obtained by me from
my partner, Senator Wilson, (now serving with the A. I. F.)
from Professor Campbell of the University of Adelaide,
Mr. G. C. Ligertwood, K. C. and their Honours Mr. Justice
Angas Parsons and Mr. Justice Napier of the Supreme Court
of South Australia at a time when I applied for the Chair
of Law at Victoria University College, Wellington, New
Zealand.

        Reference can be made to Professor Campbell or

Yours faithfully,

Mr. Ligertwood if need be.
I enclose herewith medical certificate.

The first page of John's application to the University of Sydney to lecture in law, around 1940.
Private Collection.

between, in 1946, he had applied to teach the criminal law course, but Roderic Chamberlain, the Crown Prosecutor, was appointed. He nevertheless stayed on to teach Roman Law until 1967 when he was appointed Chief Justice. John was never known as a great orator, and his students found him hard to understand if they were not in the front rows. But one of his later students and godson, Michael Abbott, discovered that the Roman law book John was quoting from in English one lecture was in fact in the original Latin.

At some point during the 1940s John began appearing on Radio 5AD, to answer questions sent in by its listeners to the show 'Information Please'. No records exist as to how John was chosen, but it is possible that it was through his family connection to the Bonythons, former owners of *The Advertiser* newspaper, which owned the radio station. The radio station also organised quizzes, and over the middle decade of the 1940s John supplied questions and answers by the hundreds.

One of his future close friends, Brian Medlin, born in 1927, was still at school in the 1940s, and he was a loyal listener of 'Information Please'. His mother, Myra, said to him: 'That Dr Bray is a bit of a character. If he doesn't know something he works it out.' Brian found out much later that there was a trade secret: all the questions that would be asked on the program were mailed out in advance so the comperes would be prepared. But even so, Myra Medlin had accurately detected that John was not just reciting prepared answers, he explained how he arrived at those answers.

With falling hopes of ever gaining an academic position, John began submitting articles and reviews for publication. One of the earliest of these is a review of a performance of Shakespeare's *Richard III*, sent in his appalling handwriting to *The Chronicle* editor, Harry Plumridge. In the accompanying letter, dated 6 April 1948, John confesses: 'I enclose herewith a very rough article done by me in great haste last night.' In the review he was grateful for the 'unique privilege' of seeing Shakespeare 'competently performed by professional actors' in Adelaide.[16] Various other manuscripts survive

---

16   Bray papers, SLSA, PRG 1098/37/1.

among his papers, some of them typed but some of them in his increasingly unreadable handwriting. One is on the Constitution of South Australia, and another on recent trends in literature.

This one is typed, mercifully, not dated, but likely to be from the same period. John gives a broad introduction to his feeling about literature at the time:

> The present age is remarkable for the fact that the productions of the press are divided into two classes – books that the public reads and the books that the literary specialists read. Literature has become divorced from the people. A small group of literary experts produce works which are practically unintelligible to everyone except themselves and one sometime doubts if they even understand and everything that appeals to the popular taste is damned as being second-rate. This was not always so. In the past great works of art were directed to and appreciated by the multitude, eg Athens, Shakespeare and the Victorian age. This tendency to make literature a matter for the specialists is not confined to writing, it being an attribute of the twentieth century.[17]

John was also writing material for radio. The earliest contribution appears to be a piece for ABC radio in 1939 on the Nazi legal system. His introductory paragraph shows what he feels:

> Some of you may have read some time ago that it had been decided that certain portions of the German law were to be applied in those countries occupied by Germany and you may have wondered what this system was which was about to be bestowed on so many millions formerly ignorant of its blessings. It is, at least in its basic principles, utterly unlike anything which the civilised world has seen for many centuries.[18]

---

17 Bray papers, SLSA, PRG 1098/37/6.
18 Bray papers, SLSA, PRG 1098/37/18.

'Truth and the Law Courts' was written for Radio 5KA and broadcast Sunday 14 June 1941 from Maugham Church on Franklin Street. John writes about the incredible difficulty for courts to find out the truth of any given matter under dispute. He outlined the tactics used in past systems, like trial by battle in feudal England and torture on the continent. He explains how juries evolved out of Norman tax commissioners and the role of cross-examination in testing witnesses' accounts of how they perceived an event.

In one of his rare writings on a contemporary theme, he wrote a piece for ABC Radio at the end of 1941, 'What Neutrality Means'. In this talk, John talks about the rules of neutrality developed during the 18th and 19th centuries. At the start of the talk he expresses his concerns that the concepts seemed to have lost its significance. He wrote that a fundamental principle of neutrality was 'that the neutral who cannot protect himself against the wrongdoing at the hands of one belligerent cannot complain against reprisals at the hands of the other'. He was particularly referring to Norway, who had not been able to prevent Germany using her territorial waters as a base of operations.

John concluded neutrality is a 'fantastic anachronism for all states are inter-dependent and every state has now realised the bitter truth that peace is indivisible'. He also condemned states that allowed their neighbours to be attacked and compared them to householder who ignores a burglar breaking into his neighbour's house and cutting the throat of his wife and children.[19]

John also wrote two more pieces for radio around that period. One was political, on the fact that until then no one had been tried for high treason in Australia. In May 1944 he escaped the war themes and wrote about a couple of French historical mysteries, the first about Marie Antoinette's diamond necklace and the second about the identity of Dumas's Man in the Iron Mask.

He also wrote a piece that is undated but judging by its format and paper, undoubtedly part of his ongoing contributions to the ABC. This one was entitled 'What is the Use of History?' He begins:

---

19   As above, PRG 1098/37/23.

What for that matter is the use of education at all. Many people think that the purpose of education is to help you earn your living. For that purpose history is of very little use. But, of course, that is not the true object of more than a small part of education and that the least important. Its real and fundamental purpose is to make you an intelligent and fully-developed human being and citizen in an intelligent and fully-developed community. The importance of history for that purpose can be hardly exaggerated.[20]

John believed that history can provide lessons about how to deal with similar situations reappearing in the present. 'History teaches us to be of good cheer: that as human beings we differ from molecules and stars because within wide limits we can control our own destinies'. He then has added considerable notes as afterthought at the end, sounding somewhat idealistic, but mindful of earlier warnings about the incomplete nature of historical records: 'The only art of history which is worthwhile reading is the work of a genuine historian, one unswervingly devoted to the truth and free from conscious bias.'

History has also taught us that even historians are shown eventually to have not quite got it right.

Meanwhile, although John's poor eyesight prevented him from any active military duty himself, some of his friends were sent overseas to fight. These included R M Gibson (Gibbie), Frank Moran and David Thomas. The regular letters from both Gibbie and David revealed the awful loneliness felt by young men sent abruptly away from families and friends to bewilderingly unfamiliar countries. Gibbie wrote in July 1941 from Syria:

Tell Mrs Bray I've only had one game of bridge since leaving Australia and I often think of the very pleasant Sunday evenings spent with Mr Bray and the others. ... I am scribbling this while doing guard duty.[21]

---

20   Catalogued as PRG 1098/37/28.
21   PRG 1098/1/1. Letter from Gibbie to John, 30/7/1941.

David Thomas wrote in September that year from Iraq:

> Oh, Monster!
>
> I have just received your letter which I found extremely amusing. ... As I write, I am seated in my little white tent not far from the banks of the Euphrates. ... At my elbow I have a mug of whisky and water.
>
> Despite the dust-laden, death-ridden, devastating, depressing, dive-bombed, dysentried, disgusting and delightful atmosphere of our former days we are holding up well. Everything is quiet now and all are asleep except the guard. It is very still and the moon is shining into the end of my tent.[22]

Bill was at the University of Adelaide studying for a chemistry degree when he joined the Royal Australian Air Force as a navigator. He wrote to John just before leaving for Germany, dating the letter with only 'Tuesday':

> First and foremost take care of mother and do what you can to comfort her in any unforeseen emergency. I say that since we are all going away with the knowledge that our hopes of seeing these shores ever again are rather slim, though for heaven's sake don't tell that to the family.[23]

Bill was shot down around April 1944 and reported as missing. There was no further news and he was assumed killed. It was quite a shock therefore when on Saturday, 5 May 1945, *The Advertiser* published a photograph of Bill large as life with none other than Field Marshal Sir Bernard Montgomery. For over a year the family had believed him dead. According to the brief caption, he had 'bailed out of a stricken Halifax bomber over Frankfurt'.[24] He was freed in April 1945 by Field Marshal Montgomery's British Fifth Army and sent to London. Frank Moran, who had been an articled clerk at Genders in

---

22   PRG 1098/1/1. Letter from David Thomas to John, 5/9/1941.
23   PRG 1098/2/1. Bill to John, undated.
24   *The Advertiser*, Saturday 5 May 1945, p. 8. The photo was supplied by Beam Wireless Picturegram.

1940 before being sent to war, wrote the following month to John, reassuring him that 'Bill is OK though still suffering from slight malnutrition'.[25]

But Bill's health was fragile and he wrote to John from London in May 1945:

> And now if you please I have lobbed myself into hospital with yellow jaundice of all things. God knows where I got it. I probably have brought it back as my last legacy of Nazidom.[26]

Bill also refers to a piece of news that John must have passed on about the very public obscenity trial that took place in Adelaide over Max Harris publishing the poems of Ern Malley: 'I hope all the details of the Max Harris versus Pat Hackett match were faithfully collected and kept.' In fact, the Ern Malley Affair would become part of Australian literary legend, and Max Harris a decade and a half later would become one of John's group of close friends.

Bill went back to Germany after demobilisation with the United Nations Relief and Rehabilitation Organisation before he returned to Adelaide to complete studies for a Bachelor of Science degree. In 1949 he left Australia permanently, joining the London School of Hygiene and Tropical Medicine as a junior lecturer in parasitology. He would become John's most regular long-term correspondent.

Rowena had never come back to Adelaide permanently after the Europe trip. In August 1939, she was working as a crew member of a yacht which ended up hitting a reef near Gladstone in North Queensland. Adelaide's *The Advertiser* asked her to write up her adventure. Ro was on night watch when she felt the boat scrape bottom:

> At 9.45 am the boat was pounding on the coral very badly. Smoke was seen in the distance and distress signals were flown, but there was no response from the passing vessel. The mainland was only about four

---

25 PRG 1098/1/1/. Frank Moran to John Bray, 4/5/1945. Colin Moodie to John Bray, 16 June 1945, same collection.

26 PRG 1098/2/1. Bill to John, 22/5/1945.

miles away, and we were never in danger of losing our lives, but in an effort to float the boat 26 tons of granite ballast was thrown overboard. That was hard work. Very little water was coming in, although the boat was crashing down six feet on to the coral at every wave.[27]

It was not really big news but it was Rowena's 15 minutes of fame. By the end of the war she had settled in King's Cross, Sydney, and a couple of her communications to John reveal a troubled temperament. A telegram dated 6 December 1945 orders: 'As my lawyer get me manpower clearance for passport identity card no. SI-F17-41398'. John began his reply, 'I duly received your friendly telegram', before confirming he had got her 500 cigarettes and sent them by rail, for which she could either pay him £1 19/- or trade some of her alcohol still remaining at Hutt Street.[28] Not long after Rowena sent another request, advising him that 'one of those little office girls can do it', and concluding: 'Please do this and send it back immediately'.

On 10 August 1944, John received a letter from the Director of Education informing him that the Governor had appointed him to the Libraries Board as from the fifth of that month. He was filling a position left vacant by the death of Mr B S Roach. Around this time lending was introduced. Jean Whyte told the story in her contribution to *Portrait of John Bray* of how one day Premier Tom Playford and Education Minister Charles Abbott arrived at the library to work out how to find books for the lending service.

It was the 26 June 1945, the Premier and the Minister were anxious about the lack of funding available for a separate collection, but keen to ensure that library users would soon be able to borrow books to take home. The solution they found that day was very simply to take books from the existing reference collection and make them available, and also to make most of the reference collection itself available in any case. According to Jean, John always remembered this day when the two government men were walking down the aisles of books with the librarians choosing which books could

27   *The Advertiser*, 16 August 1939, p. 24.
28   Bray Papers, SLSA, PRG 1098/1/1.

be borrowed. Allowing reference books to be borrowed was supposed to be temporary until the lending collection could be fully funded, but in fact that took much longer than expected – 35 years.[29] John would still be on the Library Board then; in fact he would be reappointed until February 1987.

---

29   *A Portrait of John Bray*, pp. 116–117.

Chapter 6

PAPINIAN

Come, poet, come, see if the rose,
Whose bud the morning heats unclose,
Fresh under Virgo's sign
Will have fulfilled in evening's ray
The crimson promise of the day,
That tint, you say, like mine.

John Bray, from 'Mignonne Replies to Ronsard'

John's aspirations to be a writer were partly satiated through the 1940s from his occasional contribution to Charles Jury's 'Answers' in *The Advertiser* and radio scripts. In May 1946 Oscar Mendelsohn, a magazine publisher in Heidelberg, Victoria, asked John to contribute to *View*, described as a 'journal of opinion'. He was looking for a regular column on Adelaide artistic events to be called 'The Adelaide Letter.' Mendelsohn (1896-1978) is listed in the *Australian Dictionary of Biography* as a 'polymath, bon vivant and public analyst'. His achievements stretched from being a nationally known food scientist with laboratories in Melbourne, Sydney, Brisbane and Adelaide, to writing books and composing music, and establishing literary prizes.[1]

John was at first reluctant, not believing he would be able to write well enough. He also found the editorials and articles in the April 1946 issue displayed 'a certain naïveté' and that there was a political bias. He wrote to Oscar: 'I should warn you that nothing that I write if you want me to write

---

1   Ray Marginson, 'Mendelsohn, Oscar Adolf (1896–1978)', *Australian Dictionary of Biography*, Volume 15, Melbourne University Press, 2000, pp. 349–450.

will have any bias toward the left'.[2] Correspondence went back and forth and 'The Adelaide Letter' evolved into a possible column on dining in Adelaide. John's response to this suggestion was:

> I do not know of anyone who could write a bright article about eating in Adelaide. As a matter of fact the only places one can eat at night in Adelaide are either hotels or Greek or Chinese restaurants, fish shops, etc., although I believe there are one or two other places where a grill or something can be obtained.[3]

John did not end up writing for the energetic Oscar, who in one of the last letters from him, dated 3 June 1947, accused John: 'You may be an eminent jurist but you are far from as cunning as you imagine.'

John was not directly involved with any literary groups, including Charles Jury's poetry reading circle on Friday nights. Nevertheless, he met with Charles on Saturdays at the now demolished South Australia Hotel, opposite Parliament House. In 1950, members of Charles's circle who John met there included Neil Lovett, Jean Whyte, Michael Taylor, Jock Bills, Herbert Piper, Gavin Walkley, Barbara Walkley, Audrey Muecke, Doug Muecke and Lilo Western. There was little cross-over between these literary friends and those who John met later each Saturday night at the Amateur Sports Club down the road at 178 North Terrace.

One day in 1950 Charles Jury introduced John to Brian Medlin, a fiery 23-year-old who had come back to Adelaide after living in the Northern Territory. Brian had been submitting poems to the rare literary magazines, such as that of Flexmore Hudson, and had come to the notice of Michael Taylor, who in turn introduced him to Charles Jury.

Brian was born in Adelaide in 1927, growing up in the western suburbs. His father Jack worked in a factory on Anzac Highway during the Depression years, working 12-hour days with the knowledge that outside were hundreds

---

2   Bray Papers PRG 1098/1/1. Letter from John to Oscar Mendelsohn, 8 May 1946.
3   Bray Papers PRG 1098/1/1. Letter from John to Oscar Mendelsohn, 23 August 1946.

of desperate people, and that the managing director, Mr Richards, used to sack men for as little as working with a coat on. Brian noticed the class division between the owners and the workers: 'I grew up with a sort of hatred of these bastards and I see no reason today to moderate it.'[4] After leaving school around the time the Second World War ended, Brian also worked in a factory after an attempt to train as a teacher. He then went into the outback country of South Australia and the Northern Territory, droving cattle, breaking horses and shooting kangaroos. 'But while I was there I read, as a lot of bushmen do, or used to then, and I read in a completely unguided way. … I knew, for instance, that a small brown rat got across the Channel and cleaned up all the black rats, and that brought an end to the epidemics of plague, and not many people knew that.'

John and Brian ended up having dinner at Charles's house on North Terrace, which extended until the early hours of the following morning:

> Bray and I argued. We argued like hell and had a whale of a time. … I can remember only one thing, an absurd thing to remember. As we were disputing about whether some lines might have been written by Christopher Marlowe, Bray remarked that they were certainly Marlowesque, and I rejoined that, yes, that showed that they weren't Marlowe's.

John's friendship with Charles Jury seemed to strengthen with the entry of Brian Medlin, and his friendship with both men would endure for life. In Charles's case this was just for eight more years, but Brian's, it would be for 45 years. Brian recalled:

> It was a friendship central to which was argument, dispute, disagreement, sometimes deeply serious, sometimes heated, sometimes frivolous. Disagreement just for the sake of fun, and that disagreement had a great deal to do with our backgrounds, and I'll say something which

---

4   Interview with Brian Medlin, 19 October 2002. Unless otherwise mentioned quotes following from Brian Medlin are from this interview (not available to the public).

I haven't said before: that we both came from a background in which argument and disagreement was taken for granted. I suppose in Bray's case it had a good deal to do with his being a professional lawyer. It certainly wasn't his family background, but chiacking and argument went on amongst Bray's circle of friends that I saw.

Brian joined John and Charles each Saturday at midday in the saloon bar of the South Australia Hotel. 'There was one memorable occasion in the South when Bray, who was accustomed to walking everywhere, arrived in a taxi because he'd had an attack of gout and was, as I remember, carried across the pavement into the saloon bar of the South Australian for his Saturday session by the taxi driver and myself.' In 1953, Brian married Prue Lamotte and the two of them moved into the former servants' quarters at the back of Bray House, where they lived for five years while Brian took up studying for a degree at the University of Adelaide. He eventually won a scholarship to Oxford.

The Bray home on Hutt Street was of larger dimensions than the homes with which Brian had been previously familiar:

> Early in my acquaintance with Bray, I finished up spending the night at Bray House. We used to drink enormous quantities. I woke up in the morning and looked out and my eyes hit a plain surface, and I raised them, and raised them. And, except that it was carpeted, I might well have believed I was in the middle of the Nullabor Plain because they didn't strike anything until eventually, from an immense distance, my eyes hit the bottom of the door. I was in the front living room, sleeping on the couch, in Bray House – a huge colonial structure of great decayed opulence.[5]

When Brian and Prue were living in the servants' quarters Brian had more to do with the routine of John's life. 'He would come back from the Amateur Sports Club with a bunch of blokes in various stages of leglessness

---

5   Interview with Brian Medlin, already cited.

... Amongst these was John Davey, who of course didn't drive and would often take a taxi home; O'Connell the architect, a bloke called Shepherd, a jeweller; Buster O'Loughlin I think was sometimes there.'

John would bring his friends into the front of the house, which is the grand Italianate wing with the huge rooms. His parents slept in the old wing towards the back of the house, which was far enough away not to be disturbed. Bray House has around 18 rooms. Brian was impressed: 'You could make a great deal of noise in this house without being heard throughout it.' It was also the first time he had encountered a family that had domestic help, though the days had gone of live-in staff. Having a house-keeper meant John never needed to cook, shop, clean, wash clothes, pay bills, he was insulated from day-to-day banalities, but perhaps no differently than if he had been married at that time.

John's brother, Bill, occasionally returned from overseas and joined in John's weekend sessions. He recalled one in the Amateur Sports Club with Davey and Bray: 'I was sandwiched between these two heavyweight beer drinkers and not allowed to buy a drink even to slow down the whole process. At 11.30am some eighteen full schooners of beer lined up along the bar showed how far this weak and sodden link had fallen behind.'[6]

Charles Jury and Brian Medlin each decided to write a play. Charles called his *The Administrator*, which was on the surface about Dionysius, the tyrant of Syracuse, but in reality an allegory about A P Rowe, the Vice-Chancellor of the University of Adelaide. Brian was writing *Governor Bligh*, on the colonial officer who achieved fame for the famous mutiny against him as Captain of the *Bounty* in 1789, and 15 years later for the Rum Rebellion when he was Governor of New South Wales.

John announced one day quite out of the blue that he too would write a play. His would be on the Roman lawyer, Papinian, who lived from the years 142 to 212 and was the close friend and legal adviser of Emperor Severus.

---

6   Dr R S Bray, 'Davey and Bray', Letter to the Editor, *The Adelaide Review*, [after September 1995].

Though generally forgotten, Papinian is the single most influential lawyer in Western history. He was the authoritative influence on the Roman emperor Justinian, whose codification of Roman law remains the basis of the civil law systems across continental Europe, Russia and South America.

Papinian's enduring legacy would not be the theme of John's play. Rather, John focused on the crisis Papinian faced at the age of 70 with Severus's evil son, Caracalla. Severus had died in 211 and foolishly left a stable Roman empire to both surviving sons. Before the year was out, one of them, Caracalla, killed the other, Geta. Caracalla then ordered Papinian to produce a legal defence for the assassination.

Even in the period, some members of the general population doubted Caracalla's reasons. A satire on Caracalla was performed in Alexandria in 215, very unwisely, as the emperor's response was to send in his troops and, according to contemporary historian Cassius Dio, 20,000 people were slaughtered. Jury, Medlin and Bray all wrote their plays in verse, hoping to revive the lost tradition of the English modernists. John's play, *Papinian*, begins at the very moment three slaves in the Imperial Palace in Rome learn that one of their co-emperors has killed the other. Enter Papinian and then Caracalla, who scorns 'men of words and texts' and proceeds to instruct his father's lifetime friend and legal adviser that if he wishes to keep his life:

> Also for history's sake, I want a speech
> Or statement of some sort, explaining all
> The details of the plot, how Geta found
> A death far nobler than he merited
> Upon my soldier's swords. Also to eyes
> Deliberately shut or else too bleared
> To see the sun at noon, I want it shown
> How I was justified in morals, law,
> Religion, politics, philosophy,
> In doing what I've done, do now
> And still intend to do to that squashed wasp
> And all his hive. You're honoured with the job.

Who better fitted to expound the plot
Since you were in it up to your hook nose?
Work for your pardon, you old hypocrite.[7]

Papinian expresses reluctance and as the emperor leaves, warns him to have it ready when he returns or face execution along with his family. The play becomes a debate between Papinian and other characters on the principles behind his refusal – including the emperor's mother Julia, his wife Marcia – who is not enthusiastic to be executed – and a colleague only too ready to do whatever was necessary to gain approval from Caracalla.

Brian Medlin was critical of the principles Papinian was prepared to die for, or perhaps more accurately, John's dramatisation of them. The historical reality is that Papinian refused and was executed by Caracalla's soldiers along with his wife and son. It was up to John to imagine the reasoning and debating during those last desperate hours until Caracalla returned to discover there was no justifying speech awaiting him.

Since Brian Medlin's inclusion into Charles's and John's Saturday mornings at the South Australian Hotel, discussions broadened from literary to philosophical topics, even though Brian had only just enrolled formally in philosophy at The University of Adelaide. He believed that their discussions had a considerable influence on John's play:

There were philosophical issues … moral philosophy for instance, absolutism versus relativism, and Bray's position was an absolutist: things are right just are right; that are wrong just are wrong, full stop.

Brian argued during this period towards the opposite position, subjectivism, that 'moral judgments were just an expression of one's own attitudes':

We also argued about metaphysics generally and the philosophy of mind, in particular, and there the bone of contention was materialism versus dualism. I'd have to say that Bray was a curious mixture of

---

7   *Papinian*, p. 56 (see bibliography).

absolutism and scepticism but he certainly was very uneasy about any supposition that all that exists in the world are material objects, material particles, the stuff of physics. He was certainly uneasy about a causal account of the universe as opposed to an account of the universe which didn't contain purpose, and came out, for instance, in his doubts about Darwinism.

Brian Medlin wanted John to challenge what Brian perceived as the conservative ideas of his upbringing. Certainly John's original ideas of what constituted right and wrong would have come from his Christian schooling and background, and Christians are absolutists. But John had an inquiring mind, as we saw earlier with his discovery of why some parts of Latin texts were not translated. An inquiring mind will tend to challenge, and perhaps it was this that Brian detected and labelled as scepticism. He wrote later that *Papinian* gave John the opportunity to mature:

> *Papinian* is no dramatised tract, but a powerful and subtle play. In the quiet of his own study, John was able to come out of his own corner, to attend to complexity, and to allow his own deeply sceptical, ironical nature to infuse his characterisation.[8]

Brian did not believe that the character Papinian was in any way a self-portrait of John Bray: 'Yet the ambivalences and inconsistencies of Papinian are very similar to those of John Bray himself – Chief Justice, distinguished jurist, and yet larrikin; ironical, sceptical absolutist.'[9]

Papinian is probably more about passion and character than an attempt to rationalise it into a philosophical frame. The play focuses entirely on a man prepared to die rather than give up his beliefs. But although Caracalla is a loathsome character, the play does not push its character's beliefs, it explores them. John would become known increasingly for his defence of people's basic right to their own beliefs, regardless of what they were. We will never

---

8   Brian Medlin in 'Papinian: Birth of a Poet', *Portrait of John Bray*, p. 138, see bibliography.
9   As above, p. 143.

know obviously whether he would have gone as far as Papinian as he lived in a reasonably functioning democracy. Brian Medlin recalled that around the time John was writing the play he was alert to attempts by the police of the day to overstep their authority.

The two of them were returning home to Bray House after a late night at Charles Jury's, living then in Archer Street, North Adelaide. A police car pulled up beside them and one of the officers asked, 'Don't you blokes ever sleep?'

Brian replied, 'When we feel like it.'

The officer demanded they approach the car. John went to the patrol car and began to pound its roof.

'Who are we? I am Dr Bray, the solicitor. What right have you to molest us like this?'

'We've every right in the world.'

'You may know the law better than I do, but I very much doubt it.'

'Well, the inspector told us …'

'What did the inspector tell you?'

'He told us to stop everyone after midnight.'

'Is there a curfew in this city?' John paused, before continuing. 'I'll think about this in the morning.' He warned the officers he might follow it up and to consider themselves lucky if not.[10]

Even if this anecdote is not accurate in every detail, the essence is sufficient to demonstrate John's respect for the law over-riding his normal disinclination to challenge authority. His principles would surface quickly if threatened.

Charles Jury read John's draft and on 8 March 1953 wrote him a 13-page response. 'As far as the treatment of the theme and of the ideas, I feel the big mind everywhere.'[11] But he found Papinian's moral position Stoïc but muddled and compared John's emotions with his lead role:

---

10   Interview with Brian Medlin.
11   Bray Papers, SLSA, 1/1/36.

The only place where I felt the theme lacked full development was in the treatment of Papinian's feelings about his son. But this we have discussed. I think both you and Papinian have a superiority complex about feeling or emotion. But I do think you and he are faced with the problem of saying rather more about it than exists. You succeed with Julia, why not with Papinian?[12]

Charles advised John to 'be more of an artist ... Which you ought to be capable of doing.'

Papinian is more than 900 lines of blank verse. Jury's *The Administrator* and Medlin's *Governor Bligh* were also in blank verse, yet a director was found and each of the plays was prepared for performance. The director for the three plays was Colin Ballantyne, who ran a photography business and was one of the leaders of Adelaide's amateur and semi-professional theatre tradition.[13] The first play to be performed was Charles Jury's, in April 1955, followed by Brian Medlin's in June. *Papinian* was scheduled for August. Young philosopher and amateur actor Graham Nerlich was chosen to play the title role. Colin Ballantyne set up 'The Company of Players' for the production of the three plays. The newly elected Member for Norwood, Don Dunstan, who acted in other Ballantyne productions, represented the authors on the Company's board.

Bill Bray was now in London completing a PhD at the London School of Hygiene and Tropical Medicine and lecturing the in the Department of Parasitology. He was living with his second wife, Betty. They had both been active amateur actors in Adelaide and had a few criticisms and suggestions. Bill had told John in May 1955, 'I have always taken great if unjustified pride in your scholarship. I hasten to qualify 'unjustified' by saying I can't see why, genetically, biologically, I should claim any portion

---

12   Bray Papers, PRG 1098/1/1/36. Charles Jury to John Bray, 8 March 1953.
13   Colin Ballantyne (1908–1988) founded the Arts Council of South Australia in 1948 and, among others, produced a series of large-scale productions of Shakespeare in Adelaide between 1948 and 1952.

of your kudos'.[14] He was reading the play and in July he wrote to John that he found Papinian's wife Marcia 'too lightweight' and that he wasn't swayed much by the lawyers' arguments.

Betty had much to say, particularly about Marcia, whom she was shocked to find was not sympathetic to her husband:

> On what historical basis you created her so selfish and unlovable I do not know, and suspect it was your whim to do so, influenced perhaps by a myriad of such characters met daily in the detail of your sometimes nauseating profession ... Could you not, John, even at this eleventh hour, reshape her a little, and thus deepen the tragedy of his choice?[15]

By this time the play was in rehearsal and Betty revealed prejudices against one of Colin Ballantyne's regular actors, Frank Gargro, wondering whether Adelaide has rid itself by now of some of 'those loathsome little queens'. She acknowledged that some of her friends were what she called 'tapette', 'but I can't tolerate that these unfortunate, sad apes of Gielgud and Barrault should be provided with a platform to make public their unpleasant deformities of intellect, speech and movement.' Betty obviously had never considered the idea that John may have been homosexual, nor one of his friends and co-playwright, Charles Jury. There is no record of John's reaction.

Papinian was performed in the week of the 23–27 August 1955 and received a lengthy review in the September issue of Mary's Own Paper. The reviewer was the former editor of Angry Penguins, Max Harris, now 34 years old and a partner in Mary Martin's Bookshop. The front cover announced in bold headlines, 'J J Bray springs the surprise of the Season'. In general, Max praised the script:

> Dr Bray's play is good enough not to be patronisingly discussed with clichés ... the theme was geared to an eternal problem which is far from

---

14   Bray Papers, PRG 1098/2/1. Letter from Bill Bray to John dated 17 May 1955. The following letter mentioned was dated 10 July 1955.

15   Bray Papers, PRG 1098/2/1. Letter from Betty to John, dated 14 July 1955, and for the quotes following.

Papinian being performed in 1955.
Courtesy State Library of South Australia.

irrelevant to the contemporary situation ... Dr Bray has considered a dilemma, a truly existential and no doubt hackneyed dilemma, in which a man must choose to live by sacrificing a fundamental and cherished principle or to die in upholding it. The problem was proposed in a meticulous and rigidly analytical manner. Dr Bray proceeded to argue the cases for and against. No argument, no matter how trivial, which had a bearing on the problem seemed to be omitted, and it was this completeness that provided a great part of the satisfaction I derived from the play.'[16]

Max Harris appreciated the use of the three slaves to embody the three alternative philosophies to Papinian's dilemma – stoic, Christian and opportunist – and give a clear structure to the play's argument. He found all the actors a little bit hard to hear with the exception of the lead, played by Graham Nerlich:

The writing possessed a quality we could expect from a legal litterateur – clarity and shapeliness. It reflected also a failing of the profession –

---

16   Max Harris ['MH'], reviewing *Papinian* in *Mary's Own Paper*, September 1955.

it was finicky and long-winded. But the author surprised us in other aspects. His ungainly, somewhat amateurish verse worked on stage: it came over with fluidity and freedom that endowed the play with that shadowy extra dimension which integrated verse can create in drama.

Max summed up that the three plays were an unqualified success, and that *Papinian* had opened up the workings of the legal conscience for its audiences. John received a few letters from appreciative audience members. He was inspired to write two more plays over the next few years, one would almost be performed in 1968 – *A Word in Your Ear* – but just missed out. He was also writing poetry now, and two early poems that survive in Charles Jury's papers were 'Nature Study' and 'Mignonne replies to Ronsard', both of which were published in John's first collection in 1962.

Despite John beginning to write poetry from the early 1950s, and spending Saturdays and some weeknights with Charles Jury, he was not yet a part of Charles's formal poetry group. According to Brian Medlin, Charles started the monthly poetry reading in the mid-1940s, but 'it took me a couple of years to be invited because Jury didn't want it to be a discussion group. He didn't want disputatious characters like me, and it took Bray even longer, because of Bray's hatred of Wordsworth.'[17] Charles formally wrote to John on 22 May 1957 inviting him to join the Friday night poetry at home on 210 Archer Street, North Adelaide. John accepted, not suspecting that in just over a year, he would have to take over.

---

17   Interview with Brian Medlin.

Chapter 7

SILK

'I have an obligation to the law
By which I lived and rose: transcending that
To justice, of whom law's the servitor
As I'm the law's: on me above all men
Devolves the duty not to shame the law
Nor let the law shame justice.'

John Bray, Papinian replies to Julia in *Papinian*

John walked each weekday from Hutt Street to Selbourne Chambers in Pirie Street, a gently aged Victorian building, demolished in the early 1960s. It housed groups of lawyers among its labyrinthine corridors. Genders Wilson & Bray was but one of its many firms. John's godson, Michael Abbott, born in 1940, spent some of his childhood in his father's office at Selbourne:

> I remember the chambers well from when I was young. They were at the end of what seemed a very dark and long corridor on the ground floor. My father, H L (Bunny) Abbott, had offices just before the entrance to what soon became 'Genders Wilson & Bray' and the smell of linoleum is one of the scents, together with the musty smell of books, that I relate to the practice of law in those days.[1]

Bunny Abbott later joined Genders Wilson & Bray, and Michael did his articles with John in the mid-1960s.

---

1   Michael Abbott in *Portrait of John Bray*, p 50.

The Adelaide legal profession in the post-war period numbered a few hundred lawyers, almost all of whom worked alone or in small partnerships. Most of the firms were located along corridors of buildings often known as 'chambers' either side of the intersection of King William Street and Pirie Street, but not chambers in the sense of barristers. Unlike London or Sydney, there was not an official division between the solicitor's work and the barrister's work, and Adelaide lawyers were free to prepare wills or appear in the courts as needs dictated.

In September 1955 the first sign of change appeared with a young lone barrister setting up in a tiny room in the Epworth Building at 33 Pirie Street. Christopher Legoe was then 27 years old, recently back from Cambridge and the London bar. Other lawyers such as Howard Zelling and Jack Elliott supported his move for an independent bar in Adelaide, but it would be the early 1960s before it was formally established.

The Adelaide profession had officially decided against separating as far back as 1928 when the Law Society had carried out a survey. In September 1959 a debate about dividing the profession during the annual general meeting of the Law Society of South Australia lasted until nearly eleven o'clock that night. Two months later, on 30 November, another meeting was held, and the minutes record that among those who spoke against division of the legal profession in Adelaide was John. He was among the 154 who voted against it, easily beating the 76 who were for division.[2]

These results highlight the pragmatic approach of the Adelaide profession then. The law and its practice had been imported directly from England at the time South Australia was colonised in 1836. Division into solicitors and barristers was not possible initially, but as the population of the colony grew one would have eventually expected a push to divide under the original English model. Not surprisingly, the established members of the profession, all admitted as 'barristers, solicitors, proctors and scriveners', could not see why there was any need to change.

---

2   John Emerson, *History of the Independent Bar of South Australia*, pp. 12–13.

The last of the theatrical silks still practising from the period between the wars was Frank Villeneuve Smith KC (1884–1956). He had predicted John's great future in the 1930s, but now approaching 70, appeared less in court. His regular sparring partner of the day, E E Cleland KC, who had livened up Chief Justice Murray's starchy Court when appointed in 1936, had died in 1943.

As John approached his fortieth birthday, the leaders of the bar were no less colourful. One of John's leading contemporaries, Jack Elliott (1914–2001?), in his *Memoirs of a Barrister*, provides some lively descriptions of prominent lawyers and judges of the day.[3] One of the prominent criminal lawyers was Harry Alderman (1895–1962), son of a boot-maker, who was appointed silk in 1943. According to Jack: 'among the senior bar, no one was as genuinely egalitarian as Harry Alderman. He treated everyone the same, down to the most youthful articled law clerk.' Joe Chamberlain led prosecutions, having been Crown Prosecutor from 1928 to 1949, and subsequently Crown Solicitor, and according to Jack, was too inclined to believe that anyone accused of a crime was likely to be guilty of it as well.[4] E B Scarfe (Eb) followed Joe Chamberlain as Crown Prosecutor and was quite different – Jack commented on Eb's characteristic 'focsle humour' and 'enthusiastic drinking'.

Jack Elliott juniored John in a divorce case in the 1950s and described him as a 'black-haired, burly, somewhat hunched figure, very reserved and the best read man I ever met':

> I used to see him almost daily eating a snack lunch, absorbed in reading a book. I was drawn to him because, like me, he walked everywhere, had no time for sports, was agnostic and sublimely individualistic. He was said to have a photographic memory and dabbled in poetry. He never learned to drive a motorcar, nor owned a wireless set and had no intention of acquiring a television.[5]

---

3   Elliott 2000, p. 124.
4   Elliott 2000, p. 179.
5   Elliott 2000, p. 203.

In fact John did later in life own a television set, but according to friends, would claim not to know how to turn it on.

In the days before the massive increase in legislation of the 1970s it was possible for lawyers in South Australia's small profession to practise successfully across the range of jurisdictions. Nevertheless lawyers tended to do most of their work within one or two areas and thus gain expertise. Jack Elliott built his reputation as a criminal lawyer, like Harry Alderman, while the Treloar firm focused on probate matters, for example. John would stand out for his success in any jurisdiction increasingly over the term of his professional life.

In a speech he gave to law students on the 'Art of Advocacy', John explained his broad approach to his profession. He compared the advocate to the 'taxi-driver and the prostitute, bound to accommodate all customers who can afford to pay the fare or the fee.'[6] Michael Abbott confirmed this, calling John 'the paradigm of the barrister who obeyed the cab-rank rule, since there appears to have been no jurisdiction and no case for which he was not prepared to accept a brief.'[7] As we saw earlier in the book, John's earliest reported cases before World War II were a motor vehicle collision, an alleged adultery, two divorces, an unlawful sale of liquor, and the bankruptcy of a member of parliament.[8]

John also revealed in that speech his belief that 'the aim of the advocate is victory':

> The trial has some resemblance to a formalised and bloodless combat.
> Within the rules of ethics, I repeat, the aim of the advocate is victory,
> and like the general, he adopts an overall strategy and such immediate
> tactics as he thinks best calculated to win the battle.

---

6 SLSA, PRG 1098/37/53, page 3. The subsequent references to this are found on pp. 4, 5 and 11.

7 Michael Abbott, already cited, p. 51.

8 *SASR*. In the single 1935 volume, *Deed v Liddle* at 188 and *Hopkins v Hopkins* at 295. In the 1936 volume, *Tonkin v Tonkin* at 100 and *Cotton v Cotton* at 191. In 1939, *Smith v Kite* at 79 and *Stott v Parker* at 98.

He gave some advice on the cross-examination of a witness who was trying not to avoid certain topics. His advice was to approach the topic obliquely and using pure logic: 'If x is true then x1, x2 and x3 must be true. You must approach the witness with these, to "shut the gates", and eventually he can only admit that x is true.' John also admitted himself that 'in some unhappy cases, or course, Counsel is in the same position attributed to the proverbial philosopher, a blind man in a dark room at midnight looking for a cat that isn't there.'

This dilemma may have been uncomfortably close to the truth when John appeared, in 1947, for Mr Satterley who was appealing against a conviction for theft before Justice Mayo. Mr Satterley had been convicted in the Police Court for illegally taking three containers of salvage material from his employer, Hendon Small Arms Ammunition Factory. He had told the police officer that he had not purchased them, then later attempted to convince the magistrate that he had, but producing a receipt in someone else's name. It did not seem like the most winnable of cases. Employees at Hendon Small Arms, which was owned by the Commonwealth, were not allowed to sell themselves waste material. Management overlooked transactions if they did not appear in the employee's name. Thus a receipt for the fictitious Packer and Sons was created for Mr Satterley.

Regardless of accepted practice, these transactions were illegal and for a reason not on record, someone reported them. Once charged with taking from the Commonwealth, under s 21C of the *Crimes Act* then, 'the burden of proving that the act was done with lawful authority' was on Mr Satterley. John argued firstly that his client had a receipt for the goods, but Justice Mayo was not convinced:

> How can a sale of three stainless steel containers to the appellant be evidenced by entries of sales of timber, or timber and iron, to Packer & Sons, or any other person, or persons, real or imaginary?[9]

---

9   *Satterley v Palmer* [1947] SASR 346 at 350.

Although section 21C only required a level of probability from a person accused of a theft that they had lawful authority to possess the goods, Mr Satterley's receipt fell short. It also did not help that he had initially denied any purchase had taken place when questioned by the police.

John then tried a defence based on that actual 'taking' of the goods. A truck driver called Burdett who also worked at Hendon Small Arms had delivered the containers, and so John argued that it was he who took the containers, not his client. But Justice Mayo did not accept this, answering that Mr Satterley was fully aware of the fact he did not have legal authority to take the goods – either directly or through a delivery:

> The fallacy of the appellant's contention can, I think, be demonstrated. Where an employee directs a co-employee, who is his junior, to perform an act, such as the delivery of specific goods at a stated destination, the act being within the scope of the usual duties of the subordinate, the carrying out of that direction does not clothe the mandate so given with authority and regularity, if actually these characteristics are wanting.[10]

The black cat simply was not there. The appeal was dismissed.

John had more luck the following year, 1948, when he succeeded in an appeal and won the praise of Chief Justice Sir Mellis Napier for his argument. The case was an example of many Magistrates Appeals that John would take on over the course of his career at the bar where there were signs of a police set-up. This was the period when South Australia still had extraordinarily severe laws on the sale of alcohol and the police were under pressure no doubt to reduce breaches of these laws.

The evidence of a set-up is obvious even now from the circumstances of the charge. A young part-indigenous man, Tommy Nettoon, claimed he purchased two bottles of wine from Mr Davies, who lived in a small street in the west of Adelaide's central business district. The only two witnesses to this purchase were two police officers, who were watching this happen,

---

10   *Satterley v Palmer* [1947] SASR 346 at 351–2.

apparently unnoticed. Mr Nettoon claimed to have paid for the wine with a 10/- note.

After Mr Davies allegedly handed the two bottles of wine to Mr Nettoon, who importantly did not go inside, the two police officers arrived and charged Mr Davies with selling alcohol on his premises. They found no evidence of any kind to support their allegation – no 10/- note, no stock of wine matching that in Tommy Nettoon's possession – just 11 bottles of beer and 12 bottles of port. Despite this, s 267(4) of the *Licensing Act* then in force permitted that 'the presence of two or more persons shall be *prima facie* evidence of such a sale.' Because Mr Davies's son was present, and a boarder, Mrs Benton, Mr Davies was found guilty in the Magistrate's Court.

How such an extraordinary law ever was passed is not within the scope of this biography, but John Bray immediately spotted the weakness in the whole prosecution argument when he took the appeal to the Supreme Court. Justice Mayo, who would not always agree with John's defences elsewhere, wrote:

> On the appeal to this Court, I have had the assistance of counsel, and I am indebted to Dr Bray for an interesting argument upon the construction and application of s. 267 (4). If it had been necessary to deal with all the points that were raised, I should have taken time to consider my judgment. But the one point, upon which I think that I can dispose of the appeal, is Dr Bray's submission that s. 267 is inapplicable to the circumstances of this case.[11]

At the opposite end of the bar table the Crown Solicitor, Albert Hannan KC, argued that the sale took place *on* the premises. John pointed out that Tommy Nettoon had not been inside, and therefore the sale, if there was one, could only have taken place *from* the premises, not on it. 'That may be a fine distinction', agreed Justice Herbert Mayo, 'but this is a very drastic section, and, although it must be applied according to its terms, I do not think that it ought to be extended, by a liberal construction, to any case

---

11   *Davies v O'Sullivan.* [1948] SASR 9 at 11.

that is not really within its purview.' He allowed the appeal and quashed the conviction.

That same year Justice Mayo disagreed with one of John's fine linguistic arguments in a deceased estate. John represented the eldest of the seven children of a man who in 1940 pre-deceased his mother. She had included him in her will with her other three sons, stating quite clearly: 'I give unto my sons A.T.F, W.F, F.F, and C.F all my real and personal estate which is to be sold at my death and all moneys from the said sale is to divide between my sons, namely [and she again named them each]'.[12] The dead son – 'A.T.F' – was, however, illegitimate, and under the *Wills Act* 1936–40, sons had to be legitimate.

John claimed 'that the testamentary references to "my sons" and the inclusion of the *prepositus* in that description, should be treated as meaning that the testatrix acknowledged him as her legitimate son so that all the benefits of legitimacy should apply to the gift of his share.' Justice Mayo agreed from the genetic point of view, but not from the legal one. It was not possible to legally recognise an illegitimate child just by drawing a will and including them. He went on to discuss interpretations of the 'child', of 'lapse' in cases of pre-deceasing, the evolution of the status of illegitimate children, and the notion of 'issue', drawing on a vast range of authorities dating back to the 18th century. Finally, Justice Mayo agreed with the second part of John's argument, that s 55 of the *Administration and Probate Act* 1919–1937 allowed for illegitimate children to have the same rights as if they were legitimate, and that also applied to their succession.[13] Thus he ruled finally that the children of the late 'A.T.F' were entitled to the quarter-share left to him by their grandmother.

John was again before Justice Mayo the following year in his first reported complex civil case, *Executor Trustee v Insurance Office of Australia*.[14] In November 1947 a truck with six people collided with a train near Port Germein in South Australia's mid-north. The four people on the buckboard

---

12 *Estate of E.F deceased*. [1948] SASR 97 at 98; 99–103 for the ones following.
13 As above, at 101–102.
14 *Executor Trustee v Insurance Office of Australia* [1949] SASR 337.

and the driver died. The sole survivor, the passenger in the cabin, was suing for compensation from the Commonwealth Railways Commissioner. The driver of the train had not been found negligent during the initial inquiry, but he had died from unconnected causes before the truck passengers' insurance claims against the Commonwealth Railways were settled.

The firm E J C & L M Hogan briefed John to help represent their client, The Insurance Office of Australia, who was the Railways' insurer. There were three King's Counsel and five junior Counsel at the bar table. Joe Nelligan KC and his junior, Mr Reilly, represented the deceased plaintiffs, Ernest Phillips KC and his junior, Miss Roma Mitchell, represented the surviving passenger, Mr Bettison, John juniored Mr Hogan, and Harry Alderman KC with a Mr Mills represented the Commonwealth Railways Commissioner. The trial took place in the middle of 1949 and Justice Mayo delivered his judgment at the beginning of August.

In essence, the plaintiffs were arguing that the train driver's testimony at the coronial inquiry could also demonstrate negligence by the Commonwealth Railways. Counsel for the Insurance Office of Australia argued that the testimony was only relevant to the driver. The Railways Commissioner argued that the train driver's testimony had no authority to represent the Commissioner and should not be admitted as evidence in the claims.

John argued on the finer points of the *Road Traffic Act* 1934–1936, notably s 70d(2), which looked at insurance liabilities. He had found a British case from 1747 to illustrate the way this section should be interpreted, which in turn had been on the interpretation of the *Middlesex Registry Act* in 1708. But the Judge did not believe the approaches in those cases applied:

> That the language used in Part IIA involves a consequence the legislature did not really intend (if that be so), is a matter for that body, and not for the courts. The scheme may seem "lopsided" or imperfect to persons interested. It may be faulty. Nevertheless, if it is to be rectified, that alteration is for Parliament.[15]

---

15   As cited above, at 349.

This clarification of the role of the Court would later match exactly that of John's when he was Chief Justice and faced with the same need. Justice Mayo awarded amounts for the family of the deceased members and over £4000 for the survivor.

John's reported cases for the 1950s average four or five per year and always include divorces. Despite many appearances in the High Court from the late 1950s, he has only one reported case in the CLR's, one involving his own father challenging a cousin's extraordinarily eccentric will, which we will come to later. Astonishingly, John never seems to have used his doctoral research at all during his career. With the title, 'Bankruptcy and the winding up of companies in private international law', he must have been at the time of its awarding in 1937 one of the most highly qualified international corporate lawyers in Australia.

The closest he came to a case involving private international law was a divorce case in 1955, *Morris v Morris*, in which he successfully defended his client in Adelaide against an unfavourable divorce ruling from Kenya. His client, Mr Morris, had in fact never lived in Kenya, and this was crucial to the final ruling in South Australia. He and his wife were living in England in early 1950 when they decided to emigrate to Australia. They agreed for him to go first and establish himself. She would look after the sale of their house, and then come to Australia via Kenya, where her sister Molly had lived for many years.

In Kenya Mrs Morris found her sister very ill and, with the agreement of her husband, she stayed and cared for her sister, who later died. Mrs Morris stayed on to settle Molly's affairs. In June 1951 she wrote to her husband who had now found a job in Woomera, advising him that she wished to remain in Kenya. This commenced an exchange of letters in which Mr Morris implored his wife to change her mind, and in her replies she maintained she would stay.

Mr Morris moved to Adelaide in 1953, even more hopeful no doubt of changing his wife's mind. But in March 1954 he was served with a petition for divorce issued by the Supreme Court of Nairobi, alleging desertion as the reason.[16] Mr Morris sought legal advice and his solicitors sent an objection to the jurisdiction to the Court of Nairobi. He also began his own petition for divorce, supported by the many years of letters from his wife that showed quite the opposite of what she claimed. Mr Morris repeatedly had urged her to leave Kenya and come to South Australia with him as had been their original plan.

Strangely, they heard nothing back, but Chief Justice Napier was able to discover that the Nairobi Court on 8 October 1954 had issued a decree nisi, presumably being made absolute around 6 January 1955.[17] Mr Morris appealed on December 7, 1954 with John Bray representing him. The key question to address was whether Nairobi had jurisdiction in this particular case in South Australia, as within Commonwealth countries using the common law system mutual jurisdiction is generally accepted. Mellis Napier acknowledged an earlier case in South Australia 'where the Court of Appeal held that it would be "contrary to principle and inconsistent with comity if the courts of this country were to refuse to recognise a jurisdiction which *mutatis mutandis* they claim for themselves".'[18]

The key to jurisdiction in this case was whether both parties were resident in Kenya at the time of the alleged desertion. Mr Morris had never set foot there, and they were both in England when he left for Australia. Chief Justice Napier ruled that his court could not concede jurisdiction to Nairobi in these circumstances, and having read the collection letters from Mrs Morris over the years since they parted in England, he granted an order nisi for divorce to Mr Morris on the grounds that it was he who had been deserted by his wife, not the other way round.

John was appointed Queen's Counsel on 28 March 1957. He had been in court on several days earlier that month in an appeal against a murder conviction

---

16 *Morris v Morris* [1955] SASR 80 at 82.

17 As above, at 83.

18 As above, at 84.

in February, and had been successful in having the conviction reduced to manslaughter. This was very important when the difference then was being hanged or imprisoned.

This was not only John's first win in the South Australian Court of Criminal Appeal but a rare event in the greater arena of South Australia's courts then. Michael Abbott put it into context:

> The year 1957 saw no other reported successful criminal appeal based on the errors in trial judges' ruling or directions. Indeed the Court of Criminal Appeal was then well-known for its reluctance to criticise the conduct and rulings or directions of trial judges.[19]

The Fredella appeal hung on the finest of points. He had been convicted on the probability rather than certainty of circumstantial evidence. Margaret O'Connell had been living with Mr Fredella in a precarious relationship in the same house as Mr Fredella's mother and his nine-year-old daughter from a former marriage. In the early hours of Sunday morning, 23 December 1956, Margaret was found dead in bed from injuries she had received Saturday afternoon.

She had around 50 or 60 bruises and abrasions to her body from her face to her legs, and many internal ones including to her pancreas, bladder, intestines and liver. The liver had been ruptured by a ten-centimetre tear and in the trial the two medical witnesses, Dr Dyer and Professor Cleland, disagreed strongly about how this rupture may have occurred. Dr Dyer argued that it was 'utterly impossible' that Ms O'Connell's injuries could have been caused by the repeated falls that Mr Fredella and his mother claimed to have taken place, while Professor Cleland only went as far as to say it was 'not likely'.[20] The Fredella's story was that Ms O'Connell had suffered up to ten epileptic seizures, and that she had fallen each time from her chair. Professor Cleland said the liver injury could have come from falling on a broken chair, if Ms

---

19   Michael Abbott, quoted before, *Portrait of John Bray*, p. 53.
20   *R v Fredella* [1957] SASR 102 at 109.

O'Connell had fallen from a height 60 cm in addition to her own. In court Mrs Fredella proved an 'unconvincing witness'.[21] Mr Fredella had conflicting stories about his presence at the time these injuries occurred. Both he and Ms O'Connell had been drinking heavily all day.

They had sent Mr Fredella's nine-year daughter, Sonya, by herself to the cinema and she gave unsworn evidence in the trial that she had returned home around five o'clock that Saturday afternoon. She said that she saw 'Mrs Fredella holding the appellant's hand, and saying "stop it", while the appellant was saying "let go". According to Sonya, 'there was blood and water on the deceased's dress.'[22] This was crucial to the prosecution, as except for Sonya's eye-witness account, they had little to prove beyond doubt that Mr Fredella had assaulted Ms O'Connell.

On appeal, John referred to sections 12 and 13 Evidence Act 1929–1955 that unsworn testimony from children under ten cannot be used to convict if the accused denies the charge and there is no corroborating evidence to support the child's testimony. Justice Mayo did not agree that the girl's testimony was crucial to the conclusion that Ms O'Connell's injuries could only have been caused by an assault:

> We think that it is a matter of common sense, that the blow on the back
> of the head, the rupture of the liver, and the bruising of the intestines
> and of the bladder would involve at least three separate accidents. Is it
> feasible that any one of these accidents would have left the deceased
> capable of doing what it is suggested that she did? It seems to us that
> it is not, and that common sense excludes the hypothesis suggested by
> the defence.[23]

The judge thus concluded that the only explanation for the injuries was that Mr Fredella was responsible for them, but he was less confident of the existence of 'malice aforethought' necessary for a murder conviction:

---

21   As above, at 107.
22   As above, at 104.
23   As above, at 109.

In our opinion the verdict was not unreasonable, but we gather that *Ligertwood* J. would not have regarded a verdict of 'guilty of man-slaughter' as in any way unreasonable. On that we are disposed to agree with the learned Judge. The finding of homicide proceeds upon the view that this was the violent act of a drunken man, but a man in drink may not realise or intend the natural and probable consequences of the violence that he is using, and, on this issue of intent, the unsworn testimony might have a very important bearing.[24]

From Sonya's account, the Judge inferred that Mr Fredella was in an emotional state. His life was saved, as in those days murder was still a hanging offence.

Genders Wilson & Bray appeared to be no less conservative than any other Adelaide firm of the day. All the partners were graduates not only in law from The University of Adelaide but had also been schooled at St Peter's College. Sir Keith Wilson was a founding member of the Liberal Party of Australia with Prime Minister Sir Robert Menzies and was the Member for the federal electorate of Sturt. He was, however, the only member of the Adelaide Club at that time.

Yet in 1957 Genders Wilson & Bray did the almost unthinkable at that time and employed a young female lawyer, Pam Cleland, who had just been admitted. Coincidentally, Justice Herbert Mayo decided at the same time to try a female associate and Pam had to turn down his offer. She turned 30 that year and had initially been a reluctant law student, taking it up primarily because it was not as expensive as other degrees. She completed a Bachelor of Arts after leaving school and had studied painting under Jeffrey Smart when he was still teaching in Adelaide: 'I had no intention of practising but Roma Mitchell, the star of the women lawyers, persuaded me to go into articles and with her.'[25] Pam began articles under Roma at Nelligan Mitchell and O'Grady, but was still not convinced and left for an extended trip to America:

---

24   As above at 114.
25   Pam Cleland, private correspondence to John Emerson, 2009, for all these three quotes.

That is another story and pretty disastrous but I learned my Mercantile Law Textbook almost by heart and returned with a new enthusiasm for Law. Nelligan Mitchell and O'Grady were a perfectionist firm and great teachers and great personalities.

The firm initially employed Pam Cleland for one year as a solicitor but the situation changed rapidly:

> John Bray took silk and needed a junior, Alex Genders decided he wanted to go to court as little as possible, Bunny Abbott did not go to court and Keith and Ian Wilson were in Canberra most of the time. Far from no court work, it was like jumping off the end of the jetty.

Apart from being the firm's first female lawyer, Pam stamped her artistic personality by painting her room yellow with purple skirtings, possibly a unique decorative event in the history of South Australia's law profession. She would become not just John's junior in the years to come but they would develop a friendship that would endure until John's death. More than 30 years later, she wrote to John:

> Brian is right that you are one of "the greats". It has been my desire in life to "BE" even if it tears out my hair. In Adelaide with its rectitude (so well described in one of your earliest poems) one does not receive much support for such an attitude except from people like you, Fred Thönemann and my now deceased friend Kay Collins together with correspondence with such people as C G Jung and Aldous Huxley. But to you I am grateful for your wonderful friendship. I thank you for a cheerful party; there will be lots more.[26]

The 'Brian' to whom she refers is Brian Medlin; Fred Thönemann was Pam's twice-married husband (1960 and 1990). Kay Collins assisted Pam in the yellow-painted office, adding an aquarium and a small forest of ornamental

---

26 PRG 1098/1/25. Bray Papers, SLSA. Letter from Pam Cleland to John Bray, dated 19 September 1989.

plants. The letter highlights John's fundamental acceptance of people, of individuals more correctly, perhaps subtly a sign of his awareness of his own frustrated desire to 'be' who he really was. And in turn, Pam encouraged John's development.

The year 1957 was a cornerstone year in John's life. Now he was silk he began keeping transcripts and materials from his cases. He appeared to take both his legal and literary careers much more seriously. The bulk of the papers his executors left to the State Library of South Australia are from this post-1957 period. They show he was increasingly asked to review books for national literary publications and give speeches at literary events. He began preparing a collection of his own poetry for publication. He became a fully-fledged member of Charles Jury's poetry group, and found himself an increasingly prominent member of Adelaide's literary and artistic community. And he remained a 'bachelor', living at home, showing not the slightest interest in dating or marriage. There was a Peter Pan side to John, despite him being treated more and more seriously, a side perhaps that wanted to be the boy that never had to go to boarding school.

Chapter 8

CHARLES JURY DIES

Say, Austral Muse, what kinship can be thine.
What correspondence, with the sacred nine?
The lyre empower'd Calliope's great son
To make lions tame and rivers cease to run.
Can thy child charm the lively kangaroo,
Or dam the Murray, with the didgeridoo?

John Bray, from 'Address to Various Personages'

The first half of 1958 was a happy period in John's life. His life was framed within a reassuring pattern of recurring events. The workdays began with the daily walk from Hutt Street down Pirie Street to work, and often finished with drinks at one of the 90 or more city hotels before closing time at 6 pm. He rarely worked after hours, only if a trial needed it.

Other times he walked to Charles Jury's house in Archer Street. Brian Medlin would join them after lectures at the University of Adelaide:

> He would join in these readings and discussions and was often amazed and amused by my naïve dealing with classical authors, and from there we would walk home to Hutt Street, sometimes at six o'clock, sometimes at three o'clock in the morning.[1]

Saturday mornings John lectured in Roman Law at the University of Adelaide during semesters before heading to the South Australia Hotel opposite Parliament House on North Terrace. Here he met Charles Jury,

---

1   Brian Medlin, Interview with John Emerson, see Bibliography.

Brian Medlin and passing acquaintances for pre-lunch drinks. Sometimes they would lunch at 'The South', sometimes on sardines with milk on toast at Charles Jury's flat, sometimes continue drinking until dinner time.

Friday and Saturday nights were almost a ritual, reserved for the Amateur Sports Club. John exchanged erudition for larrikinism, most often with Jack Davey. Brian Medlin recalled one incident that showed that neither of the two men cared much about the nature of what they were drinking. John had his own key and often he and Jack would let themselves in:

> Davey was blind and Bray was – what would you say – visually impaired, and they used to get a flagon of white wine and drink it. On this occasion they were drinking this flagon of wine. It was pretty strong wine. They'd drunk half the flagon and the barman came in, and he said, "What are you doing, drinking vermouth?"[2]

Peter McCusker joined Bray and Davey in later years and discovered that some of their dialogue was 'of a more serious kind'.

> They pondered the human state and their own attitudes. Bray would express annoyance at the charge that he was a promoter of the permissive society. For him human nature was imperfect. Its imperfection did not shock or outrage him though at times it would sadden him.[3]

Peter was impressed that neither Bray nor Davey were concerned whether their views conformed with popular opinion:

> They would talk of literature and poetry, Bray's great love. Bray's discussion of literature was brilliant; his recall of passage and verse Olympian. Davey's was far less than Bray's yet his knowledge was impressive. Bray would entertain with dramatic deliveries of the soliloquies of Shakespeare and the verses of Byron, Shelley, Blake or other poets whose names arose in conversation.

---

2   Brian Medlin, Interview with John Emerson, see Bibliography.
3   'Bray and Davey', Peter McCusker, *The Adelaide Review*, September 1995, p. 34.

These varied discussions would go far into the Saturday nights. Brian Medlin remembered Bray 'would drink until the wee small hours of the morning, then miraculously appear at 9.30 or 10 o'clock on the back lawn with a pile of books that many of us would have regarded as the library – and read these. He read at an enormous rate and he remembered everything he read'.[4] His photographic memory and wit needed little sleep to thrive.

Other activities repeated over a monthly cycle. There were the Library board meetings, generally sober, and the XX Club meetings, generally less so. Friday nights once a month since May 1957 were poetry nights at Charles Jury's flat in Archer Street. One the first Sunday of each month Colin and Gwenneth Ballantyne held open house at 77 Kingston Terrace, North Adelaide, beginning 5 pm. Peter Ward recalls:

> Theatre people, academics, writers, artists, journalists, some professional men and women and the occasional left-liberal politician attended the 'Dos,' with as many as 100 people turning up monthly, often bringing their own flagons of rough red, though under Gwenneth's management they were always decorous gatherings. Bray and Jury attended regularly, the young MP Don Dunstan very occasionally. It was at a 'Do' that Bray and I first met, sometime in 1956 I think.[5]

Colin Ballantyne had directed the plays of Charles Jury, John Bray and Brian Medlin in 1955, and was one of Adelaide's leading amateur theatre producers.

In March 1958 John led another major criminal case, a murder trial in Port Augusta, with a young lawyer called Len King. Bray and King, two future chief justices of South Australia, represented Malcolm Howe, 24 years old, who was charged with murder.

The trial began on the 24 March, Justice Ross finished his summing up for the jury at half-past eleven on the 27 March, and they returned at a

4   Brian Medlin, Interview with John Emerson, see Bibliography.
5   Peter Ward, *Memoir* prepared for John Emerson.

quarter-past two with a guilty verdict. They did not believe Howe's claim of self-defence entirely, but did recommend he be sentenced with mercy. Justice Ross sentenced Mr Howe to hang as the law obliged him but forwarded the recommendation for mercy to the government.

Malcolm Howe had admitted shooting Kenneth Millard in the back, stealing a large sum of money from his wallet and leaving his body by the side of a deserted road past the Port Pirie airport on 13 November 1957. Howe claimed that Millard had attempted to attack him sexually, and that in defending himself he had shot Millard in anger.

The odds were stacked against Malcolm Howe. Apart from his own word, his defence was supported only by the fact that his shirt was torn and that Kenneth Millard had been found with fly open and that for some unknown reason he was not wearing undergarments.

Howe had invited Millard to see a film at the Port Pirie drive-in theatre that Tuesday night, and before going they drove out in Howe's car to a deserted spot beyond the airport to share a bottle of wine. Howe claimed that Millard had leaned over and unzipped his fly. He told Millard to get out of the car but got out as well and it was then that Millard grabbed him and in his flight from this second attack his shirt tore.

Howe happened to have a loaded .22 repeating Remington rifle under the driver's seat from a rabbit hunt the previous night. He went back to the car, took the rifle, and shot Millard who must have been either retreating by this time or facing the other way.

Besides this, it was discovered that Mr Howe was finding it hard to repay his debts and that Mr Millard had recently both won a lottery and inherited some money. Howe stole around £80 from Millard's wallet – the equivalent of four weeks of his net wages from the local smelting plant. He admitted that he tried to put Millard's body in the boot of his car to bury it somewhere, but was not able to lift it. He went to the drive-in by himself after killing Millard and taking his money, then went to the Port Football Club and had dinner with some friends, and even remarked on the absence of Kenneth Millard.

Worse, although the jury did not know, Howe had previous convictions recorded for larceny and housebreaking. He had broken a good behaviour bond, been sent to Magill Reformatory, escaped, been sent back, and had subsequently reoffended. The Crown had argued at trial that the real motive for the killing was more probably robbery, and that the jury should reject the story of sexual attack. But even a killing in the course of a robbery may not be murder, as a murder conviction requires 'malice aforethought', or in this case, that 'the accused fired a rifle at the deceased with the intention of killing him or inflicting some serious injury'.[6]

In the trial, John had attempted unsuccessfully to convince Justice Ross to offer the jury the alternative verdict that Howe was guilty of manslaughter on the grounds of excessive self-defence. It was a novel defence that John found had been implicit in authorities dating that he cited as far back as *Cook's Case* in 1640.[7]

At the appeal in the Full Court made up of Justices Mayo, Reed and Piper, John was successful. John's copy of the transcript of the trial is available in his papers in the State Library, and large sections are underlined in blue, red, green and brown coloured pencil and occasionally coded with letters in the margin.[8] The code is lost but interested readers should feel welcome to visit the State Library and view the document and try their hand at interpreting the multicoloured system.

One paragraph underlined in brown has a large letter 'D' in the left-hand column. Another paragraph in red has an 'A' in the left column. At this point Malcolm Howe was in the witness box being examined: 'Millard lent over and grabbed my trousers and he touched my penis.'

Howe described that moment in more detail and the following is underlined in blue:

I thought it might be the effect of the wine in him.

---

6   *R v Howe* (1958) SASR at 104.

7   *Cook's Case* (1640) ER at 1063.

8   Bray Papers, SLSA, *R v Howe*, PRG 1098/33/12.

Then back to red: 'After he grabbed my penis, I didn't like any person to do that. It upset me.'[9] The next sentence is underlined in brown:

> We were outside the car, he ran at me and grabbed me by the shoulders. I struggled loose in my anger and I ran to the car. He caught me round the shoulder from behind. I started to run, I believe. He tore my shirt. Looking at the shirt – that is where he tore it. [the shirt is held up as an exhibit].

The following one is underlined in blue:

> Then I ran for the car, got the rifle out from the front seat and, in my anger I put it up and shot him."

John convinced the Full Court that the old law made a 'distinction between justifiable homicide and excusable homicide. Self-defence came into both of them, but the distinction is that in a case of justifiable homicide there is no necessity to retreat, but in the case of excusable homicide there is. Killing and resistance to felonious conduct is justifiable; killing and resistance to non-felonious conduct is excusable.'[10]

John argued that since sodomy was a felony, Malcolm Howe could justify not retreating from Kenneth Millard. But in not retreating, Howe may nevertheless have used disproportionate force in relation to the perceived threat, and if the jury decided that was the case, then he was guilty of manslaughter, not murder.

The Full Court found that Justice Ross in his directions to the jury, had directed them that if they believed Howe had been excessive in his response, then he was still guilty of murder.[11]

The Judges decided that John's argument about excessive self-defence should have been an option for the jury to consider. The Full Court did not wish to consider the facts again, and so although John had hoped they would

---

9   As above, *Howe* transcript, pp. 60–61.
10   Cited in Michael Abbott, *Portrait of John Bray*, p. 54, see bibliography.
11   *R v Howe* (1958) SASR at 124.

substitute a verdict of manslaughter for murder, they ordered a new trial instead.

The Crown appealed to the High Court of Australia to overturn this decision. John Bray and Len King appeared before five judges of the High Court in Sydney at the end of July 1958, against the Crown Solicitor Roderic Chamberlain (known as Joe).

Roderic Chamberlain was outraged by John's defence of excessive self-defence and was quoted in *The Advertiser* at the start of the High Court appeal as saying that this was 'a concept foreign to this branch of the law, and extremely dangerous.' He continued:

> It was not right, he said, for the court to allow a man's own belief that
> he was not using too much force to excuse him to the extent of making
> his crime only manslaughter.[12]

Jack Elliott gave many examples in his *Memoirs* of Chamberlain's reputation for not believing innocence existed in the criminal courts.[13] His description of excessive self-defence as being 'a concept foreign to this branch of the law' showed his limitations in understanding the common law. John had not invented anything, he had done nothing but identify a latent but existing principle and bring it to light.

Joe Chamberlain in another ten years would become John's enemy.

The High Court, led by Chief Justice Sir Owen Dixon, agreed with the Full Court's decision to order a retrial.[14] This was John's second success in the South Australian Court of Criminal Appeal whose reputation for so many years had been not to overturn verdicts, as well as being his first reported case in the *Commonwealth Law Reports*. The High Court's decision was also reported in detail in *The Advertiser* on Saturday 16 August, page 3. Mr Chamberlain's reaction is not recorded.

---

12   *The Advertiser*, Wednesday, 30 July 1958, p. 10.
13   Jack Elliott, *Memoirs of a Barrister*, p. 78.
14   *The Queen v Howe* (1958) 100 CLR 448.

Nevertheless, all did not run smoothly. John was unable to appear with Len King for Malcolm Howe as the Crown Prosecutor controlled the court listings and refused to schedule the new hearing dates to allow for John's availability. Joe Nellighan QC took John's place as Senior Counsel. Happily for Malcolm Howe he was found guilty of manslaughter and the principle of excessive self-defence John developed became known as the Howe Principle.

There was an epilogue. Twenty years later, Len King succeeded John as Chief Justice. He reclaimed control of the court listings from the Crown Prosecutor, to make sure that hearings were arranged to suit both parties.

Brian Medlin had started his tertiary study later than most students and in 1958, he turned 31 years old. He won a scholarship to study philosophy at Oxford and at the end of July, Prue and he left their humble quarters at the back of the great Bray house on Hutt Street and boarded a ship for England. They would be gone from Adelaide for eight years, until Brian was appointed the foundation professor of philosophy at the new Flinders University.

Particularly because Brian lived at Bray House, John missed him immediately, but there was some consolation that much of their time was shared with Charles Jury.

A few weeks later John found himself alone at the South Australia Hotel after his lectures on Saturday morning. There was no sign of Charles and so he walked to 210 Archer Street, knocked, and let himself in. He found Charles inside, lifeless and cold.

Charles had died the night before, Friday the 22 August. He was 65 years old. John had now lost the two friends he had met almost daily for the past seven years, and had been able to converse on any subject with that freedom that comes only with a rare few friends in the course of a life. Charles was even more than a close friend; he was nothing less than John's alter ego.

Charles was also from a wealthy Adelaide family and had gone to St Peters College. Like John he was attracted to the classic authors – Virgil, Horace, Homer, Euripides – but also English poets like Keats and Shelley.

He produced his first collection of poetry at 12 years old, and his second five years later. His parents were extraordinarily supportive, and subsidised both printings.

Unlike John, Charles did leave Adelaide and from 1913 to 1938, spending that period of his life based in England and on the European continent. He left for Oxford to study English at Magdalen College after matriculating at St Peters, then in 1914 he enlisted to fight in World War One. A hand grenade injured his leg seriously in France a year or so later and he returned. He spent months in hospital recovering.

After he obtained a First Class BA in late 1918 he returned to Adelaide briefly and his father set him up with sufficient funding so he would never have to earn his own living. This was an extraordinary sign of support for a literary vocation from a self-made wealthy father. In contrast, Harry Bray only ever tried to steer John towards conventional male pursuits, once buying him a toolkit, another time a motorcycle – neither were ever used.[15]

Charles returned to Adelaide again in 1921 and his mother endowed a chair in English at The University of Adelaide hoping to keep him in Adelaide. There is still a Jury Chair of English, but Charles only occupied it much later, after his definitive return in the 1940s. For now, he missed England.

He spent three years in Adelaide from 1930 and tutored in English. This is most likely when John met him, as a student, though the earliest record of their friendship is a letter from Charles in 1937 inviting John to meet him in Greece during his European trip.[16]

After the precocity of his pre-Oxford years, Charles became perfectionist and would only fully complete five verse plays and 50 poems during the rest of his life. They are works of art, exquisitely written, but their classical and Renaissance structures had to compete with bold new works in English by poets such as T S Elliot and Dylan Thomas.

---

15   Peter Ward, *Portrait of John Bray*, p. 4.
16   Bray Papers, PRG1098/1/36.

Charles aimed to be a Romantic poet at first. Then he changed his mind. In a letter to Ian Buttrose in 1936 Charles wrote that he tried to be the least and last of the Renaissance poets: 'I believe I can say that I have never cared a button – anyway not more than a dozen buttons – about being what is called modern, or up-to-date, or, as the word goes now, contemporary.'[17]

In 1938 when Charles returned to Adelaide his plan was to stay and continue writing poetry and try his hand at blank verse plays. As it turned out, it would be almost ten years before he would have a completely free run at full-time writing. World War II broke out and he joined an Intelligence unit until 1944, and he was based for several years in Brisbane.

After the war ended, he was finally accepted as the Jury Professor of English and remained four years before returning to full-time writing at the end of 1949. He lived in a flat on North Terrace in a building called Frome House, which was demolished to make way for Frome Street. In 1953 he moved to his final home at 210 Archer Street.

Around the time he returned to Adelaide at the end of the 1930s, he finished a long tragic play in verse, *Icarius*. This was printed in 1941 though not released until 1955.[18] It was Charles's swansong, a bold and revealing work that John discussed at an address to the University of Adelaide's English Association in 1960:

> This play is a conflagration of several myths. It handles with delicacy and pity the subject of homosexuality. The hero is a man who knows what he wants and that he can never get it. In the end he is torn to pieces by the maenads who represent here not only ecstasy but fruitfulness.[19]

According to Barbara Wall, Charles was inspired to write *Icarius* after reading Radclyffe Hall's *The Well of Loneliness*.[20] The publisher Jonathon Cape was

---

17   Letter dated 7 June 1936, cited by Barbara Wall in *Portrait of John Bray*, p. 99, see bibliography.

18   *Icarius* was printed by the Hassell Press, Adelaide, in 1941, but not released until 1955. See also Barbara Wall's article in *Portrait of John Bray*, p. 101.

19   *Emperor's Doorkeeper*, p. 29.

20   Barbara Wall, p. 100.

taken to court for publishing it; this was still 40 years before censorship of artistic works was rationalised. Charles had to subsidise the publication of *Icarius* and it was perhaps too esoteric to incite a similar reaction in Adelaide.

Over the 1950s Charles and John became equals in debates on literature. John may have been the apprentice when he wrote *Papinian* but after its performance in 1955 Charles began seeking John's advice. They met each Saturday morning, and usually during the week after work so correspondence is rare, but two or three letters survive, including one of John's of which he made a copy.

It shows the frank nature of their literary exchanges. John is blunt after receiving a manuscript from Charles in November 1956. 'I remained unconvinced', he wrote, and queried whether the work was an essay, a treatise or a brochure. Charles was classifying different rhythms in English verse. This is one of John's many queries:

> "Stricken owl" is a good case. You say (p. 6) that this is an anapaest. This means that the two syllables of "stricken" are equal to each other and together equal to "owl". I say that they are not. I say and will maintain under persecution that "strick" takes as least twice as long to say as "en". Indeed a case could be made for making "stricken" a monosyllable like "heaven".[21]

In November the following year Charles tells John he will bring along a manuscript that Saturday. There is no record of which work this was. This letter was dated 13 November 1957. John was rapid in his assessment. Just one week later, in a letter dated 20 November 1957, Charles is thanking John for his notes.

John in turn sent Charles another play he wrote for a critique, 'He that hath Ears'. This was never performed though in 1967 it got close when the University of Adelaide Footlights was considering it.

---

21   Bray Papers SLSA, PRG 1098/1/36. Letter to Charles Jury dated 8 November 1956.

Not all the correspondence was so erudite. Charles wrote to John on 27 January 1958 with instructions for looking after the house while he was away:

> Bread I'm afraid has to be bought at the shops, as described in the accompanying document. [...]

> The flagon of claret in the kitchen – the opened one – was opened yesterday evening and is still functioning quite well, but will probably begin to go off after tomorrow evening. Other flagons are in the cupboard, as described. Bottles in the living room, ditto.[22]

As far as we can gather from John's capabilities with alcoholic beverages, the opened flagon of claret did not have a chance to go off.

On the Monday after Charles's sudden death, *The Advertiser* published almost a full column and a photograph.[23] He was described as a 'distinguished poet, dramatist and scholar'. John was quoted as saying:

> He was a literary and classical scholar of profound though unostentatious erudition and a great force on the side of the angels in the cultural life of SA.

The President of the Classical Association of South Australia agreed, adding: 'hardly anybody in modern times had as high an appreciation of the relation between poetry and distinctive types of metre.'

John had only been a member of Charles's monthly poetry group since May the previous year, and he must have believed it was worth continuing. 'The Poetry' met at his home until his last year, when it moved to Barbara Wall's.

The loss of Charles and Brian looked like the end had come to the lively Saturday morning literary debates that had been part of John's life for over ten years. But in fact, it left John free to join the larger group of

---

22   PRG 1098/1/36. Letter from Charles Jury dated 27 January 1958.
23   Monday 25 August 1958, p. 3.

artists and writers that met at the Sturt Arcade Hotel on Grenfell Street. It was where John, a creature of habit, would spend each Saturday for the rest of his life.

Chapter 9

WATERSHED 1959

*'The master keys of power are held by comparatively few,
by those known collectively as the establishment'.*

John Bray, 1965

The Sturt Arcade Hotel had been built in the 1880s and stood on Grenfell Street, near the current entrance to the Regent Arcade. It had two storeys, with a wide first floor balcony extending over the footpath in the style of many Australian hotels of the period.

Colin Ballantyne was one of the champions of Adelaide's lively amateur theatre scene, and his successful photographic studio was just on the other side of Grenfell Street to the hotel. He ran the business with two partners, John Turner and Ray Templeton, and he was the official Art Gallery photographer.

> After work, Ballantyne, his partners and friends, and a number of his associates from what has been called the 'Little Theatre Movement' regularly drank in the Sturt Arcade's saloon bar at the fireplace end and the group became known as the 'Ballantyne School'. These were the days of 6 o'clock closing for hotels and the so-called '6 o'clock swill' when men – above 21 years; women were not allowed in bars and saloons – commonly sought to drink their fill before the bars closed. After 6 o'clock they were allowed about 20 minutes grace to consume all they had purchased before the hour.[1]

---

1   Peter Ward, 'A background memoir', pp. 1–2 for these quotes.

Around the corner Max Harris, the editor of *Angry Penguins* who had published the Ern Malley poems, had his own 'school' that met in the Rundle Hotel, on Rundle Street. Max was a partner with Mary Martin in the bookshop that remained one of Adelaide's leading independent bookstores until 2012. Mary was still at the bookshop, but by this time was only interested in India, and in 1962 moved there to spend the rest of her life.[2] Max had praised John's *Papinian* in the September 1955 issue of his occasional literary and cultural newssheet, *Mary's Own Paper*. Later he wrote for *The Australian* and regularly appeared on television. His daughter Samela became a journalist with *The Advertiser*.

In 1957, Mary Martin's Bookshop expanded and moved to the first floor of the Da Costa building in Grenfell Street, and the two literary schools merged at the Sturt Arcade. The following year, after Charles Jury died, John joined the group:

> I think it was at Ballantyne's invitation that he joined what was now becoming known as the 'Sturt Arcade School', attending after office hours, that is, for the swill, as well as on Saturday mornings. At this about this time the Sturt Arcade's publican, Peter Whallin, changed the ladies lounge, which was adjacent to the saloon bar, into what he called the 'Sturt Arcade Tap Room', where despite Mrs Whallin's execrable cooking, the whole group took Saturday lunch for many years until the mid-1980s.

Along with Colin Ballantyne and Max Harris, regulars included sharebroker David Tippett, Peter Ward and entrepreneur Horst Salomon. Horst later set up a restaurant opposite the Sturt Arcade Hotel, and often the group would lunch there. Horst was a vivacious German Jew who had once as a schoolboy accidentally met Adolph Hitler. In the 1970s Horst restored four two-storey terraces in Hurtle Square, one of which would become home to John, and the neighbouring one to Peter and his partner Dimitri. The Saturday group

---

2   Julie Lewis, 'Mary Maydwell Martin. *Australian Dictionary of Biography*. Online adb.anu.edu.au.

Colin Ballantyne, Max Harris and John Bray, around the mid-1960s.
Private collection.

varied by the week, and in one form or another would endure for the next 35 years. Barely had it formed when it became a centre of debate over a murder that would go on to attract international interest:

> Visitors included out-of-town writers, journalists, academics and artists – many of them participants in the then current public debates in South Australia and local notables such as Rohan Rivett and (once) Rupert Murdoch, both during the Stuart Affair. The school was agitated over the Stuart Affair and the continuation of capital punishment, and markedly over the continuing anti-democratic effects of South Australia's malapportioned electoral system, later dubbed the 'Playmander'.[3]

Max Stuart was arrested for murdering a nine-year-old girl in the last week of 1958 and the circumstances of his arrest and subsequent conviction, appeals and a Royal Commission, remain topics of debate 50 years later. He

---

3   Peter Ward, 'A background memoir', pp. 2–3, also for the preceding quote.

was an Aboriginal. It was not as simple as an example of prejudice against the indigenous peoples, who were still not counted as citizens. It exposed the cronyism of the Playford government. Stewart Cockburn, Playford's biographer, called the Stuart Affair 'the watershed of the Playford era':

> The event which marked, and still marks, it was not in itself remotely connected with politics. It was the brutal murder of a child in the State's far west. During the ensuing twelve months this killing was destined to provoke some of the most sensational developments in South Australian criminal and political history. Breaches were hacked in the wall of the hitherto impregnable Playford fortress through which disaffected opponents at last gained entry in force. They permanently destabilised the government and went on to accomplish, first, its de facto defeat in 1962 and finally its fall in 1965. The so-called Stuart Case was one of the principal catalysts which precipitated these events.[4]

By 1959, South Australia had been firmly under the control of its premier Sir Thomas Playford for 20 years. His leadership and outstanding achievements for the State seemed beyond reproach. He was responsible almost single-handedly for transforming South Australia into a modern industrial economy, from which it benefits to the current day. He was responsible for the establishment of the defence industry in Salisbury, the General Motors and Chrysler motor vehicle manufacturers, the Whyalla shipbuilding, the power plants, the Leigh Creek coal mine, major water pipelines, and public housing. Unemployment was almost non-existent, 46 people were officially unemployed out of a total population of 797,000; a figure unimaginable in the final Depression years when Playford was first elected.[5]

The economy was purring yet socially the population was not adjusting to the prosperity and mobility brought by their industrialisation. John alludes to it in an essay included in *Satura*:

4   Stewart Cockburn, *Playford: benevolent despot*. Published by Axiom: Kent Town, 1991, p. 292.
5   Stewart Cockburn, *Playford Benevolent Despot*, p. 84.

The Playford government energetically forwarded the industrialisation of the State. In so doing it prepared its ultimate defeat. [...] The difficulty of living technologically in the twentieth century and psychologically in the nineteenth century seems to have been obscurely felt.[6]

The Stuart Case exposed some of the less than fair practices behind South Australia's governing institutions. It accelerated changes already taking place that had been slowly eroding Playford's political dominance. One was the increasing challenge from Rupert Murdoch's *The News* to *The Advertiser*'s monopolisation of the media in South Australia. *The Advertiser* supported Playford's government. It also owned Radio 5AD, and between the two gave little voice to opponents to the Playford government. They had become almost invisible. But a young, ambitious Rupert Murdoch, who inherited *The News* from his father in 1952, with his editor Rohan Rivett, 'had begun to shake up and irritate the so-called Adelaide establishment.'[7]

A new medium of public communication also arrived in Adelaide that fateful year, 1959: television. Playford had been a regular radio guest but television required a visible theatrical presence, and he simply was not a theatrical personality. The young Labor Member for Norwood, Don Dunstan, was, and the Stuart Case was one of his early opportunities to use the new medium to his full advantage.

John did not have any official role in the Stuart Case itself. While those events were unfolding in the courts, John became involved in the organisation of the first Adelaide Festival of Arts.

The Advertiser's editor Sir Lloyd Dumas began seeking interest to establish a major arts festival in Adelaide similar to Edinburgh's International Festival. With John Bishop, Professor of Music at The University of Adelaide, they succeeded in gaining £15,000 of sponsorship from the Adelaide City Council and business leaders. John Bishop was appointed the first Artistic Director, and a retired army officer, Major-General R N L Hopkins, was

---

6   *Satura*, p. 170.
7   Cockburn, p. 297.

appointed CEO. The Board of Governors was mainly made up of the business leaders, whose names appeared on other boards in that time: Lancelot Hargrave (Lord Mayor), Arthur Rymill (former Lord Mayor 1950–54), Edward Hayward (owner of John Martin's department store, now a David Jones store), Roland Jacobs (Chairman of SA Brewing), Kenneth Wills (chairman of G & R Wills & Company), L C Waterman and Lloyd Dumas.

In June 1959, Major-General Hopkins invited John to submit a play for performance in the Festival. If accepted, it would run for six nights at Union Hall, and he would be paid a fee of £200. John submitted two plays, possibly 'A Word in Your Ear' and 'Not Without Honour'. In the copy John kept of the letter that accompanied the plays, we see his characteristic self-deprecation:

> I doubt, however, whether either of these plays, being in verse on historical subjects, although as the author I would naturally cherish them as literary works, are of the type which your committee is seeking.[8]

John's scepticism proved accurate and, instead of choosing his play, the Festival Board asked him instead to chair the Festival committee set up to select an Australian play. Colin Ballantyne was proposed as the producer. Other members of this committee would be Miss Margaret Day, from Rigby Publishing; Dr K W Thomson from the University of Adelaide's Geography department and Dr Brian Coghlan, from German Studies.

The Festival Board membership, although strong in its business ability, was made up of those who held 'the master keys of power', to use John's words, 'known collectively as the establishment'.[9] John would find himself in conflict with their artistic choices as a result of chairing the Australian Play committee. The Festival Board supplied his committee with 26 plays and asked them to recommend four from which the Board would choose the ultimate winner.

---

8   Letter dated 19 June 1959, Bray Papers 1098/92.
9   *Satura*, p. 173. 'The master keys of power are held by comparatively few, by those known collectively as the establishment'.

John and his three other committee members read through the plays and recommended that the winner be chosen from Alexander Hay's *Peter Abelard*, Alan Seymour's *The One Day of the Year*, Gabriel Larson's *The Beast in View* or R L Thossell's *For Salour*. Major-General Hopkins wrote back thanking the committee for their efforts.

They were therefore surprised to read in the *Sunday Mail* on 4 October 1959 and in *The Advertiser* 5 October 1959 that the Festival Board had chosen a play which had not even been among the 26 they had so dutifully read and critiqued. Instead, the Board announced that the Australian play would be Alex Symons's *Goodbye to Number Six*. John was quite shocked and wrote to Major-General Hopkins: 'I heard nothing further about the matter until I read in the press recently that it had been decided that a play by Mr Symons should be performed at the Festival, a play which was not one of those submitted to me and my fellow judges.'[10]

The problem, he said, was that the public believed that his committee were responsible for the choice of the *Goodbye to Number Six*:

> We desire that an announcement should be made stating that the play in question was not chosen by or submitted to us. We feel it is right for us to take this attitude both out of regard to our own literary and theatrical reputations and in justice to the original entrants.[11]

Major-General Hopkins replied with a letter the next day stating that he would not release anything to the press.

John and his committee were very unhappy and discussed this for the next few weeks. John wrote again to the Festival CEO:

> Unfortunately we cannot agree that there is no room for misapprehension in the public mind. Instances have already occurred when it has been assumed that Mr Symons's play was selected by our committee. [...] For reasons made plain in my last letter this situation is intolerable

---

10   Bray Papers, PRG 1098/92.
11   Letter dated 19 October 1959, Bray Papers PRG 1098/92

to us and unjust to the original entrants. We think that it is absolutely necessary that we should be dissociated from the award.

We intend to make a public statement to the effect that the play selected by the Festival Executive Committee *Goodbye to Number Six* was not among the twenty-six plays submitted to us out of which we forwarded to you the names of four plays ranked by us in order of merit.[12]

John added that the members who had read *Goodbye to Number Six* nevertheless regarded the play highly, and that their public statement would also mention this to avoid embarrassment to the author.

Major-General Hopkins wrote back on the 17 November that he 'should hate to think that anything we had done is either intolerable or unjust' and agreed to John making his public statement. On the 19 November John sent a public statement to the editor of *The Advertiser*, Lloyd Dumas. Apart from being the very founder of the Adelaide Festival of Arts, Lloyd was also on its Board of Governors, and somehow Adelaide's major daily appears not to have published John's letter, or anything else on the surprise appearance of Mr Symon's play. This affair is a perfect example of the way the Adelaide Establishment operated.

The Festival opened in March 1960 and was such a success it has been held each second year since. It redefined Adelaide as the arts capital of Australia, and lifted Australia's arts profile firmly and permanently onto the world arts map. The Adelaide Festival of Arts retains its slightly stuffy image, which inspired the alternative Adelaide Fringe Festival, since grown to become the largest alternative arts festival in the world.

John reflected on the Festival at the end of an article 1965, published in the *Current Affairs Bulletin*:

And then astonishingly enough there is the Festival. Adelaide now holds a biennial Festival of Arts. There were festivals in 1960, 1962 and 1964. The claim to be the Athens of Australia has been not too seriously

---

12   Bray Papers as above, letter dated 13 November 1959.

advanced from time to time in the past, but it has now been made in earnest on a quasi-official level. Much has been said; more no doubt will in time be said, about the inner history of these festivals. To bring them about needed the combination of two factors: the establishment figures who provided the official organisation and the financial backing and the wilful, difficult, temperamental figures from the *terra incognita* of the arts who directed the artistic planning and execution.[13]

John concluded that it was 'a quirk of fate that the city of the respectable Dissenting and Benthamite dream, the city, the keynote of whose society Douglas Pike found to be a "nobly depressing rectitude", should turn out to be the sponsor of a recurring Festival of Arts on such an ambitious scale.' Up until 1994, John never missed a Festival, and was usually among the poets who gave readings during the accompanying Writers' Week.

Meanwhile that year, the Stuart Case had grown to catch the world's attention, unheard of in South Australian legal history. The crime was horrific. Nine-year-old Mary Hattam's body was found battered, sexually violated and callously abandoned in a cave near Ceduna, 800 km north-west of Adelaide. She had gone missing mid-afternoon on Saturday, 20 December 1958. Police arrived the next day from Adelaide, and elsewhere, to hunt the murderer. Police arrested Rupert Max Stuart on Monday 22 December, who on Saturday had been working with a travelling circus, since departed.

The trial was founded almost entirely on the confession police had obtained; on 24 April 1959 the jury pronounced Stuart guilty and Justice Reed sentenced him to hang. An appeal was heard in the Court of Criminal Appeal on 6 May based on the unreliability of the confession and the circumstances in which it was taken. Having failed, an application for special leave to appeal was made to the High Court, whose refusal was handed down on 19 June.

---

13   *Satura*, p. 177, and p. 178 for the following quote.

But how did it get past the Police Court with the glaring inconsistency in the time that Stuart was supposed to commit the murder? In the confession given to Police, Stuart states that he killed Mary Hattam before he went to work on Saturday at 2 pm. But Mary did not go to the beach until 2.30 pm, confirmed by her father Rupert Hattam who was the first witness to appear in the trial in the Supreme Court. Stuart was at work at that time.

The Crown Solicitor Joe Chamberlain KC, who had been the senior prosecutor in the trial, breached fundamental processes in his zeal to secure the successful prosecution of Max Stuart. The High Court in their reasons against hearing the appeal, criticised Chamberlain's behaviour twice. Firstly, about a negative comment he made to the jury about Stuart's refusal to give evidence and be cross-examined, describing 'such a comment as is forbidden by statute.'[14] Secondly, about a letter that Chamberlain had sent them about his personal opinion of Stuart's English ability while they considered the application for special leave: 'This communication we have entirely ignored and we do not think it ought to have been made.' The comments from the High Court inspired the Leader of the Australian Federal Opposition, Dr H V Evatt, himself a former High Court judge, to send a 600-word telegram to Tom Playford recommending an appeal to the Privy Council.

At the same time, the South Australian Police Association published a statement defending the police officers who had interrogated Stuart in Ceduna and obtained a confession in educated English. The President of the Association, Detective-Sergeant Paul Turner, also happened to be one of the six interrogating officers. The President of the South Australian Law Society, Leo Travers QC, issued a public statement stating that he was 'simply appalled' by the Police Association statement.[15] But, like Chamberlain, the police also let zeal guide them, and their single biggest error was that they did not, as required by law, have Ceduna's Aboriginal welfare officer present during their interrogation of Stuart.

---

14   Ken Inglis, *The Stuart Case*. Melbourne, Melbourne University Press, 1961, p. 49, and p. 50 for the following quote.
15   Cockburn, p. 294.

The two main players in Adelaide's *News* were its Editor-in-Chief Rohan Rivett and Rupert Murdoch. Both had been to Oxford. Rohan Deakin Rivett was the grandson of Australia's second Prime Minister Arthur Deakin, a close political ally of Premier Playford's grandfather who was a Minister in the first Federal parliament. Rohan's father Sir David Rivett had been Head of the CSIRO. After surviving the infamous Changi prisoner of war camp in World War II, Rohan joined Keith Murdoch's papers and was based in London, before his appointment in Adelaide. Rupert came to Adelaide directly from Oxford in 1952 after his father Keith died and left him the *News*. He lived just around the corner from the Brays, at 114 East Terrace.

In July 1959, just after the High Court rejected special leave to appeal, Rohan Rivett and Father Thomas Dixon met for lunch at the University of Adelaide staff club. Father Dixon was Stuart's prison chaplain and had come to seriously doubt that Stuart was guilty of the murder. Astonishingly, the defence at the trial of Stuart had not called any witnesses from the Funland Carnival with whom Stuart was working that fateful Saturday to confirm that he was working at the time that Mary Hattam was on the beach. The Carnival had moved on to Whyalla on Sunday and the Court had been content with the statements police took from its staff there. Father Dixon believed that the Funland proprietors and workers might, however, provide Stuart with an alibi at the time of the murder. Dixon was convincing enough for Rohan to offer him a flight to Queensland where the Carnival was now located, together with a *News* journalist, Jack Clark.[16]

This was the beginning of Rohan Rivett's personal interest in the plight of Rupert Max Stuart, and the *News* ramped up its coverage of the case:

> Dixon's journey was being logged on the front pages of every state. Everybody knew about it, except people who depended for news on the Adelaide *Advertiser*, in which the priest's name did not appear until after the Privy Council hearing. Until late July the *Advertiser* and the

---

16   Inglis, pp. 69–70.

News had given the case fairly similar treatment. The approaches now diverged widely.[17]

The *News* began publishing the statements Father Dixon and Jack Clark obtained from the proprietors of the Funfair Carnival, Norman Gieseman, and one of the girls, Betty Hopes. They most urgently were hoping to find Allan Moir, who had spent much of Saturday 20 December 1958 with Max Stuart, both working together at the Funfair and drinking together in between. He was with a separate part of the carnival but they found him in a remote little town in North Queensland.

Sometimes there would be four pages in the *News* dedicated to the Stuart Case. Headings included 'Priest: "Stuart has Perfect Alibi" Murder Case Bombshell' and captions like: 'Will he die?' During this time Rupert Max Stuart was about to be hanged after two reprieves and the pressure was to obtain a third reprieve. Stuart would obtain seven reprieves from hanging before the death sentence was eventually commuted to life imprisonment. At the same time, the editorials – written mostly by Rohan Rivett and occasionally by Rupert Murdoch – made it quite clear the *News* 'had no brief for keeping alive whoever committed the dastardly crime at Thevenard', they just wanted to do their bit to ensure that it was the right person.

On 30 July 1959 the South Australian government, under pressure from the unprecedented media attention, called a Royal Commission into the Stuart Case, and appointed Chief Justice Sir Mellis Napier to lead it with Justice Geoffrey Reed. But Justice Reed had been the trial judge and Justice Napier had sat on the Court of Criminal Appeal. The South Australian government was to immediately regret this short-sighted attempt to contain the Royal Commission's findings. The *News* editorial the following day criticised the choice of commissioners, the narrowness of the terms of reference, and included a cartoon depicting Tom Playford with two identical doctors under the heading 'Previous Judicial Opinion' and three more doctors identical to

---

17   Inglis, p. 74.

the first two under the heading 'Proposed Judicial Opinion'. The caption read: 'Blimey! Tom's not calling in the same docs again, is he?'

Ken Inglis in *The Stuart Case* believed that such a strong criticism of government in a South Australian editorial could have been unique. Newspapers normally avoid serious criticism of governments in office for the simple reason that if more readers voted for the government than not, good business means not alienating that majority. Inglis was a lecturer in History at The University of Adelaide and published *The Stuart Case* in 1961. John proof-read the manuscript and checked for any potential defamation risk. Ken Inglis later became Vice-Chancellor of the University of Papua and New Guinea and a Professor of History at the Australian National University.

The Royal Commission was due to begin hearing witnesses on the 17 August 1959. The single most important witness apart from Max Stuart was Allan Moir, who had only just turned 16 years old. He had worked with Stuart on the day Mary Hattam was murdered, and he had also been with Stuart on a number of drinking bouts. Police had only interviewed him once, and this was in Whyalla on the Monday after the murder, the 22 December 1958. This interview would turn out to be the catalyst that led to Sydney barrister Jack Shand QC, who represented Rupert, quitting and the *News* editor Rohan Rivett being sued for the way the paper reported the walk-out.

There was a great deal of nervousness when it came to Allan Moir. He was brought over from Queensland as a defence witness. Father Dixon and Helen Devaney, the second of Stuart's lawyers, booked a motel room for Allan and came to Adelaide airport to meet him. They were astonished to see two men cross the tarmac, and take Allan away by car instead of coming through the terminal:

> According to a reporter from the Melbourne *Sun*, a cameraman trying to photograph Moir was ordered off by one of Moir's escorts, who pushed him aside and trod heavily on his foot. Neither Stuart's lawyers

nor Moir's elder brother, who had flown from Western Australia to see him, could reach the boy on Sunday.[18]

The *News* the following day, the first day of the Royal Commission, responded with headlines: 'Action over Allan Moir called "denial of rights". Government Seizure of Stuart Witness Denounced'.

Jack Shand was one of Australia's most successful and respected barristers across all jurisdictions. First thing Monday morning after the Royal Commission began, he asked for an explanation as to why the defence had been not permitted to interview Allan Moir. Counsel for the Royal Commission, Jim Brazel QC took responsibility, explaining that he did not want Moir interviewed by anyone before his appearance. Shand was naturally not impressed, and even Sir Mellis Napier agreed that the defence should have been allowed to see Moir.

Moir's *de facto* abduction was another example of how the government at that time was quite ready to breach fundamental legal rights. On Tuesday, Don Dunstan asked in Parliament whether the Royal Commission had this right to take persons into custody. Playford disagreed that Moir had been in custody, but the *News* the next day asked 'under what law of this land was this action taken?' On Wednesday in Parliament again Don Dunstan pushed the question and Playford denied that Moir had been unlawfully detained.[19] But the fact is that he had been.

John was also present on the first day of the Royal Commission. He applied to represent Stuart's lawyer David O'Sullivan with Charles Bright, but was told the application was premature, and he could ask again when O'Sullivan's turn came for examining.[20] This was reported in the *News* on Wednesday 19 August with a photo of John. The first witness to be examined was Norman Giesemen, who owned the fun fair. After he spoke, John again rose and asked this time if he could question Mr Gieseman. Sir

---

18   Inglis, p. 101.
19   Inglis, p. 102.
20   Inglis, p. 103.

Mellis Napier asked him what questions he would be interested to ask, and John replied on Mr Gieseman's movements since the murder. Sir Mellis refused, saying: 'I cannot see how that affects you. Later on we will take it into consideration.'[21]

John tried at least twice to contribute to the Stuart Royal Commission without success. He probably never imagined that Jack Shand would quit the first Friday, and that the government would sue the *News* for their reporting of this, and that John would take the case and successfully defend them against incredible odds. He certainly never would have imagined that as a result of this success he would have a police file kept on him, that one day this file would be used to try and stop his appointment as Chief Justice, and ultimately contribute to the sacking of a future Police Commissioner.

Jack Shand's stated aim was to ensure Rupert Max Stuart had been treated fairly by the legal system, and that no doubt remained about his guilt. He made it clear at the start that the role of the Royal Commission was to find 'whether a man should die or whether he should not'.[22] Shand's cross-examinations of both Allan Moir and Sergeant Alexander Phin were crucial, as the statement Phin had obtained from Allan Moir in Whyalla led directly to Stuart's arrest.

Shand demonstrated that neither Moir nor Phin were reliable. Moir seemed incapable of providing a consistent account of the fateful day, and changing his account of several details back and forth. One of his most serious inconsistencies was his confused belief that Stuart had told him he had 'done someone in' called Lennie and wanted to take the body out to sea.[23] But as Ken Inglis pointed out in his book, no one – not Sergeant Phin, nor anyone else at any point in the rest of the Stuart Case, including during the Royal Commission – ever followed up who the mysterious Lennie was.

---

21   Inglis, p. 109.
22   Inglis, p. 104.
23   Inglis, p. 129.

Phin had very kindly given Allan Moir ten shillings and a cigar after he obtained his statement. But between his recollection of his conversation with Moir on Sunday night on 21 December 1958, which he did not take notes from, the statement he prepared for the illiterate Moir to sign on Tuesday 23 December, and the statement Sergeant Phin had prepared for the Royal Commission, there was a noticeable number of inconsistencies and omissions. One was about the timing of Moir's story of Stuart indecently assaulting a pregnant 'half-caste' woman at the cinema. This varied from Friday night to Saturday morning.

The fact that Phin had not taken notes of his initial conversation with Allan Moir worried Jack Shand, particularly as after this Phin rang Ceduna police and suggested Max Stuart as a suspect. Stuart's subsequent arrest was based on the flimsiest of foundations:

> Shand: I supposed you have sometime made a statement about your recollection of this conversation?
>
> Phin: Yes.
>
> Shand: When did you make that?
>
> Phin: Here in the city, just recently the 30th of last month [30 July 1959]
>
> Shand: Did you have anything to help you?
>
> Phin: No.
>
> Shand: You had nothing to refer to to help you at all?
>
> Phin: No, I had to rely on my memory.[24]

Phin had earlier used the seven-month delay to excuse discrepancies. But he also did not record another interesting piece of conversation with Allan Moir, this time on the Tuesday after Allan had signed his statutory declaration.

---

24 Transcript of the Stuart Royal Commission, pages 358–359, sourced from the Bray Papers, PRG 1098/30.

Phin told Moir that Stuart had confessed to killing the little girl and that he could hang:

Shand: What did he seem like then?

Phin: Then he seemed to realise the seriousness of the position. He put his hands over his face, and head forward and said 'Maxie, Maxie. I am sorry now I told you so much.'

Shand: 'I am sorry now I told you so much?'

Phin: Yes.

Shand: Was that all that was said?

Phin: Yes, as far as I can remember.

Shand: [...] You thought that was a genuine kind of remark?

Phin: Yes.

Shand: Did you ask him to add it to the statement?

Phin: No.

Shand: Have you made any notes of your conversation with him?

Phin: No.

Shand: You didn't make any at all?

Phin: No.

Shand: Did you consider when he had given you the whole of his statement it might bear on the murder of the little girl?

Phin: Yes.[25]

Shand shortly after suggested to Sergeant Phin:

---

25   Royal Commission into the Stuart Case, transcript p. 357.

Shand: For all you know he might have been the guilty person or one of the guilty persons?

Phin: Anyhow, I did not suspect him.

Shand: I am not asking that. For all you know he might have been one of the guilty persons?

Phin: Possibly so.[26]

John Bray had listed Allan Moir's comment in his own notes, 'Maxie, Maxie, I'm sorry now I told you so much' but without any note. Alexander Phin was quoted in a Whyalla paper that year as having said: 'When I was told that a little child's body was found foully murdered, and that the head had been battered in [...] I did not for a moment consider that outrage the work of a white man. I immediately thought it was the work of a darky.'[27]

Around a quarter past three on Thursday afternoon as Shand pursued his cross-examination of Phin, Sir Mellis Napier interrupted him. The Stuart Case was already daily front page headlines; this led to a whole new affair altogether:

Shand [to Phin]: Is that the one you say is the real explanation?

Napier: He is not obliged to explain anything.

Shand: If he says he can't explain it ...

Napier: It is for him to say whether he wishes to go any further or whether he wishes to leave his evidence where it is.

Shand: If you want me to stop cross-examining I will stop.

Napier: I have not the slightest intention of stopping you but as far as I am concerned I have heard enough of this.

---

26   Royal Commission into the Stuart Case, transcript p. 360.
27   Inglis, p. 12, fn 1.

The exchange between the two men went from bad to worse when Napier then said 'everybody makes mistakes'. After three more questions to Phin, Jack Shand asked for an adjournment 'to consider my own position as to what I intend to do'. That fateful Thursday, 20 August 1959, the Stuart Royal Commission closed for the day one hour early.

John and Cairns Villeneuve Smith, son of Frank who almost 30 years earlier had written to John foreseeing a great future for him, spent the evening with Jack Shand, encouraging him not to quit, but it was too late. He had made up his mind and he would announce it Friday first thing.

Friday morning's *Advertiser* covered the adjournment of the Royal Commission, but made a mistake about the reason Jack Shand had asked to consider his position. Just after Shand completed his three final questions to Sergeant Phin, Jim Brazel had introduced witness statements challenging gossip that Shand heard had been circulating in Ceduna that the police had bashed the confession out of Stuart. The *Advertiser* stated that because of these statements Shand had called for the adjournment. Their reporters did not understand the importance of Shand's reaction to Napier's interruption.[28]

The adjournment mid-Thursday afternoon happened too late for the Adelaide *News* that day. But they would be the first paper to report Friday morning's events, and the result would change the destinies of John, the newspaper's proprietor Rupert Murdoch and the newspaper's editor, Rohan Rivett.

---

28   Inglis, pp. 134–135.

Chapter 10

DEFENDING
RUPERT MURDOCH

I decline to answer that question on the grounds it may incriminate me.

Rupert Murdoch, repeated 28 times, in
R v News limited and Rohan Deakin Rivett

Jack Shand's exit just after 10 am from the Stuart Royal Commission Friday, 21 August 1959, was in itself brief and undramatic. Ken Inglis was among those present:

> When the Commissioners entered on Friday morning, Shand and his colleagues Miss Devaney and Smith sat in their places, but the table in front of them – covered the previous day with an untidy pile of papers and books – was bare, except for a copy of the *Advertiser* and a single sheet of paper.[1]

Shand firstly corrected the *Advertiser*'s reporting of him adjourning because of the changed witness statements and reminded the Commission that it had been only because of the interruption to his cross-examination. He then read his prepared statement, finally declaring 'the particulars have established that this Commission is unable properly to consider the problems before it and we therefore withdraw.'[2]

---

1   Inglis, p. 134.
2   Inglis, p. 135, and p. 375 of the Stuart Royal Commission Report.

Napier then chose to lecture one of Australia's leading Queen's Counsel, defending his interruption of Shand's cross-examination of Sergeant Phin as a means of 'omitting to waste our time on irrelevant matters'.[3] Shand must have wondered why he had come over to South Australia. He ended the exchange with the following sentence before walking out:

> Time and time again it happens, what might be considered severe cross-examination brings out the truth in other respects, and personally – in the cross-examination which no one suggests was unfair and which had some object – I have never in my career been stopped before.

Jack Shand flew out of Adelaide that same afternoon and, incidentally, was dead in six weeks from bowel cancer. The Stuart Royal Commission adjourned to allow a replacement Counsel for Stuart to be appointed.

Although he did not know it at the time, that afternoon would have a profound impact on John's life. It would also be a turning point in the direction of both the lives of Rupert Murdoch and Rohan Rivett. It began with two posters advertising that afternoon's issue of the *News*:

SHAND QUITS

"YOU WON'T GIVE STUART

FAIR GO"

and:

COMMISSION BREAKS UP

SHAND BLASTS NAPIER

The front page was dominated by a headline:

Mr Shand, QC, indicts Sir Mellis Napier

"THESE COMMISSIONERS CANNOT DO THE JOB"[4]

---

3   As above, and for the following quote from Shand.
4   The *News*, 21 August 1959, p. 1. John kept clippings from the entire Stuart Royal Commission in PRG 1098/30/7. See also Ken Inglis's comments, pp. 135–39.

On Monday, 24 August 1959, Shand's walkout filled the front pages of all the major Australian newspapers of the time, which included the *Sydney Morning Herald*, the Melbourne *Herald*, and Sydney's *Daily Telegraph*. Ken Inglis observed that not only was it 'unusual for the Sydney and Melbourne press to be devoting so much editorial attention to a single matter outside party politics', but also that these papers were all 'anti-Labor in policy'. Almost all criticism referred to the appointment of Napier and Reed as commissioners. Ken Inglis also noted that at no point did the *Advertiser* report any critical remarks of the Royal Commission, and in fact, 'Adelaide's only morning paper was giving less space than any morning paper in Melbourne and Sydney to an affair in its own city'. Inglis could not help but note that the 'solidarity of interstate comment, now and later, may have owed something to an unholy satisfaction that all this was happening in the holy city of Adelaide.'[5]

Monday's front-page headline of the *News* was 'QC's ATTACK JUDGES NAPIER AND REED, Mr Shand supported'. The accompanying article noted the interstate reactions:

> A group of Sydney barristers including two QC's issued a statement today which attacked statements made by two judges on the Stuart Royal Commission. A number of major Australian newspapers today carried editorials on the Stuart case questioning the composition of the Commission.[6]

The day ended with a personal tragedy for Sir Mellis Napier: his wife of over 50 years, Dorothy, died that night. She had been rushed to hospital the previous Wednesday and had not regained consciousness.

The Royal Commission was adjourned until Monday 31 August to discuss a replacement for Shand. The President of the Law Society, J L Travers QC, who had already written to the Premier complaining about the conduct of police early in the Royal Commission, now wrote again about his concerns for David O'Sullivan:

---

5   Inglis, p. 139.
6   *News*, 24 August 1959, p. 1.

He had expressed the personal view that the Society would take no part "in an enquiry which may be designed in some way to pillory one of its members after he had done a few thousand pounds worth of free work for the Government". He had mentioned that Dr J J Bray QC and Mr C H Bright were already attending the enquiry on behalf of O'Sullivan.[7]

He suggested Bray and Bright to represent Stuart. But Jack Shand advised Stuart through David O'Sullivan and his solicitor Helen Devaney not to be represented. That week was crucial to Stuart as he was due to be hanged on Monday, 31 August. The Government for the sixth time granted a respite, this time until September 30.

The Commission recommenced on 31 August, but pressure was building on Premier Playford. This included a letter, part of which was published, from the former Chief Justice of the High Court Sir John Latham, recommending a retrial. On Tuesday, in Parliament, the Opposition Leader Mr O'Halloran asked Playford for a debate on the Royal Commission and Playford refused.

Parliament sat at 2 pm on Wednesday and Mick O'Halloran introduced the first motion of no-confidence that the Playford government had faced in its 21-year rule. Don Dunstan, Labor member for Norwood, criticised the fact that the Stuart Royal Commission included three judges who had sat on the Stuart Case.

But Playford countered with his own attack. He produced copies of the posters and the day's paper from the previous Friday's *News*. He declared:

> These words were never spoken, yet they are put in inverted commas, and that is the sort of thing that has been used to try and drag our judges down. These words, or anything like them, were never spoken. They are the gravest libel ever made against any judge in this state.[8]

---

7   Inglis, p. 141, and pp. 142–144 for subsequent information.
8   Inglis, p. 162, and pp. 162–163 for the following.

Frank Walsh, a Labor member, asked: 'Why wasn't a libel action taken against them?' Playford replied that the government would 'consider action at the appropriate time to protect our judges, make no mistake about that.' He recommended 'a resolution of commendation to Sir Mellis Napier, who, in one of the most tragic times of his life, has been subject to the vilest abuse and yet has carried on his duties manfully, and, I believe, with great dignity.'

The debate lasted four hours and the following day, Wednesday 7 September 1959, the *News* published a very strong editorial in response, in addition to several articles on the previous day's developments in Parliament. The battle had begun:

> Let's set the record straight. [headline]
>
> Yesterday Sir Thomas Playford charged that we had engaged in a campaign to discredit the members of the Supreme Court who are sitting on the Royal Commission.
>
> Worse still, Sir Thomas Playford, under Parliamentary privilege, accused the *News* of alleging 'the vilest crimes' by his government and the judges.
>
> The *News* is quite prepared to defend itself at the appropriate time and in the appropriate place, as may be directed.[9]

The editorial made that point that the *News* had never argued that Stuart was innocent, only that he must be proven guilty beyond all doubt. The editorial concluded in italics and capitals:

> The News sees it as its duty to fight always not only for justice to be done, but for justice to appear to be done.
>
> WE MAINTAIN THIS STAND, AND WILL CONTINUE, WITH PRIDE, TO FIGHT FOR THIS IDEAL.

---

9   The *News*, Wednesday, 3 September 1959.

The Stuart Royal Commission would continue. The President of the Law Society, J L Travers QC, appeared on Wednesday 16 September, ostensibly to represent Rupert Max Stuart but he withdrew immediately: 'I can come to no other conclusion than that for some reason my presence in the Commission is not at all welcome.' The defence then produced John Starke QC from Victoria, who represented Stuart until the Royal Commission was completed.

On 5 October, South Australia's State cabinet commuted Stuart's death sentence to life imprisonment. The news made BBC headlines. Eventually, on 3 December the Royal Commission produced a report that, unsurprisingly, confirmed the verdict of guilty, that Stuart's alibi was not proven, and that the police had obtained the confession correctly.

A transcript of the entire Royal Commission is available at the South Australian Supreme Court library, or in John Bray's publicly available papers. Sir Mellis Napier's hostility to Jack Shand and any other matter concerning Stuart's defence steams off the pages. His attitude was appallingly biased. His appointment was the most serious error of judgment in both his and Playford's career. Many years, later, in 1977 Sir Thomas Playford admitted to Sir Walter Crocker:

> One decision I made in 1959 gave me considerable cause for concern. I consulted the Chief Justice about certain procedures. That was wrong of me. It would have been better if the Chief Justice was not involved. He should not have been my advisor.[10]

Sir Thomas would not give Sir Walter more details, but one can easily surmise that Sir Mellis had suggested himself to lead the Stuart Royal Commission.

In November that year, Charles Bright, who had sat with John each day of the Commission hearings recorded his personal observations on a dozen or so foolscap pages, and embargoed them until all the senior people had died.

---

10   Cockburn, p. 300.

They were accessed the first time only in January 2011. Charles Bright was born in 1912, the same year as John, and although he did his secondary studies at Scotch College he had known of John at St Peters College. Charles was appointed a Queen's Counsel in May 1960 and a judge of the Supreme Court of South Australia in 1963. He was a judge on the court all the way through John's tenure as Chief Justice, and retired just after him in 1978.

The first person Charles discussed was Sir Mellis Napier. He confirmed that Sir Mellis had a habit of interrupting Counsel in mid-address, but that it was not malicious. Charles was a member of the Adelaide Club and knew Sir Mellis. One day just as the Stuart Commission was beginning he was walking back to it from the Club with Napier:

> He said something about not knowing whether to let Shand appear. I said there would be more uproar if he were kept out than if he were left in. The Chief laughed and agreed. After Shand walked out the Chief was very bitter about him.[11]

During the course of the Royal Commission Charles noticed that Napier and the other judges sitting on it would regularly be 'in the smoke room of the Adelaide Club laughing and joking with Sir Lloyd Dumas, editor-in-chief of the *Advertiser*. No senior executive officer of the *News* is a member of the Club.'

This explains the fact that the *Advertiser* only reported the Stuart Royal Commission from a perspective favourable to Napier and the Playford government. Charles Bright was also critical of Napier for putting too much faith in the police and believed it was one of the problems of a long judicial career:

> The chief police detective in this case Turner cannot be regarded as certainly pure. On at least one occasion there was the greatest suspicion that he had beaten up an accused – indeed the judge directed an acquittal.

---

11   Legal Notes of Sir Charles Bright, SLSA D 6452(L), for all his quotes.

Charles thought that Justice Geoffrey Reed had 'aged considerably' over the Stuart trials and Royal Commission, believing that although he was honest he was intellectually small. He felt strongly against Jim Brazel, Counsel assisting the Royal Commission and found him increasingly pompous and biased:

> He has frequently read set statements in which he has appeared to give voice to the views of the judges, and their enthusiastic support of his views has added colour to this belief.

> These things do not matter much, but far worse has been his very obvious conjunction with Chamberlain, the Crown Solicitor. They sat together, frequently whispered together, often chuckled together, and outside court commonly stayed together.

> [...]

> It was common gossip among lawyers and court officials that Chamberlain and Brazel were both looking to be appointed judges, and both lost no opportunity of ingratiating themselves with the existing judges.

Charles apologised for his strong assessment of Brazel: 'What a note this is! I am sorry, posterity, to have inflicted it on you.'

He wrote these notes in early November 1959, after the Royal Commission had finished sitting but before its report was delivered to Parliament on 3 December. As it turned out, both Reginald Roderic St Clair Chamberlain and James Francis Brazel were appointed to the Supreme Court of South Australia on 16 November 1959. Not only had Charles guessed correctly but their simultaneous appointments timed at the end of the Stuart Royal Commission can lead to speculation that they were rewards.

Of Chamberlain, Charles Bright had mixed feelings: 'In the Adelaide Club he is smiling and apparently benign – but he has a resentment which I cannot explain towards the profession.' Charles thought Chamberlain as Crown Solicitor mistakenly considered the police like clients, and 'has demonstrated a ferocity, a single-minded determination to condemn Stuart and to protect the police, that any observer could not fail to detect.' Charles Bright wondered if Chamberlain had some grievances in recent years from the High Court of Australia. They had questioned constitutional cases in which he had drafted the legislation. Charles also mentioned that three murder appeals knocked back by the High Court, which had previously done little to tamper with appeals against South Australian Court of Criminal Appeal decisions. One of these was *R v Howe*, in which John had successfully obtained a new trial and Chamberlain had publicly condemned him for the notion of excessive self-defence (see Howe, chapter 8).

Charles did not believe Chamberlain was effective in the Royal Commission:

> I thought that his closing address was so charged with emotion as to be fairly incompetent. He had much to say about the allegations of police violence but very oddly he said not one word about the fun fair people who backed Stuart's alibi. It's a great pity that a man of such respectable if not outstanding ability should have built a wall of prejudice around himself.

Charles left John Bray until last in his list of character sketches of those present at the Stuart Royal Commission and here it is in full:

> He has a fine academic mind and writes some poetry. He was called 'pansy' at St Peters but despite rumours to the contrary I think this refers merely to his early weakness. He is fond of wining and dining and has a ferocious appetite.

> He is a fairly successful barrister, but seems to regard advocacy as a parade of legal points.

> He says that he will never be put on the Bench as he will not become respectable enough. I think he takes an exalted view of his

Bohemianism, which to my mind is fairly harmless. He frequents the company of younger men.

In the Commission he erred in my opinion by becoming committed. He prepared a timetable as to the alibi and in many ways closely associated himself with Stuart's advisers. He should not have identified himself with them. I felt myself increasingly out of touch with him as the Commission progressed. He probably thinks me pompous and far to the right. He repeatedly joined in conferences of Stuart's Counsel to which I was not invited. He has quite an association with Rupert Murdoch.

He is of large build, a little stooped, with a shock of hair now going grey on which he never sports a hat. He is extremely short-sighted and speaks in a low semi-audible manner with no air of conviction.

Charles Bright came back to his notes in 1980 and revised his view of John's approach to law. By then he had seen the impact of John's approach to the common law, it was not merely a 'parade of legal points'. But this shows how even the top Queen's Counsel like Charles Bright and Roderic Chamberlain did not grasp the level of advocacy that John was striving for.

Around this time John dined on Friday nights with Peter Ward, whom he had met through his literary activities. Peter and would become a life-long friend of John's and would be an executor and beneficiary in his will. At the time, however, Peter was 20 years old, and perhaps this accounted for the 'rumours' about John being in the company of young men. A few years earlier John regularly spent time with Brian Medlin, 15 years younger than him, and at the same time with Charles Jury, who was 18 years older than John.

But in relation to the Stuart Royal Commission, it is perhaps justifiable that John was interested in Rupert Max Stuart's alibi as it was the key to proving his guilt. There was a conflict with it as we have mentioned, since several witnesses confirmed he was at the circus the whole time that Mary Hattam was at the beach. But the Counsel assisting the Commission, Jim

Brazel, had picked up on a crucial point during the course of the Royal Commission which had never been explored during Stuart's trial.

The Gieseman's travelling fun fair had come from Western Australia, which since May 1899 has been one and half hours behind South Australia in time. Brazel discovered in examination of the Giesemans and their workers, including Allan Moir, that although they knew there was a time difference they were unsure by how much. The fun fair had six clocks and no one could remember whether they had been advanced to South Australian time. They also needed daily winding. The fun fair owner Norman Gieseman stated that he used his own watch to check the time, and that he had used a radio station to set it.[12] There was also a question of when the South Australian time zone came into effect. From the transcript it appears that people followed Western Australian time until 3 miles west of Ceduna, the first major settlement from the State border.

If for example, Norman Gieseman, the only reliable witness from the fun fair, only advanced his watch by half an hour, he may have believed it to be 2 pm when he opened the fair that Saturday when it fact it was 3 pm. Max Stuart in this case could have been at the beach when Mary was there. Regardless, the single greatest fault of the South Australian justice system then was not to have called the Giesemans at the start, either for the very first hearing of the Stuart trial at the Police Court, or at the trial in the Supreme Court. Perhaps David O'Sullivan should have had a Queen's Counsel such as John Bray to lead him.

The editor-in-chief of the *News*, Rohan Rivett was in his office in the newspaper's building on North Terrace as usual on Monday afternoon, 4 January 1960. At a quarter to three some police arrived, led by Inspector Edwin Calder. He wanted to interview Rohan about the headlines and posters that had been published back in August about Jack Shand's walk-out. Rohan may have been surprised at the unannounced visit, but he was prepared. He

---

12   Royal Commission Transcript, PRG 1098/30/2, p. 42; pp. 312–313

refused to answer any questions without legal advice and called the company's solicitor Mr Bob Clark, at Alderman, Brazel, Clark and Ligertwood. The interview was immediately arranged to take place in Bob Clark's office at 3.30. Mr Clark's advice on almost all the questions put to Rohan was 'I advise you not to answer'.

Inspector Calder interviewed Rupert Murdoch's assistant Kenneth May on 13 January. They interviewed the 29-year-old managing director in Bob Clark's office at 8.45 on Friday 15 January. Rupert Murdoch, as with all the staff interviewed, declined on advice from Mr Clark to answer any question Inspector Calder put about the headlines and posters published on 21 August 1959.

One of Rupert Murdoch's biographers, William Shawcross, wrote that Murdoch 'saw the case as a weapon with which to attack the Playford administration and the Establishment of Adelaide which he so detested.'[13] In 1959 he had tried to buy the *Advertiser* and failed: 'This scheme was rejected with a paragraph in the *Advertiser* suggesting that the paper was best run by local patriots and that Rupert was not one of these.'[14]

But Murdoch was already often away from Adelaide, looking further afield to extend the breadth of his media business. He was frequently in America and England looking for new newspapers and investigating the establishment of television in Australia. Not long after the Rivett trial he bought one of Sydney's daily evening papers, the *Daily Mirror*. Later that year Murdoch moved to Sydney to make his mark in territory that had until then been firmly under control by the Packer and Fairfax families.[15]

No record unfortunately exists of the conversations that must have taken place later that Friday and over the weekend between the Police, the Crown Prosecutor and the Premier. On Monday, 18 January 1960, a summons was delivered to the *News* offices charging the paper and Rohan Rivett jointly with nine counts of libel for the three offending headlines and posters. The

---

13   William Shawcross, Rupert Murdoch, London, Chatto & Windus, 1992, p. 100.
14   Bruce Page, *The Murdoch Archipelago*, London, Simon & Schuster, 2003, p. 101.
15   Bruce Page, p. 102.

extraordinary feature of the summons was the listing of three charges of seditious libel. It is the only time anyone in the history of South Australia has been charged with seditious libel. Stewart Cockburn in *Playford* mentions:

> an apocryphal story of the day had it that Playford personally sifted through law statutes to identify appropriate charges which could be brought against Rivett. When he came to the section of the Act dealing with seditious libel he is said to have jabbed his fingers at it and exclaimed: 'That's it. We'll have a go at him on this. The penalty's death![16]

Britain's infamous Star Chamber had invented the crime of seditious libel around 1606 to punish public criticism of monarchs and governments. The crime was 'based on the need to maintain public respect for the government and its agents, truth could not be a defence against a seditious libel charge'.[17] Playford's choice of such an extreme charge revealed a personal vendetta against the *News* and because of its extremity also made countering it easy.

The charges brought against News Limited and Rohan Deakin Rivett were to be heard at the Adelaide Police Court on Monday, 25 January 1960, before R J Coombes Esq. There were nine charges in total. Each of the two posters and front-page headline from Friday, 21 August 1959, faced one charge of seditious libel under common law; one of defamatory libel contrary to s 246 of the *Criminal Law Consolidation Act, 1935–1956*; and one of defamatory libel contrary to s 247 of the Act. Each charge also gave the reason the government was offended.

The first charge read:

> On the 21st day of August 1959 at Adelaide, published a seditious libel concerning the Hon. Sir Mellis Napier Chief Justice, the Hon. Sir Geoffrey Reed and the Hon. Mr Justice Ross, Judges of the Supreme Court of the said State, in a News poster reading:

---

16   Stewart Cockburn, p. 308.
17   James H Landman. 'Trying Beliefs: The Law of Cultural Orthodoxy and Dissent', in *Insights on Law and Society*, Winter 2002, p. 5.

"Shand quits 'You won't give Stuart a fair go'"

meaning thereby that the Chief Justice and Judges were biased and unfair in carrying out their duties as Royal Commissioners enquiring into matters connected with the trail and conviction of one Rupert Max Stuart and that they were unfitted for judicial office.[18]

(Common law)

The reasoning was the same for the other two charges for the 'Shand quits' poster. The reasoning for the three charges for the poster 'Commission breaks up Shand blasts Napier' was that 'the Hon. Sir Mellis Napier, Chief Justice of the Supreme Court of the said State, was unfitted for his office and had carried out his duties as a Royal Commissioner improperly'. The three charges for the headline 'Mr Shand QC indicts Sir Mellis Napier "These Commissioners cannot do the job"' each read that the 'Chief Justice and Judges were incompetent and unfitted to properly carry out their duties as Royal Commissioners enquiring into matters connected with the trial'.

John had no official role in the case when it was heard at the Adelaide Police Court during the last week of January 1960. Journalists and secretarial staff were called to give details about the newspaper's operations on the fateful Friday, 21 August 1959. Rupert Murdoch was called on Friday 29 January. He admitted only to being the Managing Director of the paper, but to 29 further questions about the production of the *News* that day he declined to answer.

The Magistrate decided the case could go to the Supreme Court and John took the brief to lead the defence of Rohan Rivett with Clarence Hermes as his junior. Harry Alderman QC and Neil Ligertwood would defend the *News*. Leo Travers QC, with J R Kearnan and Mr Lynch, would lead the prosecution. The only judge who could hear the case was Justice Mayo. The rest of the Supreme Court bench in 1960 had either sat on one of the Stuart

---

18   Bray Papers, PRG 1098/31, including the subsequent quotes.

hearings as judges or been involved the case before their appointment – Napier, Reed, Ross, Chamberlain and Brazel.

The *Rivett* case would be unique in John's career due to the extent of his prior experience in it. It is unusual for barristers to have had any knowledge or participation in a brief. But John was actually a witness himself to the two key events in the Stuart Royal Commission that led to the *News* publications at the centre of the libel charges – Napier's interruption of Shand's cross examination of Sergeant Phin and Shand's walk-out on the fatal Friday.

John kept the transcripts of both the Police Court and Supreme Court trials, now available at the State Library of South Australia. Together with the transcripts – already a rare treat for a biographer – are John's trial preparation papers complete with a typed list of his 'Lines of Defence'. Firstly, he wished to make the point that the Commissioners were not sitting as judges when sitting on the Royal Commission. That point was crucial to the charges of seditious libel. He listed *Reg. v Sullivan* Cox 44 at 49 as confirming: 'An attack on judges in their private capacity is not seditious. Such an attack does not bring the administration of justice into hatred or contempt.'

Secondly, he intended to argue that the statements were not libellous, notably 'Shand blasts Napier', which he considered would be more likely libellous of Shand.

Thirdly, he wanted to make the jury familiar with newspaper practice. In Travers' opening address to the Police Court he had highlighted the fact that the words in quotes were not exact, implying dishonesty, so John would have to show that it was established practice to summarise speech and newspaper readers accepted and understood that. Fourthly, he would spend time on the exact processes taking place at the newspaper and draw attention to the speed and urgency that would make it hard to accuse Rohan Rivett as having a malicious state of mind. The telephone call that Shand had walked out of the Royal Commission was around ten in the morning when the day's edition has been almost finalised. The posters, headlines and articles were written just before the deadline to send the plates to the printers and the schedules were not flexible.

John had a copy of Leo Travers's address to the Police Court jury and he began his defence with this, since it outlined the Prosecution's battle strategy. In the Supreme Court, Travers would continue to argue that the Stuart Royal Commissioners had treated Shand fairly and had no reason to quit. He also wanted to argue that the cross-examination of Sergeant Phin was of no importance to the Royal Commission and thus Sir Mellis Napier's interruption was proper. In addition, Travers wanted to show that regardless of the interruption; Napier had invited him to continue regardless. He concluded in the address that 'the incident was seized on by the defendants as the background for serious libels. It was as I shall show grossly and altogether dishonestly misrepresented by the defendants.' John underlined this sentence and also several others, some quite emotionally charged, for example: 'The cunning mischief of it!' and 'it was the product of a mind that was either unbalanced or so seething with malice it was unable to give the truth.'[19]

John would seize upon this latter allegation in particular during the Supreme Court trial. He would challenge the assertion that Sergeant Phin's interview with Allan Moir was remote to the Stuart affair. It was surprising that Travers exposed himself in this way. Jack Shand, one of Australia's leading criminal counsel, would hardly waste his time examining a witness unless it was essential. Though Shand had since died, he had sent a letter shortly before his death, dated 4 September 1959, addressed to David O'Sullivan and Helen Devaney's offices. He made it clear that 'until Your Honour, the Chief Justice made the remarks which just as effectively stopped my examination as if Your Honour had directly so ordered, the suggestion of withdrawing from the commission had never even been thought of, let alone discussed by us, Stuart's Counsel.'

The Supreme Court trial of *R v News and Rohan Deakin Rivett* began before Justice Mayo on 7 March 1960. The first days were spent examining *News* staff and meticulously establishing the details of the normal processes each day to get the paper out by 3 pm each afternoon. The Prosecution

---

19   Bray Papers, PRG 1098/31/3, and for the letter from Jack Shand.

wanted to be able to show a deviation from the daily routine on the day of the offending posters and headlines, and the Defence aimed to show that everything happened just like any other day.

On Thursday, 10 March 1960, the jury was sent out for legal discussions and John began his argument that there was distinction between the words enclosed in quotation marks, and those that were not:

> Dr Bray: I submit firstly that all the alleged libels here are in the nature of report and not comment.

> Justice Mayo: That is a matter for the jury to say, but I am to direct them.

> Dr Bray: The words in quotation marks can never purport to be comment by the newspaper itself, but a summary of what Mr Shand said. As to the words not in quotation marks, the argument would range around the words 'blasts' and 'indicts' and those words are merely descriptive.

> Justice Mayo: These words, in so far as they are not an exact reproduction which purports to be a summarisation, contain comment.

> Harry Alderman: I disagree with that. I think that will have to be for the jury.

> Justice Mayo: I am not saying I have to decide; I have to tell the jury whether there is comment there for them to consider or what they can treat as comment and not as report.

> Dr Bray: It is my contention that these words are report and not comment.

> Justice Mayo: You ask me to direct the jury that they are report and not comment?

> Dr Bray: Yes. Secondly, I say that if they are comment, then they are fair comment of Mr Shand's statements and behavior.

At this point the argument had been distilled down to the two key words 'blasts' and 'indicts'. The importance of these words being treated as fair comment was that under common law fair comment is a defence for libel. Justice Mayo asked for a judicial lead on distinguishing comment from report, but John introduced a new angle, that a heading could also be considered as an index to the content of the article appearing below it, and in this case it would be classified as report. He cited *Grand Theatre v Outram* from 1909, and Justice Mayo proposed to examine the newspaper article.[20] John agreed:

> Dr Bray: Yes, and I say that words like 'blast' and 'indict'.

> Justice Mayo: 'Indict' is an unfortunate word.

> Dr Bray: Yes, but I think the approach of lawyers to it might be coloured by our understanding of its meaning. If Yr Hon. thinks it is open to the jury to hold that any of these words are comment and not report, I would contend they are fair comment in that they are Mr Shand's words summarised.

> Justice Mayo: 'Commission breaks up' – that is not a true statement; that is a comment on what is going to happen, what the future holds, and not what had happened – comment.

> Dr Bray: I submit it is like 'school breaks up' – it does not necessarily imply a permanent end. I submit that phrase can mean a permanent or temporary cessation of activities, and it is for the jury to say here what it means. It will be very difficult to contend that the phrase 'commission breaks up' can be defamatory standing by itself.

> Justice Mayo: But it does not stand by itself. 'Shand blasts Napier'. What does 'blast' mean – high explosive?

---

20   Bray Papers, PRG 1098/31/3. Transcript page 'E', Sess. Cas. 1018 Hals. 3 ed. Vol. 24 page 66 paragraph 116. The following block quote is from Transcript page E.

Dr Bray: Also to blow a loud blast on a trumpet – according to dictionary definition.

Leo Travers discussed the implications of truth not being a defence in cases of seditious libel, as the offence was based on the idea that the published material brings the reputation of government into question. Justice Mayo was uncomfortable, replying: 'if truth is no defence that makes it an impossible situation in the common law.'[21] It indeed seems extraordinary that any legal system would disallow truth.

The difficulties presented by the charges of seditious libel and the lack of evidence led to further lengthy legal arguments a week later after the Crown case had been heard. Justice Mayo wanted Counsels' views about how he should frame his summing up to the jury. Over 50 pages of argument for Wednesday 16 March 1960, and the following day, report the intense discussion between four leading legal minds of the time: Leo Travers QC for the Crown, Harry Alderman QC for the *News*, John Bray QC for Rivett, and of course Justice Herbert Mayo.

Both John's and Harry Alderman's principal intention was to convince Justice Mayo to drop the charges for seditious libel – namely charges 1, 4 and 7 – and not present them to the jury:

> Mr A. I say that on a sedition charge there is no evidence here on which it can be found that as a fact there was ever any intention here to interfere with the administration of justice in any way at all. The judges were sitting as Royal Commissioners, but that does not mean they are judges. The most that can be said is that if there was an attack it was on these gentlemen as Royal Commissioners and not otherwise, and cannot from that infer that in some indirect oblique way that there was any intention to undermine the administration of justice, and it was not

---

21 PRG 1098/31/2. Transcript of the Supreme Court trial of *R v News Limited and Rohan Deakin Rivett*. Page R. Both groups of pages in the transcript reporting legal argument in the absence of the jury use identical A–Z pagination. This is the first group for 10 March 1960.

undermining the Executive, which was not referred to in any way. That is a matter of law, I submit.[22]

John joined forces citing one of Leo Travers's authorities, *Stephens' Digest of the Criminal Law*, 9th Edition, p. 93:

> Dr B. Stephens has the definition of seditious libel as Mr Travers has alleged. I don't know when the first edition was. He has a long list of intentions which are seditious, and one is to bring into hatred and contempt the administration of justice. That is the intention which is alleged. On the submission brought by Mr Alderman, I submit it cannot be seditious libel on a Commissioner in his judicial capacity even if it reflects on his capacity to hold judicial office.

John argued further that the Stuart Royal Commission was set up 'for the guidance of Executive as to whether the penalty of death should be carried out; that has nothing to do with the administration of justice, but as to mercy. It is axiomatic that it has passed out of the administration of justice and the only matter is whether the representative of the Crown should exercise the prerogative of mercy.'

On Thursday the argument continued even stronger:

> Dr B. I endeavoured to show to your Honour that originally, if Royal Commissions had anything to do with ---
>
> H.H. [Justice Mayo] I am very impressed with what you put on that.
>
> Dr B. It has been pointed out to me that during the sitting of the Royal Commission itself, His Honour Mr Justice Ross said "We are sitting here not as a court but as a Royal Commission and we could just as easily have been three laymen or one layman."
>
> H.H. I am not bound by that.

---

22   PRG 1098/31/2, p. R, 16 March 1960.

Dr B. No. But it cannot be contended inferentially, in the way Mr Travers wants it, that any remark made by a person who happens to be a Judge in some capacity other than the judicial, may reflect upon the administration of justice because it may show that that person may not be a fit and proper person to be a Judge. I cannot submit to that proposition.[23]

John argued even further that none of the words in any of the counts could be understood without reading the contents of the paper, which were not under scrutiny, and therefore were not capable of either defamatory nor seditious meaning: 'Here is a hot item in the News. Find out what it says.'[24] Justice Mayo did not agree, so John focused immediately on the three seditious charges:

H.H. As I understand it, you put it that on the facts before the court, the seditious intention is not proved. No evidence whatever.

Dr B. Yes, and the words are not capable of conveying the meanings and innuendoes so far as 'fit to occupy judicial office', and therefore apart from the question of intention there is no case to go to the jury on seditious libel anyhow[...]

John added not only was there no case to answer on the seditious charges, nor was there on any of the others. Mr Alderman agreed with him. Mr Travers did not, and spoke at length on how the Royal Commission could be classified as the administration of justice. The problem was that although he argued that 'the administration of justice includes any executive act', he could not find that definition in any legislation or case. He emphasised that even if three blacksmiths had led the Stuart Royal Commission, it was still the administration of justice.[25]

---

23   Ibid., p. Z.
24   Ibid., p. KK, and p. LL for the one following in block.
25   Ibid., p. OO for the first quote and p. UU for the blacksmiths one.

John's final plea to Justice Mayo reiterated his argument as strongly as he could put it:

> Dr Bray. [...] Each of the counts here contains the words 'wickedly, maliciously and seditiously' etc. and 'seditious'. Evidently they are essential ingredients of the offence.
>
> I make these formal submissions: 1) That there is no case to go to the jury on counts 1, 4 and 7 on the ground that the words are not capable of any seditious meaning, and that there is no evidence of any seditious intent; 2) No case to go to the jury on any of the remaining accounts on the ground that the words are not capable of defamatory meaning and 3) That there is no case for the jury on counts 2, 5 and 8 on the grounds that there is no evidence that Rivett knew any of the words to be false.
>
> Mr Travers. I join issue.
>
> H. H. I will consider the matter.[26]

When the jury returned Justice Mayo informed them that there was no case to answer on the three seditious charges. He said that they still had to decide as a jury on the issue of defamation on the other six charges.

John chose not to call any witnesses nor tender any documents in order to preserve his right to the last address to the jury. This meant that Rupert Murdoch, who had been a witness in the Police Court, would have no involvement in the Supreme Court. He made use of the allowance for two character witnesses, a Methodist minister and a bank officer who both vouched for Rohan's integrity and honesty. Rohan himself only appeared in the dock once, to read an unsworn statement. He confirmed that in his belief, the entire wording used in the headings and posters under investigation was fair and accurate, and that he did not have any intention of defaming anyone, most particularly the Chief Justice.

---

26   Ibid., page ZZ.

A full copy of his statement is available in John's papers at the State Library of South Australia (PRG 1098/31/2), and there is also a hand-altered draft. John kept no record of his closing address to the jury, but fortunately Ken Inglis had access to it for *The Stuart Case* and he recorded:

> The jury was given a clear invitation by Bray to see the prosecution as politically inspired. It had been conducted, he said, with immoderation. It was the result of a fit of pique on the part of the government. The Premier had said that the *News* accused the judges of the vilest crimes. This gross exaggeration showed a mind carried away by wounded pride. Why were there nine counts? The fact that charges of sedition, since withdrawn, were ever included, suggested the hysteria of those behind the prosecution.[27]

John went on to claim that 20th-century journalism was on trial here and that the South Australian press had the right to summarise lengthy statements in the language of its readers.

Reg Kearnan had addressed the jury before John for the prosecution, and of course argued that Rohan Rivett had deliberately distorted Shand's words:

> If Murdoch, as Rivett claimed, had suggested the headline and one of the posters, it would have been of great interest to hear him say so as a witness for the defence. If Murdoch was their author, then in the editorial of September 3 he seemed not only ashamed, but frightened for himself [...] The fact that Murdoch and Rivett put their heads together to contrive libels did not exclude the editor from his responsibility.

The jury needed almost five hours to consider their verdicts on the remaining six charges. They found Rohan not guilty on all counts except one upon which they could not agree. This was the charge of defamatory libel for the poster "Shand Quits: 'You won't give Stuart a fair go'." This outstanding charge was withdrawn only ten weeks later on 6 June 1960. Three weeks later

---

27   Inglis, pp. 288–289; and p. 288 for the quote from Reg Kearnan.

Rupert Murdoch moved to Sydney to run his new newspaper there, the *Daily Mirror*. Five weeks after this last charge was dropped, Rupert Murdoch sacked Rohan Rivett, who took a year off and then moved to Zürich as director of the International Press Institute, eventually returning to live in Melbourne, his home city. He remained a friend of John's until his death in 1977.

The aftershocks from the Stuart Case and the trial of the afternoon paper would cause tremors in Adelaide for many years to come. The legal profession ostracised the three lawyers involved in the Stuart Case – J D O'Sullivan, Helen Devaney and Cairns Villeneuve Smith: all were made to feel unwelcome and moved to Melbourne. In Cairns Villeneuve Smith's case, being the son of the late Frank Villeneuve Smith meant nothing.

The legal profession would continue hold John in the highest regard, and his career never suffered for his involvement in the Stuart Case, nor for successfully defending Rohan Rivett against charges of libelling the State's chief justice. The ramifications for him would instead be far more subtle, and far more damaging to him personally. From 1960 onwards, he was subject to police surveillance, their patrol reports would one day be used to try and prevent his appointment as Chief Justice, later again their existence would lead to the sacking of a South Australian police commissioner in the year of John's resignation as Chief Justice of South Australia. At an even more insidious level would be rumours of criminal behaviour that continue to the day of the writing of this book, rumours that have fed on no other source than the lingering spite and revenge from John's successful defence of Rohan Rivett.

Chapter 11

THE POET LAWYER

Not look behind. Surely a harsh injunction,
Thus to restrain the freedom of direction
And block the major springs of inspiration.
Three fourths of poetry is retrospection.

John Bray, from 'Orpheus Ascending', in *Poems*, published 1962

In 1962, John published his first collection of poems with Cheshire Press in Melbourne. He subsidised the publication, and he would do this with all his books.

It is a small book, 48 pages, selling for 17*s* 6*d*, and the selection of material could be described equally as eclectic or eccentric. It includes 15 of John's own poems, a few translations from French ones, and the choruses both from his play *Papinian* and another one that is unnamed. John had published some of the poems in earlier anthologies, such as R M Morrison's *A Book of South Australian Verse*.[1] The selection of material in the collection is a vivid illustration of John's forceful individualism, but the material itself illustrates his conservative side, if not better described as sentimentalism for a period long passed before his own life. Classical references dominate the works, with frequent references to the Romantic period, which was inspired so fundamentally by the classics. John seems bent on trying to resolve the fact that he is doubly removed from the classics, both in time and in place. He attempts continually to knit a fragile thread between the themes and

---

1   Adelaide, Mary Martin, 1957.

characters of classical mythology to the late 20th-century Australia he lives in. It is good to remember that this period was still when literature taught in Australian schools and universities was only classical or European, Australian authors and poets were still not considered to be capable of the same quality

All the poems are in traditional verse forms, usually rhyming. John often employs arcane vocabulary. The poems are permeated with the dry wit that characterised John's personality and would also later frequently flavour the most unlikely of writings, his judgments as South Australian Chief Justice.

For the reason of their traditional forms, the works stand out for their indifference to the poetic movements of his day. One of his two reviewers, K B Magarey, noted that John follows Charles Jury's example and 'does not avail himself at all of post-Eliotian poetic diction.'[2]

For the biographer, the poems provide some insights into John's daily preoccupations. In *Hymn to Chance* he addresses a mythological incarnation of chance and asks her 'that you forbear your teasing / And spin the world ignoring my existence';[3] in *The Chariot of Pluto* he labels conformity a 'scabby wall-eyed camel'; and *Autumnal Reflection* is his reflection on mid-life, finding himself on the 'downward swoop':

> And I know that my hair will fall and my teeth and my body grow
> gross,
> And later dry up with my wits of call a convention of pains,
> Or deflate like a pricked balloon at the touch of a cancerous pin,
> [...][4]

He sounds grim but ends it with a twist of wit and irony:

> Do I mourn for the death of desire? Do I drape the urn of my youth?
> Or do I reflect with complacency, how uncertain it was, how raw,

---

2   K B Magarey, in *WEA Bookroom Bulletin*, Vol. 2, no. 2, pp. 1–3.
3   *Poems*, p. 4.
4   'Autumnal Reflection' in *Poems*, p. 14.

> And now I command status, and politeness at the bank? If so, is this the
>   worst of all?

In the third and final section of the collection John scatters his preoccupations far and wide. In the relatively long *Prelude to a Modern Epic*, he wonders if it is possible in Australia to follow Keats's example in Europe of being inspired by the classics:

> Why not to us in Adelaide or Sydney
> As once in Greece to Sappho and her kidney?

The catalogue of classical characters shows his deep immersion in the period. He seems sometimes regretful, if not apologetic, for living in a new country on the other side of the world. He names Virgil as his favourite classical poet, and questions the wisdom of publishing poetry in Australia:

> 'If you'd get published here you're writing faultily,
> Our ewes aren't piped by Corydon or Thyrisis.
> Unless they're written wittily or naughtily
> Australia won't take quasi-classic verses
> This is no way to get into a quarterly,
> Or make the CLF demoth their purses.
> In Quadrant or Meanjin watch your betters,
> Or you won't make *Australian Letters*.[5]

John admits that 'conceit, no doubt, or some such psychic ailment, makes me ignore the signals of the critic' and invites 'derailment'. The critics are particularly targeted:

> I find the trade a trifle parasitic.
> Their nipping keeps our bards so lean and yelpy –
> Like the rich flea who bought himself a kelpie.

---

5   'Prelude to a Modern Epic' in *Poems*, p. 30; p. 29 for the preceding excerpt; p. 31 for the
     following excerpt.

In the poem following, *Address to Various Personages*, John continues his reflection and asks his mythological mentors how three poets in Adelaide might gain access to the *Austral Muse*. His three poets are noted above the poem as 'B H Medlin, M G Taylor and the late C R Jury':

> And he must drink, who would thy favours share,
> The waters, not of Helicon, but Eyre.
> > Yet not alone, fam'd sisters of the well,
> Septrional swains obey your spell.
> Where swan-deck'd Torrens hugs her weedy strand
> You number still a small devoted band.[6]

We see John's imitation of the English of Keats's time two centuries earlier, identifying himself perhaps as in the same position, and hoping for the same result:

> Give them their due and give it not by stealth
> And bid old Plutus dig his buried wealth.
> Let cornucopias shower on all their days,
> And loud-tongued Rumour fill the streets with praise!

The muses were perhaps not as kind as John had hoped, at least with the praise. Not just for his chosen candidates, but half a century later Australia has not been guilty of filling the streets with praise for all but a handful of her poets.

In *Virgilian Reflection*, John tackles the theme of falling in love and the resulting loss of rational thought. There is a strong sense of pessimism, but he offers a solution: yielding so:

---

6   *Poems*, p. 33; p. 35 for the following one, and p. 36 for 'Virgilian Reflection'.

We engineer the tyrant's overthrow,
And like Antaeus as we touch the ground
Derive new strength our captor to confound.

John kept his experiences of love very private, but we can be reasonably sure that none led to a conventional long-term partnership. The following poem, *Nature Study*, may throw light on a fear of commitment, due in turn to a fear of women:

The male mosquito sups on sap:
The female dines on gore.
Jack is a vegetarian
And Jill a carnivore.

The male mosquito scarcely speaks:
The female drones till dawn.
Jack is a distant violin
And Jill a motor horn.

And John concludes:

Blest Mother Nature who instructs
Through entomology
In Hive and anthill modelling
The insect world to be,

With Diptera for characters,
From age to age she pens
This cautionary pantomime
For homo sapiens.[7]

A little later in *Jack and Jill* John also takes on the theme of men and women:

Of woman's frailty write the cynic's worst:
She only falls when man has fallen first.

---

7   *Poems*, p. 37; p. 42 for 'Jack and Jill'.

A third Jack and Jill poem is called *Wordsworth*, curiously overlooked in the contents page, though according to Brian Medlin, John hated Wordsworth. He parodies the English poet's style, mocking the famous poet's poems, and suggests that the great poet went round looking for trivial 'pap', such as the Jack and Jill story, to quickly write up and send off to his undiscerning readers.

One of the poems held in Charles Jury's papers, *Mignonne Replies to Ronsard*, mocks a melodramatic poem by French poet Pierre de Ronsard, written in 1545, *Mignonne*. The poet was then 20 and had met the 13-year-old daughter of an Italian banker. In the poem, he offers to take the girl to see a rose and show how quickly it loses its beautiful bloom, warning her to make the most of her youth. Ronsard was a poet in the court of King François I, and the poem became well known for this image of the transitory nature of love.

The French word 'mignonne' is a term of endearment, roughly equivalent to 'sweetheart'. Bray completely neutralises the seriousness of the original, giving the girl the opportunity to reply and tell the poet that a grub would have eaten the rose before it even had the chance to fade. She concludes in the final lines, critical of poets themselves:

> Then, poet, if you catch my trend,
> Be mindful of your latter end,
> Pick cypress, palms and yew.
> The rose let blossom where she stands,
> Or else be plucked by suppler hands,
> Not gnarled and ink-stained blue.[8]

By this period, John was in his early fifties and boasting of not having a romantic attachment to anyone; he was the proud bachelor. His challenge to Ronsard shows a light-hearted scepticism of the notion of romance and no doubt as a consequence, distaste for overly serious romantic poetry. These early two poems also show a type of poetry that John would pursue, responding to existing poems, often tongue-in-cheek.

---

8   *Poems*, 1962, p. 45.

John Bray reading poetry in Elder Park, 1961.
Seated L-R: Ian Mudie, Colin Thiele, Norville Morris, Flexmore Hudson.
The Advertiser, with permission.

Two other poems are of biographical interest in John's first published collection, one of the most unusual he published in his lifetime, *Ballad of the Future*. Complementing the bulk of his poems, including later some speeches, that show a keen yearning for past historical periods, particularly the classical ones, is this pessimistic view of the future.

The poem shows signs John has read George Orwell's *1984* and considered the space travel just beginning around the 1960s. John tells the story of a man in the future whom a computer chose to be the guinea pig for a new space ship:

> He was seen to read a book last year,
>   His IQ's one six three
> And the thought police say he goes to sleep
>   At compulsory TV.

Shot out into space, the luckless hero passes the moon and the planets and then meets Venus, the goddess of love, and she takes him away with her.

John might be suggesting there that he still prefers the values and mythology of the classical period to the increasingly technological society he found himself in.

The last poem in the collection is *Hymn to Respectability*, John's all-encompassing vision of Adelaide. He pokes fun at the River Torrens that 'hardly flows' and the liquor laws that shut hotels at 6 pm but allowed private clubs to remain open. John was a member of three of these clubs, the Amateur Sports, the Savage and the XX:

> I see thee with thy august brood
> In drowsy session,
> Snug Solvency, starch Rectitude
> And shy Repression.
>
> Goddess, straight backed and straiter laced
> Be thou my fort.
> Preserve me sober, grave and chaste
> Or else uncaught.[9]

Reviewer K B Magarey's found this first collection of John's 'intensely readable; but it is perhaps rather slight.' But he elaborated his view:

> This fine product of the experiments of what we might call for a moment the Jury school with classical metres (the lines are semi-quantitative hexameters) is poetry, it is true, partly because the metre and syntax successfully enact the thought: but the thought has a drama, almost a brilliance of its own.[10]

And then K B Magarey gets to the heart of John's poetry:

> It might be simpler to call it wit. Dr Bray's poetry is certainly witty: it is less certain whether the wit is essential to the poetry – whether it is, in any of the current specialised senses, poetic wit.

---

9   *Poems*, p. 47.
10 K B Magarey, as before, p. 1, for these three quotes.

Sturt Arcade Hotel, 1967.
(Unknown,) Colin Ballantyne, Max Harris, Peter Whallin (standing), Neil Lovett, John Bray.
Private collection. *The Advertiser*, with permission.

He wonders about the wisdom of John's choice to publish a small collection of poems in a large number of genres and of his themes: 'anti-marriage, anti-science, anti-conformity, pro-Virgil'. He also wonders if John is 'dodging between the full blaze of two spotlights, irony and tragedy, wit and the grand manner, and the result is sometimes a flicker.' But overall he is positive:

> There is a great deal of poetry in this volume, and Dr Bray has the essential equipment – the genuine inner ear for the rhymes of image and thought – to write (not to gimmick) more. But he has also a dangerous talent for making it immediately enjoyable: dangerous not only to himself but also to his assessment by the 'solemn fools', the literary snobs and puritans led by the 'scabby wall-eyed camel called Conformity'; and by the worshippers of Respectability.

The mention of 'literary snobs' is relevant as because K B Magarey did speculate about 'an influence from Professor A D Hope: organ-voiced like some of his, though less organ-conscious. In these, the language is in a Miltonic and Romantic, rather than a metaphysical, Augustan or Australian strain, and one would expect wit to play little part.'[11]

John had in fact given a speech two years earlier on 17 May 1960 on Hope's poetry and introduced it by admitting that he was 'an admirer of his poetry':

> I admire Hope's poetry for many reasons. [...] First of all it is intelligent and witty; you get the feeling of a mind at work both competent by nature and trained by experience and scholarship.[12]

John added that he found Hope's poetry civilised, ironic and metrically successful. He defended it against a criticism of Hope's metrical errors published earlier in *Australian Letters* by Bryn Davies. John's detailed response gives us an insight into the extent of his technical skills:

> He [Davies] singles out the poem *Imperial Adam* as his example and compares it unfavourably with Pope for metrical variety. This poem has 44 lines and I took the last 44 lines of the Dunciad as a test case. Hope has 9 trochaic inversions in the first foot, Pope 9, equal. Hope has 12 anapaests in substitution for iambs, Pope 8 – 4 up to Hope. In Hope I found 8 examples of consecutive syllables with strong speech stresses giving a quasi-spondaic effect – in Pope only 3 – 10 up to Hope in all.

Bryn Davies may not have anticipated such a detailed analysis of his accusation.

Professor A D Hope also reviewed John's collection, and seemed unfortunately unaware that John had defended him so meticulously. He was condescending. Hope's review was published in the *Australian Book Review*, April 1962, and was entitled 'Hope for Bray'. Alec Hope was the

---

11   W A Magarey, p. 2.
12   Bray papers, PRG 1098/37/12.

first English professor at the Australian National University and in the 1950s developed a reputation for controversial poetry and acidic reviews. He begins by distinguishing poetry as 'serious profession or it may be a pleasant hobby':

> I get the impression that Dr J J Bray, for whom poetry is obviously just such an entertaining and absorbing hobby, is also rather a lonely man in Adelaide. He has been forced to publish and very entertaining some of his poetry is. For all that it is very plainly the sort of poetry which falls into the hobby class.[13]

Hope continues and acknowledges John's gift for parody, but maintains his condescension. He thinks the poems might merit a third prize in the *New Statesman*, and sometimes have a second-hand ring. He quotes some lines from *To Magellan* and admits that though some lines are 'flat and not very perspicuous', there is 'an echo of Milton coming in splendidly'. In concluding:

> One cannot help feeling a pang for the hobbyist. Here are plenty of good things, a possible good poet, but no poem that has the quite professional touch throughout.[14]

Twenty-five years later Alec Hope rediscovered John's poetry when Christopher Pearson succeeded in getting him to write the introduction to John's collection of poems *Satura* published by Wakefield Press in 1988. Now retired, Emeritus Professor Hope admitted in turn that he had always admired John Bray:

> But until I came to read the material assembled for this book, I had no idea what a remarkable man and what an unusual Australian was living among us in the genteel, limited – and shall I say it? – rather dull little city where he spent his boyhood, and practised his profession of law until his recent retirement as Chief Justice.[15]

---

13 A D Hope, *Australian Book Review*, April 1962.
14 A D Hope, as above.
15 Preface to *Satura*, unpaged, 1988.

Writers' Week, Adelaide, possibly 1968. John, (unknown), Peter Ward.
Private collection. *The Advertiser*, with permission.

Hope found that in *Satura*, John presents himself as 'the strange, strangely diverse and yet thorough integral personality that he is'. The book includes an introductory section of John's then unpublished biography of Roman emperor Gallienus and Alec Hope mused on why John chose this obscure historical figure. He remembered that in 1972 he was in Adelaide for Writers' Week at the Adelaide Festival:

> I appeared rather late to a poetry reading on the lawns of North Terrace to be greeted by the sight of the chief justice of the State in a crowd of beards, bare feet, long hair and weird costumes calmly reading his poems as though this was the most natural thing in the world to be doing at a lunch-time gathering. True, his hair was short and his feet were not bare, in fact he was wearing Greek sandals on them, but I knew this was due to the gout from which he suffered acutely and not to eccentricity.[16]

---

16   *Satura*, preface (not numbered); same for the following quote.

Alec Hope suspected that Emperor Gallienus had attracted John's interest because 'neither of them paid much attention to conventional ideas of propriety', but he regretted that the space in *Satura* allocated to Gallienus may have been at the cost of more poems. But Alec Hope also noted John's literary criticism:

> The essay on Shakespeare's *Coriolanus* which follows [Gallienus] is one of the most profound analyses of the subject I have come across and poses a new view of Shakespeare's major tragedies and the dramatist's intentions in them.

This essay is certainly a candidate as one of John's most accomplished works of scholarship. In the opening paragraphs he compares ten of Shakespeare's plays with a confidence and dexterity that reveals the extent and depth of his reading. It is one of those rare gems of literary criticism that immediately illuminate the reader's understanding of a topic previously thought familiar. In one example, John is contrasting the lack of theoretical and metaphysical background in *Coriolanus* to the other tragedies, beginning with *Macbeth*:

> The play speaks in familiar terms of Christian theology, from Banquo's description of the witches as instruments of darkness in the first act to the invocation by Malcolm of the grace of Grace in the finale. In *Hamlet* too, though the hero is a Renaissance intellectual, we live in a world of purgatory and ghosts, the maimed rites of the suicide's burial and the primal eldest curse of a brother's blood. Othello is far more of this world than the other two; but here also the background, though fainter and more removed, is the Christian worldview of chastity and slander, murder and damnation.[17]

The essay is an extraordinary work of scholarship and eloquent writing.

The publication of *Poems* did not earn back John the money he had invested in its publication and wisely he continued his legal career.

---

17   *Satura*, p. 142.

Chapter 12

THE LAST MAN HANGED IN
SOUTH AUSTRALIA

Then as they shoved her, stumbling up the scaffold steps,
One prolonged deep animal bellow broke out of her breast ...

John Bray, from 'The Execution of Madame du Barry'

After the *News* and Rivett trial, the *South Australian State Reports* show the sheer range of John's cases, even allowing for their selectivity. John appeared across the criminal and civil jurisdictions, in land disputes, estate claims, Constitutional challenges, divorce settlements, fraud charges, child custody settlements, motor vehicle accident claims, and in 1963, even an unusual estate dispute with his own father, Harry, acting as a defendant for the next of kin against the Attorney-General. This case was reported as *In re Hodge deceased* at the South Australian Supreme Court level and at appeal to the High Court of Australia as *Attorney-General (SA) v Bray*, where the defendant's son, John, won it.[1]

Harry Bray's cousin, May Annie Sarah Hodge, died in Somerton Park on 30 October 1957, leaving an estate worth just over £21,000. She was a widow without any children, and in her will she expressed her desire to use the whole of her estate to set up and fund a home for 'homeless, stray and unwanted animals'. She also allowed her trustees to postpone the home if they needed to accumulate more funds on her estate.

---

1   [1963] SASR 173, and (1964) 111 CLR 402.

In Mrs Hodge's will she appointed *Bagot's Executor and Trustee Company* her executor and they raised the question about the viability of setting up the stray animals home with the funds that she had left, or whether the will could be interpreted as having a general charitable intention that could be carried out 'cy-près' – or as closely as possible to Mrs Hodge's intentions so that it did not fail entirely. The Chief Justice Sir Mellis Napier ordered an inquiry by the Master of the Supreme Court, who found that it would be impractical to set up a stray animals home. The Attorney-General took the case back to the Court and argued that the funds should instead be given to the existing *Lost Dogs Society*.

The Deputy Master of the South Australian Supreme Court appointed Harry Bray to represent the next of kin and Chief Justice Sir Mellis Napier heard the case in May 1960. John appeared for Harry, assisted by Pam Cleland, arguing that the will was too vague and did not disclose any 'valid charitable trusts' at all.

Sir Mellis disagreed with the Attorney-General's argument:

> The evidence is that the testatrix was a member of the *Lost Dogs Society Incorporated*, and that she had, in her lifetime, given it substantial support. It seems to me that there was no reason why she should not have given the bequest to the *Society*, either conditionally or unconditionally, if that would have served the purpose that she had in mind. But her will – as she has declared it – is that her trustees are to do something else, namely, to "purchase and equip a home" that is, *ex hypothesi*, another home and to maintain it.[2]

The Chief Justice then ordered that the funds be distributed as an intestacy. The Attorney-General appealed to the Full Court in South Australia, and Harry Bray counter-appealed, arguing that Mrs Hodge's charitable intentions were too vague to be held as valid. The Full Court dismissed the Attorney-

---

2   [1963] SASR 173 at 175. Pages 178 and 179 for the Full Court decision.

General's appeal, and confirmed that the gift had failed and the estate should be treated as intestate.

The Attorney-General appealed to the High Court, where it was heard in Melbourne in February 1964. John represented Harry again and Andrew Wells QC represented the Attorney-General. The five judges included Chief Justice Owen Dixon, and Justices Kitto, Taylor, Menzies and Windeyer. They decided collectively that the estate was valid and that if there were not sufficient funds to set up the stray animals facility immediately, then as per Mrs Hodge's wishes, the funds should accumulate until they are sufficient.[3]

Including the *Bray/Hodge* case, John appeared in up to seven reported High Court appeals: *R v Howe* 100 CLR 448 (1958); *Adami v R* 108 CLR 605 (1959); *Schumann v Schumann* 106 CLR 561 (1961); *Teubner v Humble* 108 CLR 491 (1963); *McHale v Watson* 111 CLR 384 (1964); and (on appeal to the Full High Court) *McHale v Watson* 115 CLR 199 (1966). His own papers include transcripts and occasionally his hand-written notes are available in the State Library of South Australia for *Howe, Adami* and *Schumann*.

We discussed *Howe* in chapter 8, and John's winning argument of excessive self-defence which saved Malcolm Howe's neck with a conviction of manslaughter instead or murder. The *Adami* case in 1959 was an appeal from sentences on four counts of forgery. John lost this appeal from the South Australian Supreme Court due to a curious omission on his behalf. His client, Ersilio Adami, lived in shared accommodation with other Italian single men in a city boarding house. He had been convicted of forging up to five withdrawal slips on an account belonging to another of the men living in the boarding house, Giovanni Cazzaro. The bank clerk who had authorised the withdrawals – for several hundred pounds at a time – was unable to identify Mr Adami specifically from a line-up. Mr Adami denied making the withdrawals but his writing samples matched at least two the withdrawal slips. Nevertheless, a handwriting expert was not called.[4] At trial

---

3   *Attorney-General (SA) v Bray.* (1964) 111 CLR 402, at 428.
4   *R v Adami.* [1959] SASR 81 at 89.

in the Supreme Court the judge, Justice Abbott, warned the jury to consider this but they convicted Adami anyway. John appealed to the Full Court and lost, and then to the High Court.

At the High Court special leave to appeal was refused. The judges weighed up all the evidence and were curious about one of John's strategies, in the light of the fact that the bank staff could not conclusively identify Adami:

> The observations made by the learned judge as to the possible reason why Dr. Bray did not ask the detective why he sought out the prisoner Adami have troubled us not a little. It is evident that to a juryman alive to what such a reference might imply, the inference might be highly prejudicial to the prisoner. There is little doubt that the learned judge did not intend to convey to the jury that Dr. Bray had knowledge of some fact concerning the prisoner too damaging to make the question possible. But it was clearly a very unfortunate observation from which the prisoner might suffer. However, having considered the whole case we do not think it is a ground on which we should in all the circumstances grant special leave to appeal.[5]

Schumann v Schumann only reached the High Court after two years of messy and persisting litigation in the South Australian Courts.[6] John kept the transcripts and document copies, but he was not brought into the case until the High Court appeal stage, when the case was referred back to Justice Geoffrey Reed's original trial judgment. At the original trial, Roma Mitchell represented Mr Schumann, F G Hicks represented Mrs Schumann and Len King represented one of Mrs Schumann's alleged lovers.

The *Teubner* case was a tragic 'running-down', as pedestrian accidents were known. On 12 May 1960, a photographer from the *News* was hit by a car during a stormy night while taking photographs, and left permanently disabled and unable to work again. John represented Mr Teubner with Pam

---

5   *Adami v R.* (1959) 108 CLR 605 at 619.
6   *Schumann v Schumann.* [1961] SASR 242; *Schumann v Schumann* (1961) 106 CLR 566.

Cleland as his junior. The principle question was to decide the apportioning of blame, in order to arrive at the total sum to be awarded for damages. Justice Joe Chamberlain awarded Mr Teubner £21,419 in the State Supreme Court on 27 July 1962, but deducted 50 per cent for an equal contribution to the blame for the accident.[7] John appealed to the High Court. His client remembered nothing of the accident, having been left unconscious, but the man who hit him, Mr Humble, made two admissions on which John relied in the Supreme Court and the High Court:

> In the first place, approaching the scene, he was not conscious of the presence of a street light and in fact he believed that because of the lateness of the hour the lights were off. In the second place, some time after the accident he had made a statement to an insurance adjuster (representing a conflicting interest) in which he expressed some doubt as to whether he had his headlights alight or merely his parking lights.[8]

As it turned out the High Court relied less on John's specific arguments than their critical assessment of Justice Chamberlain's reasoning. All four judges disagreed with the trial judge's apportionment and increased it to two-thirds from 50 per cent and lifted the total damages to £24,848. As a result, Mr Teubner received £16,565 instead of £10,709 – still of course not worth the loss of a leg and the mental capacity to even read the paper at which once he had been the lead photographer. *The News*, still under Rupert Murdoch's direct management when the accident happened, had continued to pay Mr Teubner's salary as if he had been at work.

McHale v Watson was an original trial in the High Court, due to the plaintiff and defendant being permanent residents of different States. On 21 January 1957 in Portland, Victoria, a 12-year-old boy called Barry Watson was making darts out of metal rods. He threw one and it accidentally pierced the right eye of nine-year-old Susan McHale. She was immediately taken to

---

7   *Teubner v Humble*. SASR [1962] 117 at 126.
8   *Teubner v Humble*. SASR [1962] 117 at 119–20; 108 CLR 491 at 497.

Mt Gambier and then Adelaide for emergency treatment but lost the sight of the eye.

Over the course of the following seven years the Watsons contributed significantly to the medical costs of treating Susan, but eventually the McHales decided to sue the boy for negligence, along with his mother and father. John represented them when the High Court was sitting in Adelaide in September 1964. There had been a suggestion that Barry Watson's father may have made the darts. The case was brought before Justice Windeyer as one action against the three Watsons:

> The claim against Barry Watson is framed both in trespass to the person and in negligence. It is alleged that he threw the article, however it be described, at the plaintiff intending that it should hit her; alternatively it is said that he was negligent in throwing it as he did. It is alleged against the parents that they were negligent in permitting their child to have the article, or alternatively in failing to supervise and control him in the use of it.[9]

Justice Windeyer pointed out that in the common law a parent is not legally liable for their child's wrongdoing, unless they actively contributed to it themselves:

> But, although the proper upbringing and control of a child is commonly regarded as the responsibility of both parents when they share his custody, I do not think that one becomes implicated in the acts or omissions amounting to negligence of the other unless he or she in some way participated or concurred in them. They do not, because they are parents, become joint tortfeasors.

The fact that Barry had thrown the home-made dart and unintentionally hit Susan's eye was not disputed. What was at stake was if he had done so negligently, and if his parents should have been supervising him. There was

---

9   *McHale v Watson*. (1964) CLR 384 at 386, and 387 for the following quote.

also the question of whether, as a result of her injury, Susan had been left permanently disfigured and without the possibility of leading a normal life.

John referred to a very old and well-known case in his argument – *Weaver and Ward*. The two were soldiers who were giving a demonstration in front of King Charles I using muskets. Ward's musket accidentally discharged and injured Weaver, who sued him for trespass. Weaver won his case, which was recorded in King's Bench in 1616. But Justice Windeyer distinguished the case from John's:

> The law in such cases is still, I think, as stated in the old and constantly quoted words in Weaver v. Ward (8), on which Doctor Bray relied, that "No man shall be excused of a trespass except it be adjudged utterly without his fault". But I should add that this was said in a report of a successful demurrer by the plaintiff to a plea in answer to a count in trespass which plea had alleged that the defendant had accidentally, by misadventure and involuntarily (*casualiter et per infortunium et contra voluntatem suam*) discharged his musket. It should have stated facts negativing negligence or showing how the act was involuntary. I read *contra voluntatem* as relating there to volition rather than intent; but there is no need to pursue the refined distinctions of later times. The words "utterly without his fault" mean, as the context and later decisions make clear, not an absence of all ground for blame and censure of any kind but an absence of such negligence as constitutes fault in law. In Bacon's Abridgement, 6th ed. (1807) under the heading "Trespass (D)" it is said: "If one man have received corporal injury from the voluntary act of another, an action of trespass lies, provided there was a neglect or want of due caution in the person who did the injury, although there were no design to injure".[10]

---

10   *McHale v Watson*. (1964) CLR 384 at 389.

The Judge was impressed by the 'careful and learned arguments' but could not find the defendants, including Barry, guilty of any negligence or trespass and dismissed the case.

John appealed on two grounds:

> first that his Honour was in error in holding that the liability or degree of responsibility of the defendant Barry Watson or the standard of care to be exercised by him in any way differed from the liability degree of responsibility or standard of care which would have been proper had he been over the age of twenty-one years; and secondly that his Honour should have made a finding of negligence whether he applied the standard of the ordinary reasonable man or the standard (whatever it might be) appropriate to a twelve-year-old boy.[11]

The appeal was heard before Justices McTiernan, Kitto, Menzies and Owen in Adelaide in September 1965 and in Melbourne the following year in March. Only Justice Menzies was convinced of John's arguments, allowing the appeal and ordering a retrial. He was outnumbered unfortunately, and the appeal was dismissed with costs.

John's overall win rate at the High Court was therefore not even 50 per cent, but still better than the tiger's hunt success rate of 5 per cent. He also lost his final criminal case, a murder conviction, and his client would become the last man to hang in South Australia.

Glenn Sabre Valance had an appalling childhood. He was born around 1943 to an unmarried mother who left him in the care of her own mother until he was seven years old. He was sent to Morialta Children's Home for two years and at nine he went to live with his mother for the first time since he was a baby. By this time without the slightest sign of love from another human being, he was already showing serious behavioural troubles. He saw

---

11   *McHale v Watson [1966]*. (1966) 115 CLR 199 at 204.

his first psychologist at nine years old, a Mr Whitfird, who referred him to a psychiatrist, Dr Douglas Salter.[12]

Unwanted by his mother or grandmother, Glenn lived at Kumanka, the North Adelaide child welfare hostel for boys, before setting out in his teens as an itinerant worker. He was not entirely ignored by his immediate family. An uncle during this time took him to see a hypnotist, Mr Reginald Francis, but Glenn remained troubled.

In November 1963 Glenn Valance found farm hand work at Richard Strang's property near Senior, near Bordertown in South Australia's south-east. He was only there a month. In his unsworn statement, he said that Strang treated him 'pretty abominably'. We are using John's copy of the trial transcript and showing his underlining:

> He had me get up one morning at 4 am knocking off at 6.30 pm.
> Another night I was there until 2 am loading grain into a shed – I never
> worked less than 11 – 12 hours a day. At the time or just before the time
> I had been friendly with a girl called Susan and I had a diary in which I
> had written about my association with the girl. I burnt this diary when
> I left the Strangs. Mr Strang read that at some time in the quarters. A
> few days before I left he made references to it – he was ribbing me about
> various parts of it. I lost my temper and it ended in a fight.

Richard Strang accused Glenn of improper behaviour with a girl helping in the house, and Glenn decided to leave that very night. He was owed a week and a half's wages, so he took a car heater, some records and two seat covers. With a fellow worker he drove through New South Wales up to Brisbane. There Glenn was arrested for unlawful possession of those goods – Mr Strang having dutifully notified the police of the grand theft, forgetting to mention no doubt the unpaid wages owing.

Glenn was back in Adelaide the day after Christmas 1963, even staying with his mother. A few weeks later he found a job near Burra as a tractor

---

12   Transcript of Glenn Valance's unsworn statement at the Supreme Court of South Australia trial, Bray Papers, SLSA PRG 1098/33/24.

driver. Mr Strang meanwhile had also rung the finance company with whom Glenn had his car and told them he had taken the car outside the State. This was apparently not permitted under the contract, so they dutifully came and repossessed it.

In hindsight, Richard Strang might have been better off forgetting Glenn Valance. The petty revenge from his former employer was expected, but the loss of Glenn's car was a real blow as an itinerant rural farm labourer. Glenn grew increasingly despondent. He managed to borrow for another one and went to see his mother one weekend in Adelaide:

> About this time I decided to end my life and jumped into the Port River off a wharf late one evening after I had left my mother's to drive home to Burra. I didn't expect to get to the other side but I did and didn't have the courage to try again.[13]

Glenn consulted a doctor in Burra who referred him to a psychiatrist in Adelaide.

> He gave me a prescription for tablets which I got at Burra. I took them but they didn't help at all and I was still tormented by the same things. I thought of killing myself again about this time and went up to Norton Summit with a view to putting the car over a cliff, but another car came up and I stopped in time.

On 11 June 1964 the Port Pirie police came up to Burra and arrested Glenn for the theft of the record player. He was locked up in Burra on Thursday night and released on Friday:

> On the Friday night I was feeling right down, as far down as I could get, and I pointed the rifle at myself and fired. It kicked and missed. I came to Adelaide on the Sunday and went down to the Strangs on Monday night. My idea was to frighten Mr Strang into dropping the charge.

---

13   As above, p. 35.

Glenn Valance left Adelaide around 7.30 pm, taking a hitchhiker and also helping tow a car to Keith. He arrived at the Strang's farm around 3.30 am on Tuesday 16 June 1964. First he tied up the three station hands in their bedrooms.

> I had no intention of shooting Strang at that stage. I never had any money or fuel to come back a second time. I had to be back at Burra at 7 am to start work.

He entered the Strang's house through the back door with his rifle and a torch. He entered the Strang's bedroom and shone the torch on the bed:

> I was only about five feet away – she screamed and dived under the blankets. I had no intention of killing Strang at all – my purpose in going there was to frighten him into withdrawing the charge. Only one shot was fired. I don't know what I thought at the time but thinking back now I think I was justified in shooting Mr Strang.

Glenn Valance may well have put his head straight into the noose with that last statement, read out in court as part of his unsworn statement. He may have still ended up on a manslaughter conviction but what he did next was horrific and certainly not justified, even in his own tragic logic. He raped Mrs Strang next to her dead husband.

He then left the property, intending to return to Norton Summit and drive off the cliffs. Instead he was arrested in a road block at Murray Bridge and taken to Mt Gambier.

Justice was swift in these pre-forensic evidence days. Glenn Valance was arraigned in Adelaide before Chief Justice Sir Mellis Napier at 10 am on Tuesday 15 September 1964, and the trial was over by the end of the following afternoon. The transcript, including 25 pages of photographs, is only just over 100 pages in total length. After lunch on Wednesday, Chief Justice Napier addressed the jury, and they retired to consider their verdict at 3.30 pm that same afternoon. The next day they returned a verdict of guilty and the Chief Justice pronounced a sentence of death by hanging.[14]

John was not involved in the case yet, Glenn Valance's sole lawyer was Roderick Matheson, who would have taken the case on legal aid or pro bono. The day after the verdict, Roderick Matheson appealed to the Full Court of the Supreme Court of South Australia. His principal grounds of appeal were that Glenn Valance should have been found not guilty of murder on the ground of insanity. The facts were not disputed. Roderick Matheson also challenged the photographic evidence shown in court as being irrelevant to the central question of Valance's state of mind and mental condition. John kept copies of these photographs and they would have indeed shocked ordinary members of the public finding themselves in a jury. One of them shows quite clearly the massive injury to Richard Strang's head.

The appeal was heard before Justices Mayo, Chamberlain and Travers two weeks later, on 2 and 5 October. It was dismissed, the judges finding that the appeal against conviction on the grounds of insanity was not supported. Much of the short trial had been spent questioning two psychiatrists about the classification of insanity and the test for insanity in law. One of them was Dr Dennis Barker, the psychiatrist called by the defence who had seen Glenn Valance after his suicide attempt in the Port River a few months earlier.

Dr Barker considered that Valance had a 'psychopathic personality disorder' and had prescribed Stalazine for him, a drug which controlled 'anger and excited behaviour'.[15] In his examination, Prosecutor Andrew Wells QC attempted to find out if the psychiatrist believed that Glenn Valance had known what he was doing that fateful night was not only illegal, but wrong, in the application of the McNaughton Rules.[16] The psychiatrist faltered:

Q (Mr Wells): Was there a defect of reason in your opinion?

---

14   As above, p. 11 and p. 95.
15   As above, pp. 40–41; and p. 46 for the examination.
16   *M'Naghton's Case* 1843 10 C & F 200. This case was used to test if a defendant can be judged insane and therefore not guilty by reason of it.

A (Dr Barker): From my examination I feel he wasn't able to reason normally about his former employer Strang.

Q: Anything else?

A: I think this is the most important one.

Q: Is it not important to decide whether as a result of a defect of reason due to a disease of the mind he was unable to know the nature and quality of his act or if he did not know that, then due to the same defect he didn't know if it was wrong?

A: Yes, I considered the whole of that.

The problem for Valance's mental state was that according to Mrs Strang's testimony, he told her he 'may as well swing for two as one'. He had implied that he knew what he had done was wrong, and that he was contemplating killing her as well. After he raped her, he even suggested killing her would save her the embarrassment later in court of discussing what he had just done to her. Dr Barker had to concede that those statements demonstrated that Glenn Valance realised after the killing and the rape that what he had done was wrong, but he would not commit to saying that Glenn Valance knew it at the very moment of the shooting and the rape.

The Crown called Dr William Salter from Hillcrest Hospital for the prosecution. He had assessed Glenn Valance as having a moderate to severe 'psychopathic personality'. He could not find any defect of reason under the McNaughton Rules that would classify Valance as insane, and spoke at length about the difference between a mental illness and having a psychopathic personality.

John Bray was called in after the Full Court appeal was dismissed, and prepared his grounds of appeal to the High Court. The appeal was heard in Sydney on 9 November. In essence John maintained the same grounds as Roderick Matheson, that the trial judge failed to direct the jury adequately about the application of the McNaughten Rules, that his comments about the unsworn statement were more unfavourable than the law permits, and that he should not have allowed the photographs to be admitted as evidence. John omitted Roderick Matheson's ground that the jury's verdict was unreasonable, instead placing the entire responsibility on Chief Justice Napier. He asked the High Court to allow a verdict of not guilty on the ground of insanity, or alternatively to order a new trial.[17] The High Court dismissed his appeal and Glenn Valance was hanged at Adelaide Gaol on 24 November 1964, just 15 days later.

17　As above, pp. 3–4.

Chapter 13

DUNSTAN'S CHOICE

In fact, this was the lighting of a slow-burning fuse.

Peter Ward, background memoir, 2009

While Roderick Matheson was in court attempting to prove Glenn Valance's insanity during mid-September 1964, John was not far away before Justice Travers in another murder trial. The front page of *The Advertiser* of Friday 18 September reported both Valance's sentence of death and Carbone's acquittal of a murder charge in adjacent columns. Giovanni Carbone's verdict is of the most extraordinary and sympathetic in South Australian history, being found neither guilty of murder, nor of manslaughter.

With a not guilty verdict, the case is not recorded in the State Reports, nor the South Australian Judgement Scheme, and John did not keep a copy of the transcript. The front page of Adelaide's *The Advertiser* reveals the incredible reporting bias the killing provoked: 'HORRIFIED CROWD SEES SLAYING', and in the largest font of all the front page articles: 'YOUTH STABBED IN CITY STREET'.

The report at this point could only take the face value view of what happened, and it did shock a city where street violence was almost unheard of. On Monday night, 27 July 1964, Giovanni Carbone left work and walked down Rundle Street on his way home. He stabbed Leon Kiley at around 5.20 pm, up to 12 times, outside Myers on the corner of Rundle Street and Stephens Place. The paper at this point could only report the aftermath, which was that Leon Kiley collapsed in a pool of blood and died on the way to hospital, and Giovanni Carbone was found unconscious not far away, and taken to the Royal Adelaide Hospital with abrasions to the face and placed under police guard.

Nothing was said about Carbone's personal circumstances. Four paragraphs were devoted to Leon Kiley who lived with his grandparents in Toorak Gardens, and his plans to finish his secondary studies at night school and go to university.

Kiley, in fact, had drunk at least five schooners of beer and according to his friends was looking for a fight. When he saw Giovanni Carbone he stopped him and prevented him from continuing along Rundle Street. There were many witnesses to the event, and they would confirm in court that Kiley had then begun to punch Carbone.

Michael Abbott was just starting his career as a lawyer with John's firm, Genders Wilson & Bray, and he accompanied John to court, along with Frank Moran and Brian Stanley. Michael wrote about the Magistrate's Committal proceedings, which began on 18 August 1964 in *Portrait of John Bray*:

> Bray extensively cross-examined the eye-witnesses to highlight the disparity in size and weight between Carbone and his assailant (the deceased was much bigger than the slightly built Carbone). [...] Crucial to the defence was the questioning of the accused by the first police officer on the scene, one Constable Rufus. I well remember Bray's cross-examination highlighting the cultural gap between a young immigrant Italian labourer and the archetypal Anglo-Saxon police constable, who could not even spell Giovanni. Bray highlighted the officer's inability to understand what the accused said, while enlarging on the accused's excitability and gesticulations. Finally he succeeded in getting the policemen to admit that he had misled the court in giving evidence that the accused had said, "I did it, I did it," and likewise that the notes recorded in his note book could well be incorrect.[1]

---

1   In ' Bray as Barrister', *Portrait of John Bray*, ed. Wilfrid Prest, Adelaide: Wakefield Press, 1997, pp. 60–61.

Michael Abbott himself is highlighting the key issue behind this tragedy, and that is racial prejudice. John's ultimate challenge was to demonstrate the sequence of linguistic and cultural breakdowns, from Carbone's panicked response to Kiley's attack, to the way this was noted to police, and this to an all male Anglo-Saxon jury.

Later in September that year in the Supreme Court, *The Advertiser* devoted many columns to the trial. They reported Carbone's unsworn statement in court, which he read in Italian, and was translated by an interpreter:

> I was very much afraid of Kiley. I was afraid of him when he blocked my path but after he hit me I became more afraid. I could not get away from him. He was holding me all the time. I had no intention of getting into a fight that day.[2]

Kiley was also backed up by several friends, one of whom Carbone heard say 'we are here'. He tried time and time again to convince Kiley to let him continue, and when he found himself forced to flee, Kiley 'hit him on the right side of the face just in front of his ear. It was a very heavy blow with a closed fist. Carbone had almost blacked out.' Carbone tried again to flee, but one of Kiley's friends grabbed his hair and Kiley continued to punch him, several blows on the chest, abdomen, face, in the kidneys and then a kick in the shins. At this stage Carbone blacked out and cannot remember what happened.

He had a pocket knife. According to one of the witnesses, Kiley's response to seeing it was 'The little man's got a knife.' The same witness confirmed Kiley's regular indulgence in picking fights. Dr Dwyer, carried out the post-mortem examination on Kiley's body:

> There was much blood about the clothes and tunic which had at least 12 holes in it as from a sharp instrument. Numerous stab wounds were present on the body and arms but only two of these entered the cavities.

---

2   *The Advertiser*, Thursday 17 September, 1964, p. 3, both quotes.

> There were 12 stab wounds to the body and one shallow wound on the
> left finger – 13 wounds in all.[3]

Justice Travers advised the jury on the Thursday that he did not think the facts of the case would lead to a guilty of murder verdict, but that they should consider provocation, whether Carbone's self-defence was excessive, and automatism – a term then in use for actions performed under great stress and not remembered.

The jury was out just three hours and their return of a verdict of not guilty of murder nor of manslaughter was undoubtedly John Bray's greatest criminal success. It was also a defining moment in the multicultural society that South Australia was fast becoming after 120 years of being primarily Anglo-Celtic. At that time, Australians still had British passports and were very unaccustomed to different cultures living in proximity to each other.

John also prepared a large number of legal opinions, an important part of the work of a barrister. Opinions advise clients often on a range of potentially complex legal matters, often on strategies to avoid the risk of future litigation, or if litigation became imminent, what the client's chances of success would be. John kept many of his opinions and they became part of his papers in the State Library of South Australia. In the folder labelled PRG 1098/29/6 IV (1965) there opinions on right of way in the Adelaide Arcade; the claim of a husband to compensation from his wife from a car crash in which she died and he survived; a wrongful dismissal claim that may have been more a contract by one doctor to buy another's practice; a dispute between Sturt Football Club and West Torrens Football Club over clearance for a footballer; a dispute between an oil refinery and a shipping company over who was liable to compensation in a mooring incident; the liability of an injured speeding driver when he hit an electrical supply pole; whether a proposed football pools competition would constitute a lottery (in the days in South Australia

---

3   *The Advertiser*, Wednesday, 16 September 1964, p. 3.

when lotteries were banned); a trademark dispute between a UK company and a South Australian company bearing the same name (Wimpy's); the wisdom of the Bay Motel appealing against a Licensing Court's decision in favour of its rival the Broadway Hotel (9 June 1965); a commercial real estate transaction where the vendor misrepresented an existing lease; and a dispute against the State government of South Australia over the value of land being compulsorily acquired.

This small selection illustrates the extensive range of legal problems to which John advised. In the case of the Bay Motel, John's final advice was:

> I can only repeat that I think that an appeal would be worthwhile with a reasonable chance of success but that the result is not predictable in view of the fact that the matters involved depend to a large extent on questions of policy on which the Supreme Court has not previously pronounced.[4]

The Bay Motel decided to appeal to the Full Court of the South Australian Supreme Court. John represented them. Not only did they win the appeal and obtain a licence to sell alcohol, the resulting judgments from Chief Justice Napier and Justices Chamberlain and Bright triggered a Royal Commission into South Australia's liquor licensing laws. Napier noted firstly the resolution of a poll carried out in Glenelg in 1961 that the electors favoured the issue of two more publican's licences:

> In support of his contention that the Magistrate had failed to give due weight to this resolution, Dr Bray directed our attention to three sections in the Act, which, certainly, call for some reconciliation.[5]

Sir Mellis Napier went into great historical detail and could only conclude that the *Licensing Act* 1932–1963 had not accommodated the massive impact

---

4   Bray Papers PRG 1098/29, 'Re Bay Hotel; Opinion of Dr J J Bray, Shakespeare Chambers, 123 Waymouth Street, Adelaide.'

5   [1965] SASR *Bay Hotel Motel v Broadway Hotel* 249 at 251; at 254 for the 'horse and buggy age' quote.

of the motor car on people's travelling and accommodation needs. The motel had evolved to meet the need for travellers in cars and hotels had not. The Bay Hotel Motel, with around 40 rooms, more than met the accommodation requirements of the Act for two rooms to be available for travellers. The Broadway Hotel, being just directly opposite, felt threatened, but Sir Mellis pointed out that its clientele were the local people, whereas the motel was catering only for travellers. The hotel only kept the minimum two rooms required by the Act for a liquor licence, and tended to let them out to lodgers, not travellers.

Sir Mellis made perhaps the strongest assertion of over 40 years as a judge:

> Speaking generally, it is no part of our function to criticise the law that we administer, or to suggest how it should be amended; but it seems to me that we should call attention to the fact that this legislation, which was designed to meet the needs of a "horse and buggy age", is hopelessly out of touch with the needs of the present day.

The Royal Commission would take much of John's time during 1966, in which he represented this time the interests of the established hotels. They were very keen to see an end to the six-o'clock closing that had been their burden since 1915, but at the same time, they were nervous about liquor licences being extended to restaurants, clubs, cellar doors in wineries, theatres and cabarets. The resulting *Licensing Act* 1967 remains the foundation of South Australia's evolving liquor licensing regulations.

Among John's papers appear to be an increasing number of speeches and papers given to various groups for the 1960s period. The topics are wide-ranging, on Constitutions, poetry, classical personalities, treason, legal education and censorship. In one he discusses the key skills of good advocacy, for example about answering questions from a judge:

> The advocate has to think quickly on his feet and to answer the judge. If he evades an answer the court will think there is no answer. It is

no good if he thinks of the answer on his way out of court, unless of course, that happens during an adjournment before he has concluded his address.[6]

He also advised that you should mention all your points in court, but spend time on the strong ones, and less on the weak ones. On the other hand, 'it may well turn out that the ones you think are strong the court thinks are weak, and vice versa. If so, without giving away your own points, deal with the matters the court is interested in even if you are not, because the court decides the case and not you.'

Another of John's papers was titled *Possible Guidance from Roman Law*, and shows the depth of his knowledge:

> I shall take the Roman law as it existed under Justinian as the standard of comparison, though not without occasional glances at the subsequent history of Roman law during the millennium and a half which has elapsed since his death and during which Roman Law became in a sense the common law of Western Europe.[7]

He then establishes the historical comparison against the common law:

> There have, of course, been continuous, if often unacknowledged borrowings from Roman Law during the whole history of the common law. The contrast between the two systems is by no means as sharp as it was, say, as recently as 1800. There was in that year in England, to take only a few examples from the field of family law, no divorce except by private Act of Parliament, no adoption, no legitimation, unlimited freedom of testation, a different system of succession on intestacy for real and personal property, involving in the case of real property the right of primogeniture, the inability of married women to contract and, by virtue of the doctrine of the unity of the spouses, the acquisition by

---

6   PRG 1098/37/53.
7   PRG 1098/37/72, p. 1; pp. 1–2 for the following quote on the common law.

the husband at common law of all the wife's property whether owned
at the time of marriage or subsequently acquired.

John then discusses the contrasts in methodology and breaks up the different
jurisdictions. There are almost 90 typescripts for such papers and speeches in
the Bray papers on legal, classical and literature topics. In addition, there are
another 40 or more typescripts of reviews of books that he published in the
mid-1960s. One early typescript is a review of a rare published biography of
a South Australian judge – R.M Hague's *Sir John Jeffcott: portrait of a colonial
judge*, published by Melbourne University Press in 1963. John summarised it
as an 'urbane and scholarly book glinting here and there with a demure irony
eminently appropriate to some of the subject matter'.[8]

Just to illustrate John's humour, the review copy had been sent to him
from a literary review of that time called *Nation*, but with no attached letter.
John wrote to them on 5 November 1963, noting receipt of the book:

> I presume that this was sent to me not for my *beaux yeux* but in order
> that I should review it. I am quite happy to do this but could you let me
> know what size review you want and when you want it?

T M Fitzgerald, editor of *Nation*, replied three days later apologising and
suggested around 850 words.

Among John's other reviews were Colin Howard's *Australian Criminal
Law*, Law Book Co., 1966; Enid Campbell and Harry Whitemore's *Freedom
in Australia*, Sydney University Press, 1966; and *Four Poets: David Malouf,
Don Maynard, Judith Green and Rodney Hall*, for Max Harris's *Australian Book
Review* in 1962. David Malouf was not yet 30 years old that year. John was
critical of the other three but of Malouf:

> To me he is the most appealing of the four. His range of sympathy
> is greater, his framework of reference wider. The poem *Epitaph for a
> monster of our times* is a portrait of Eichmann, or someone like him, in

---

8   PRG 1098/38/5, p. 1.

regular quatrains of trimeters reflecting the precision and efficiency of his subject.[9]

John also reviewed Peter Coleman's *Obscenity, Blasphemy and Sedition* published by Jacaranda Press in 1962, for the *Australian Book Review*. John was not convinced that Peter Coleman had succeeded entirely in his exploration of such a 'thorny field, thick with jurisdictional briars and all the rich tangles of a federal system', but he commended the book for its recording of 'fascinating specimens of official ineptitude and crack-pot eccentricity'.[10] The censorship in the British Commonwealth and the United States in the early 1960s was still relying on 19th century interpretation of what people should be allowed to read and it was a topic of some frustration to John. We can recall his discovery of the workings of censorship in his youth of the works in the untranslated Latin sections of the Loeb Classics, which illustrated the extent of what was officially kept from sight. He gave a talk on Censorship and Pornography at the Adelaide Writers' Week in 1964, and subsequently published this as 'Censorship' in *The Australian Library Journal*, June 1964.

John traces the history of censorship in Rome and on to England, then finally to 1964. There was in fact no official censorship, and had not been since 1694.[11] That created a problem as publishers and authors could still be prosecuted under the common law for offences such as sedition, obscenity, blasphemy and defamation without there being a clear policy in place guiding them. He details the incredible complications caused between the Federal Customs and the State laws and finally sums up the situation of the day in four detailed points. One of these mentions the Hicklin test, which later as Chief Justice, one of John's judgments would help not only remove as the test, but be a catalyst for the establishment of South Australia's, and eventually much of Australia's present system of the classification of literature and film.

---

9   PRG 1098/38/25.

10   PRG 1098/38/3.

11   J J Bray, LLD, 'Censorship', *The Australian Library Journal*, June 1964, Vol. 13, p. 61; p. 68 for the following quotes about Denmark and the perusal of Ovid and others.

The Hicklin test came from the English Lord Chief Justice Cockburn in 1868 who defined a test for obscenity for published materials or theatrical plays as 'whether the tendency of the matter is to deprave and corrupt those whose minds are open to such immoral influences', which, although unclear and circular, had been the principal authority used in courts ever since.[12]

John humorously notes that 'there is no obscene literature law in Denmark and that mass rape and Neronic orgies are no more prevalent in Copenhagen than in Adelaide'. His serious interest is the banning of works of literature:

> It has fallen to my lot to discuss with a good many offenders, juvenile and adult, the reasons for their acts but I have never known any of them to ascribe his downfall to a perusal of the works of Ovid, Petronius, Chaucer, Rabelais, Joyce, D H Lawrence, Norman Lindsay, Erskine Caldwell or Henry Miller.

John argues for a complete recasting of both Federal and State legislation, but at the same time argues that classifying published material should be a matter for the States to avoid the inevitable conservatism of a uniform Commonwealth law:

> At the present time *God's Little Acre* is taboo in Melbourne but you can read it in Adelaide. The recent Penguin about the Ern Malley controversy can only be sold at peril by an Adelaide bookseller but you can buy it in Sydney and Melbourne with impunity. Uniformity would probably mean the total disappearance of both of them from libraries and bookshops all over Australia. Diversity is the shelter of liberty.[13]

By chance before John discusses the contemporary censorship situation in 1964 he summarises his view of the common law in its totality:

> First of all, remember the law, particularly English law, is at any given time never a logically coherent whole. At any one time it consists of a

---

12   *R v Hicklin* (1868) Law Reports, 3 Queen's Bench, 360Q.
13   As above, pp. 69–70.

collection of rules of different dates. The law on any given subject stays as it is till Parliament changes it: and Parliament is apt to change it piecemeal. It passes a statute dealing with one topic: but the law on an analogous topic remains as it was. The old and the new look awkward side by side: and people get indignant and say; "This law is absurd." It appears absurd if you think of it as all proceeding from one brain at one time: but it never does. Critics of this kind fall into the same error as does a man who looks at a patched coat and assumes the tailor made it that way deliberately.[14]

John's social life never appeared to wane. Peter Ward was a weekly diner with John, often down Hindley Street on a Friday night, 'regarded as very undesirably "foreign" and suspect by many conventional older Anglo-South Australians.' Most of the migrants were from the Mediterranean countries and had some difficulty comprehending South Australia's draconian liquor and gambling laws, outdated even in their time:

> Sometimes after Saturday lunches or on long weekend holidays Bray, Tippett and others would go on 'pub-crawls' through the city or suburbs, setting certain goals such as drink at every hotel in, say, Hindley and Rundle Street (there were almost 20 hotels in the strip). In the case of the Hindley-Rundle crawls, this ultimately stumbling happy parade would habitually end up in a hotel on East Terrace where the half-hour or so before the six o'clock close would be spent in final rounds of drinks and competitive games at electronic pin-ball machines, no less. Bray would then repair to the Amateur Sports Club where for many years he and the blind lawyer John Davey were the only Saturday diners. After dinner other members of the club, including Tippett and later Peter McCusker and Maurice Crotti, would join them. The carousing would continue and sometimes

---

14   As above, p. 62.

conclude in summer at night on a beach, swimming, or at Bray House in Hutt Street.[15]

As members of the South Australian branch of the Fellowship of Australian Writers, John and Peter were also involved in organising the Adelaide Festival of Arts Writers' Weeks in the early 1960s. They organised Writers' Weeks for the 1964 and 1966 Festivals at the Royal Admiral Hotel. They invited Soviet writers one year and in those years of the peak of the cold war tensions, and Peter Ward suspected that this may have attracted the attention of local Special Branch and ASIO agents:

> Other regular activities that may have interested authorities on the lookout for Reds under or in beds included parties, especially New Year's Eve parties, at the family house of the artist and theatre director Wladyslaw Dutkiewicz, who with his artist brother Ludwic had arrived in Adelaide from Poland in 1949.

Peter remembers that although most members of the Sturt Arcade School would regularly attend parties at the Dutkiewicz home in Dulwich, notable exceptions were Max Harris and Brian Medlin. In the author's interview with Brian Medlin in 2002 for an earlier book on the chief justices, Brian did mention a 'Polish limpet who sort of stuck to the company and couldn't be got rid of'.[16]

In 1964, Peter Ward rented a house at 75 Kingston Terrace, North Adelaide with his partner Dimitri Theodoratos. It was owned by Colin and Gwenneth Ballantyne, who lived next door at number 75: 'Members of the Sturt Arcade School were regular visitors, as was Bray especially, eventually nearly every week for dinner'.[17]

---

15   'Events leading to the Salisbury Royal Commission and its aftermath'. Unpublished memoir for John Emerson by Peter Ward, 2009; and for the quote about the parties.

16   Interview by John Emerson of Brian Medlin.

17   'Events leading to the Salisbury Royal Commission and its aftermath', see above, p. 6; and for the quote about the Royal Commission into licensing and liquor trading.

Peter Ward joined the North Adelaide sub-branch of the Australian Labor Party, and later met Don Dunstan next door at the Ballantynes at a private celebration of the ALP's election win in 1965. Dunstan was initially Attorney-General and Mick Walsh was Premier, but Dunstan had the portfolios covering social reform:

> Among Dunstan's early moves as Attorney-General was the establishment of a Royal Commission into licensing and liquor trading. Bray QC appeared before the Commission representing the Australian Hotels Association, whose president then was Peter Whallin, publican of the Sturt Arcade. On behalf of the AHA Bray forcefully and successfully argued for the continuation of many of the privileges hotels then enjoyed. It was a brief close to his heart.

The year 1965 was a watershed year for South Australia. The Liberal and Country Party had been in government for a quarter of a century, and Premier Sir Thomas Playford attracted industries and built infrastructure that to this day gives the State's citizens water, power, paved roads and jobs that they may never have had. He built over 50,000 public houses so that Adelaide did not have the slums of other cities. But Sir Thomas had mostly left social issues aside. With the increasing number of immigrants from southern Europe, with women wishing to join the work force, with Aboriginal people demanding recognition, and the rise of individual identity, his post-Victorian colony was long in need of a new broom, and that new broom was Don Dunstan.

That year, 1965, Dunstan appointed the first female Supreme Court judge in Australia, Roma Mitchell. The symbolic power of that single appointment cannot be under-estimated. Women nationwide overnight saw their career possibilities expand like a new universe, from the two choices of typing pool or primary school teaching, to the full range of possibilities available to men.

The past two years at home had been difficult for the three Brays. Harry was diagnosed with lung cancer around 1963, but refused treatment. He died in October 1965 at the age of 76. John kept many of the letters and cards of condolence: not all gave surnames, or ones that could be read. They included Lindley in Stirling East, Margaret in Toorak Gardens, Sue Willcox in Longwood, Mortimer Marsh in Gilberton, Gwenneth Ballantyne, the President of the XX Club, Justice Roma Mitchell, Robert Napier in Stirling East, Justice Herbert Mayo, Justice David Hogarth, the Professor of French Jim Cornell who missed John's absence at the Savage Club, and Howard Zelling.

In the Parliament, though, Dunstan's de facto leadership was causing friction among the Labor ranks. Peter Ward had a front row seat on party politics through the weekly recording day that took place each Monday at the 5KA studios where he worked as a writer/producer:

> The Methodist Church and the Labor Party jointly owned the station and while it operated as an independent commercial entity, both owners enjoyed special broadcasting rights. In the case of the ALP that included a number of weekly five-minute political talks by prominent Labor identities. Dunstan, with his cultivated Oxbridge accent, was regarded as a good broadcaster and was thus a regular visitor to the station.

Peter noted the division between those who supported Dunstan – Jim Toohey, Clyde Cameron (Federal Member for Hindmarsh 1949–1980), Geoff Virgo (State ALP Secretary) – and those who supported the more conservative former army officer Des Corcoran – Premier Frank Walsh, Gabe Bywaters (Minister for Agriculture) and Bert Shard (Chief Secretary of SA and Police Minister). The State Cabinet of six members was split 50:50 on many issues Dunstan brought up. One of these was the matter of who would replace Sir Mellis Napier, who turned 83 in 1965 and had no intention of retiring. Dunstan had broken with tradition that year with both Supreme Court appointments. George Walters was the first magistrate to be appointed a judge, and of course, Roma Mitchell was the first female appointed in Australia. In *Felicia*, Don Dunstan explained the next challenge:

> We had, on Napier's resignation, to appoint a new Chief Justice. There is a custom, not always observed in English law, that appointments to Superior courts should be final, and that one should not appoint a puisne (ie an ordinary judge) to be Chief Justice because, it being important to maintain the complete independence of the judiciary, no judge should feel he had anything further to gain from the Executive by acting or giving judgments in a way of which they might not approve. But in Australia, more often that not, a puisne judge was appointed Chief Justice. And in South Australia, the senior puisne judge was Roderick Chamberlain. It was clear that from what he had been told by the Playford government, he expected appointment as Chief Justice. I believed that the Court needed someone very different.[18]

Sir Mellis Napier and Sir Herbert Mayo were both the same age and had both, many years before, been the last judges able to opt for a life appointment instead of retiring at 70 with contributory superannuation. Sir Herbert retired in 1965 and Don Dunstan had only Napier to convince. Three of Napier's predecessors had died in office – Richard Hanson in 1876, Samuel Way in 1916 and George Murray in 1942. The only exception was South Australia's first Chief Justice Sir Charles Cooper, who retired in 1861 with a life pension.

Over the course of 1965 and 1966 Dunstan discovered finally that Sir Mellis could not afford to retire. He was effectively supporting his son Robert's practice, a penance for appointing Robert to Queen's Counsel in 1960 without considering whether he was suitably qualified. Robert lost his basic solicitors' work and other solicitors would not trust him with complex briefs. Finally, Dunstan received a letter from Sir Mellis dated 26 January 1967, in which he agreed conditionally to retire on or after 1 March 1967,

---

18   Don Dunstan, *Felicia*, p. 115.

when he would have been a Supreme Court judge in South Australia for exactly 43 years:

> Replying to your enquiry, I cannot say that I am conscious of any disability or difficulty in coping with the duties of my office as Chief Justice but I realise that what seems clear to me may not be obvious to others, and I am prepared to fall in with what I understand to be the views of the Ministry.[19]

Sir Mellis requested six months paid leave after his retirement, that the government purchase his law library in two annual instalments after that, and that he stay on as Lieutenant-Governor. The Labour government resolved his obvious financial stress by awarding him an annual income for life similar to that which he would have received had he originally opted for retirement at 70.[20] The path was clear for the appointment of a new Chief Justice, but when word got out early in 1967 that Dunstan was planning to appoint Bray, hell broke loose in one of the chambers of the Supreme Court.

---

19   Letter from Sir Mellis Napier to the Attorney-General, 26 January 1967, private collection.
20   Don Dunstan, *Felicia*, p. 116.

Chapter 14

CHIEF JUSTICE 1967–1978

I have thought it wise however to record the matter because of the fallibility of
human memory and in order that it should, if I still think fit, be preserved for
history after the present generation is dead as a reminder of the brazenness, the
meanness and the malignancy of men and that
the price of liberty is eternal vigilance.

John Bray, from his unpublished account of an attempt to
sabotage his appointment as Chief Justice

The first hint of trouble at rumours that Don Dunstan planned to appoint
John as Chief Justice was in early 1967. Don Dunstan arrived at Peter Ward's
office at 5KA, agitated, and asked Peter to follow him outside into Franklin
Street:

> He didn't want to speak in my office in case of being overheard; the
> matter, he said, was serious. In the street he told me that a member of the
> State Executive had at its most recent meeting voiced strong misgivings
> about any government preferment being given to Bray because of the
> kind of people he associated with. He did not say who the member was
> nor whether I had been named as undesirable associate; the implication
> however was pretty obvious.[1]

Peter immediately walked round to Shakespeare Chambers in Waymouth
Street to tell John, who 'laughed the matter off and told me to do the same'.

---

1   Unpublished memoir by Peter Ward, 2009, p. 8; and pp. 8–9 for the following quote.

John's reaction changed a week later. When Peter arrived at the Sturt Arcade Friday in early February 1967 for the usual drink, he found John in an agitated state. Don Dunstan had told him that Police Commissioner McKinna had given Cabinet an adverse briefing on John's character. The members of Cabinet were sceptical, but had given the Police Commissioner the weekend to provide evidence for his allegations. As far as Peter could tell, he seemed to be the problem, living openly in a homosexual relationship in 1960s Adelaide, when homosexual activity was still illegal.

Peter hurried over to Don Dunstan's home in George Street, Norwood:

> His house was in an uproar. The phones – listed and unlisted lines – were ringing constantly. Jerry Crease met me, shook my hand, and welcomed me to "the club" saying "they've been saying it about me for years". I took him to mean homosexual. The three Dunstan children were standing about, startled and excited on-lookers. Dunstan's wife, Gretel, had taken to bed claiming nervous exhaustion and in that bedroom with her, listening and proffering advice and commiserations, a very wrought Dunstan confirmed all that Bray had said and added that he had told Cabinet that he intended to resign if his recommendation of Bray for Chief Justice was not accepted.

Don Dunstan had come face to face with the mighty conservative forces of Adelaide at that time, which controlled State politics through powerful strings pulled from the Adelaide Club in North Terrace and the Naval, Military and Air Force Club in Hutt Street, just opposite Bray House.

Police Commissioner John McKinna also held the rank of Brigadier from five years service in the Second World War and subsequent military service. He was never a police officer, but when he was appointed Commissioner in 1957, he dedicated himself to the professionalisation of the police. He set up Fort Largs Academy near Port Adelaide for cadet training, and the training area in Mylor in the hills initially began on his own small property. He raised police morale in a way subsequent commissioners were unable to achieve, and over 40 years after his retirement, John McKinna's time as Commissioner is highly regarded.[2]

John McKinna was also a close friend of Justice Roderic Chamberlain, a long-time adversary of John's from the days when he was Crown Prosecutor and John successfully defended Malcolm Howe. The judge and the commiss-ioner both attended the same church in the city of Adelaide. John's successes in criminal defences subsequently, particularly in the *Rivett* case, would hardly have warmed Justice Chamberlain's feelings, particularly if he had been promised the succession to Sir Mellis.

The South Australian police regularly raided homes of known homo-sexuals during this period in the State's history, and Peter Ward feared a police raid that weekend. David Tippett, the stockbroker, offered his home in Mitcham as a safe house, and along with David's wife Jill, John Bray, Brian Medlin and Dimitri Theodoratos spent the weekend there. Peter Ward was traumatised by the experience:

> We were all left feeling indignant variously about civil libertarian issues, misused police power and misapplied surveillance. In fact, this was the lighting of a slow-burning fuse.[3]

That slow-burning fuse would lead eventually to the sacking of Police Com-missioner McKinna' successor, Harold Salisbury, in 1978.

Cabinet met Monday morning and discussed the police surveillance reports that Commissioner McKinna had produced. John rang Peter to tell him that 'it had all been a complete nonsense and that cabinet had scorned the inanity and the banality of McKinna's report. John also was shown this report, and he wrote several hand-written pages. He summarises the process of his appointment and addresses each of four alleged incidents.

This is the full text of John's document:

---

2 Refer to the SA Police History website http://www.sapolicehistory.org/mckinna.html.

3 Background memoir for John Emerson by Peter Ward, 2009.

In about August 1965 the Attorney-General (D.A. Dunstan) sent for me. He told me he was making some appointments to the bench. He explained that he was not issuing any invitation to me because he desired to appoint me as Chief Justice after the retirement of Sir Mellis Napier which he expected to take place in April 1966. I pointed out that my Bohemian and unconventional temperament and manner of life made me perhaps a dubious choice for the post. He demurred. He said that he saw no reason why I should not continue to indulge in such activities as drinking in hotels, swimming at the beach and associating with my present circle of friends. I said that for example a Chief Justice should not break the Licensing Act by drinking after 6 o'clock at night. He agreed. I said that I would not at that stage give him a definite acceptance.

In April 1966 he informed me that the Chief Justice was postponing his retirement until December 1966. In December 1966 he told me that the Chief Justice was going to retire as from 1st March 1967. On Thursday 23rd February 1967 he rang me and said that there would be an announcement in the afternoon press of Sir Mellis's retirement as from 1st March and that I was to be sworn in on Thursday 2nd March.

On Tuesday the 7th of February I called on him. I asked him if he was sure he wanted me for the post. I reiterated my refusal to become a father figure or to embody the values of ambition. As far as I can recall I used those words. He reiterated his lack of concern. Indeed he seemed to welcome the arrangement. I then indicated my definite acceptance. This was the result of a long period of thought on the matter since it was first broached.

On Friday the 24th February the Attorney General asked me to see him urgently. I did so. He said that some members of the Cabinet were opposed to the appointment. He said that the Chief Secretary had received a report from the Commissioner of Police that I had undesirable associates including some of whom a police officer had said that he would not permit his son to associate with such people. He said that he had insisted that definite details of any such charges should be checked. He said that the police had at that stage made no specific charges at all. I gathered from his remarks and I think he was under the same impression, at it was my present friends and associates who were implicated. He said that the Commissioner was to give Cabinet details of these matters on the following Monday.

On Monday 27th February he rang me and said that there was nothing in these charges and that the appointment was to proceed as planned.

On Tuesday 28th February he gave me the details. I set out the four matters with my comments:

(1) It was said that at some time, apparently many years ago, police officers touring the parklands at night had seen two men sitting in a car. I was one of them. They passed on and took no further action. I cannot recall if the exact year was mentioned.

Comment: I have no recollection of this incident. It might well have occurred. I have on many occasions had a drink in a car in the parklands at night with friends and acquaintances. There was indeed nowhere else in Adelaide outside a private house where one could have a drink with one's friends in the 'forties and 'fifties after midnight.

(2) It was said that on one occasion, apparently also many years ago, a police officer was questioning a youth in Hutt Street near my parents' residence where I was living. He saw me and a bearded man apparently rise up from the ground behind the front fence of the premises, brush our clothing and walk away.

Comment: This might well have happened on several occasions. The bearded man would have been J R Davey who is blind, massive in build, and often unsteady on his feet. On many occasions he would come with me for a drink to 56 Hutt Street after the Amateur Sports Club closed. On many such occasions I have refused to take the risk of endeavouring to help him up the front steps of the premises. If he had fallen over I might not unaided have been able to save him. On such occasions in the summer we would sit on the verandah itself and have a drink. While seated we would from some angles have been hidden from view from the street by the fence. The verandah is constructed of stone. On rising from it one naturally brushed one's clothes. When he was ready to go I would summon a taxi. On occasions I would give him my arm so that he could walk up to the fence, which in parts was then and still is to a lesser extent supplemented by a hedge, and relieve himself. I was not told the precise date of this alleged episode either but again I received the impression that it was supposed to have happened many years ago.

(3) It was said that on at least one occasion during the years 1959–1960 the vice squad was summoned to certain premises at 56 Hutt Street where a number of lesbians and homosexuals including transvestites were observed. It was not alleged that I was present at any such occasions.

Comment: This might well have happened. At about this time my mother was prevailed upon out of sympathy evoked by a story of emergency homelessness to let the flat at the rear of the premises to three girls without references. I willingly believe that at least one of them was a Lesbian. Their visitors were many and often bizarre in appearance. The occupants of the flat changed from time to time. They failed to pay the rent and were eventually evicted by my firm. At that time there were still some obstacles to the speedy removal of tenants and I believe in the event these girls had some form of agreement. To the best of my recollection I never entered the flat during the tenancy.

(4) The first three accusations were apparently made by the Commissioner of Police. In addition it was said that the Chief Secretary had

been informed that I was to be seen on most evenings after 5 o'clock drinking in a city hotel with my "types".

Comment: It is undoubtedly true that at this time and for many years before it I was in the habit of drinking after work at the Sturt Arcade Hotel with a group of friends and acquaintances. Indeed I still do this though with less frequency. The Sturt Arcade Hotel is a highly respectable hotel though not patronised extensively by the social elite. I do not know precisely what accusation is meant to be conveyed by the use of the word "types" but my friends were and are also reputable citizens engaged in lawful occupations. Certainly many of them were and are connected with literature, the theatre, the fine arts, the teaching profession and the universities but I cannot suppose that even a police officer or the informants of a Cabinet Minister regard this us a disqualification.

I can only conclude from this lamentable episode that either the police keep a dossier on everyone, or everyone of any degree of prominence, or else that I have been singled out for special attention. As the charges seem to centre round a period during which I was professionally engaged in litigation which was likely to be displeasing to the government of the day I am inclined to prefer the latter supposition. If that is correct it can hardly be thought that the police would have had me watched and my activities noted on their own initiative.

Equally I find it almost impossible to believe that the Commissioner of Police would have approached the Chief Secretary spontaneously. I believe that he was prompted to do this. Various suggestions have been made to me and I have engaged in speculation of my own as to the identity of the prompter. I have decided however to pursue the matter no further unless and until subsequent events should make it necessary to do so. I have thought it wise however to record the matter because of the fallibility of human memory and in order that it should, if I still think fit, be preserved for history after the present generation is dead as a reminder of the brazenness, the meanness and the malignancy of men and that the price of liberty is eternal vigilance.

I must not omit to record here also the courage, the affection and the comradeship of my friends whom I was obliged to take into my confidence at a time when I thought that my present associates were aimed at and which are more than sufficient counterbalance to the qualities referred to in the last sentence of the last paragraph.

(six lines are then obliterated)

Dated this 15th day of October 1967

(Signed) J J Bray

This account stands as I wrote it in 1967 except that I have excised the last paragraphs. That paragraph contains comments which faithfully reflect my attitudes in 1967 but I no longer hold the same attitudes and the paragraph became inappropriate. 27 January 1980 (Signed) J J Bray.

John deleted six lines that may have confirmed the complete absence of homosexual experience at that time. Brian Medlin did not believe John had any homosexual experiences until some time around his sixtieth birthday, in 1972.[4] John wrote the original account six months into his chief justice-ship, and therefore after a long period of reflection. It tells us how early Don Dunstan approached him about considering the office of Chief Justice, and that he spent two years reluctantly considering the offer. John was not ambitious. He valued scholarship and wisdom over the white noise of courtesanship. Having finally decided to accept, he suddenly found himself face to face with the dark reality of conservative Adelaide politics.

John speculates about the identity of the 'prompter', and that he had ruled out both the Chief Secretary, Bert Shard, and the Police Commissioner, John

---

4   Interview with Brian Medlin, October 2002.

First day as Chief Justice of South Australia, 1 March 1967.
The Advertiser, with permission.

McKinna. This leads back to one person, Justice Roderic Chamberlain, long before promised the appointment to Chief Justice by Playford.[5]

Between the time of John's first day as Chief Justice and the time of writing about the police reports, there had also been a further attack on him. Sir Mellis Napier was trying to convince John to join the Adelaide Club, but even Sir Mellis was not prepared for the subsequent blackballing. He first wrote to John on 28 March:

---

5   Don Dunstan in *Felicia*, already cited, p. 115.

My dear John, I have a note to the effect that the Committee were "unanimous in that they would very much like to see you as a member" of the Club.

The next thing is to find a seconder. Is there anyone whom you know well enough to ask him to act in that capacity?[6]

Sir Mellis suggested that 'there might be some questions raised but the only way to test the issue is to put in the proposal'. There no further correspondence in the papers, but John must have acquiesced to allow his name to be put forward for membership of the Adelaide Club. One of the members, name unknown of course, blackballed his nomination.

Sir Mellis Napier was still extremely keen for John to be a member of the Adelaide Club, and he tried again on John's behalf. In the next letter present in John's papers, dated 7 August 1967, it sounds as if John has tried to talk him out of it. Sir Mellis writes:

I am sorry that we shall not have the common ground in which to meet on North Terrace, but I am not surprised by your decision. Indeed, it is, I think, what I should have said in the circumstances. […] I am writing to the Secretary, notifying him of the fact that you are not disposed to consent to a renewal of the nomination.

The Adelaide Club Committee itself now took it upon itself to support John's membership and Sir Mellis wrote again on 27 September, quoting his own letter from the Secretary:

"The Committee suggest that if it is your wish to proceed with the matter of nomination now will you kindly have the enclosed nomination form completed".

---

6   Sir Mellis Napier to John Bray, 28 March 1967. Private Collection; same for the letter dated
     7 August 1967.

From this I gather that the Committee feel as I do that there should be little, if any, risk of an adverse vote; but of course there can be no guarantee.

That nomination form remains with Sir Mellis's letter to this day, blank.

John replied to Sir Mellis on 29 September, expressing his gratitude for his 'trouble' and 'kindness', and that he was reluctant to expose the office he held to the risk of a public rebuff, 'a risk which may be small but which in view of what has happened cannot be regarded as negligible':

> But more compelling to me it seems that there would be some element of humiliation in going on as things stand. I do not want to be a member on sufferance. I do not want to ask people with whom I am only distantly acquainted to second my nomination in the hope that they may be more acceptable than the man who was previously kind enough to do me this honour. It is plain that there are those to whom my presence in the Adelaide Club would be very unwelcome and I think that ought to preclude me from trying to subject them to it. The Chief Justice ought not to be a suppliant.[7]

Peter Ward later observed:

> For Chamberlain, the bitter chagrin he felt over Bray's appointment lingered on. It was he who had described the members of the Sturt Arcade School as 'types' and Bray as 'that bachelor' and when, in support of long-standing judicial tradition, Napier sponsored Bray's membership of the Adelaide Club, Chamberlain black-balled it (Bray ultimately declined the invitation – on my strong advice, as it happened, which was that it was demeaning to his office and to him that he should wait on the grace and favour of the Club's membership). From that time on both Chamberlain and McKinna also pointedly cut Bray in public and were often openly hostile to the Dunstan government.

---

7   John Bray to Sir Mellis Napier, 29 September 1967, privately held.

Given the bitter, prejudicial emotions involved I believe it is probable that McKinna later briefed Salisbury on the whole matter and on those involved.[8]

Don Dunstan also noted in *Felicia*:

The appointment of Bray was greeted with delight by the younger members of the profession, with gloom and muttering from the Establishment, and with fury by Chamberlain who has never again spoken to me, whose remaining days on the bench were punctuated by remarks from the bench critical of government policy and whose retirement has featured letters to the newspaper expressing the most extreme of conservative views in condemnation of what a Labor government, or I, might have been about.[9]

Both Peter Ward's and Don Dunstan's recollections are supported by the fact that three years later, John attended a small function at the Adelaide Club, and was openly abused. The then President of the Club, Peter Morgan, wrote as quickly as he could:

9 June 1970

My dear Chief Justice, it has been reported to me that when you were dining in the annexe of the Adelaide Club last Friday a man who was also dining there said some things in your hearing which must have been offensive to you.

As President of the Club this has caused me very great concern, and I write to apologise to you and to tell you how sorry I am. I am told that the man who made the remarks had been drinking – probably an understatement.[10]

---

8   Peter Ward, already cited, p. 9.
9   Don Dunstan, *Felicia*, p. 117.
10   Letter from Peter Morgan to John Bray, dated 9 June 1970. Private Collection.

The 'Bray Court' in 1969. John is 3rd to the left.
On his right is Justice Chamberlain and second from his left, Justice Roma Mitchell.
Private Collection.

Mr Morgan hoped that the drinking may have explained the outburst and that John would regard that as a 'mitigating circumstance'. It is not known if the behaviour was from a Club member or not.

Since the days of Sir Samuel Way, the Chief Justice had also been the Lieutenant-Governor, but John told Don Dunstan that he did not want that position as well. Sir Mellis would in fact happily stay on in that role for several more years.

In the Press at the time of John's appointment, there was not a whiff of the corridor intrigues. John's appointment as Chief Justice featured on the front pages of both *The Advertiser* and *The News*. Stewart Cockburn described John as 'besides being a notable lawyer, is a poet, playwright, classical scholar – a humanist – and one of the most deeply-read professional men in the Commonwealth'.[11] Later that year in *The News*, Samela Harris described how the performance of John's play *Papinian* had introduced him into the world of theatre and literature in Adelaide.[12]

---

11 *The Advertiser*, 1 March 1967, p. 1.
12 *The News*, 28 August 1967.

At the time of John's first meeting with the other judges on the Supreme Court bench in his chambers, he is reported to have told them:

> What you do is of course for you, but I think that judges of this court have for too long subjected themselves to far too many self-denying ordinances. So I shall tell you what I shall do. I have never worn a hat and shall not begin now. I am dyslectic, do not drive a car and when I choose, from time to time, will go by public transport. I do not propose to join the Adelaide Club. And when I wish, during lawful trading hours, to meet my friends in a licensed public house, I shall do so. In fact (looking at his watch) I'm going there now.[13]

This speech, though reported indirectly, matches what we understand of John's habits and personality. Not wearing a hat in the early 21st century seems hardly worth mentioning, but in 1967, all men wore hats as a normal item of clothing. For John not to wear one he was immediately distinguished on a city street. He did not elaborate on the black-balling of his membership nomination for the Adelaide Club, but he had no wish to join anyway. His brief speech is also the language of a lawyer, and he is couching his individual freedom in terms of his most basic legal rights. John was no rebel or radical, he simply believed in the right of the individual to their own choices.

A few months later, in July 1967, John presented his views on the role of the Courts to a symposium of Justices of the Peace held in the Police Head-quarters in Angas Street, now demolished and the site of the Federal Court building. *The Advertiser*'s front page reported his speech with several quotes on 3 July under the heading 'Not Courts of Morals'. The opening paragraph read: 'No court had any legal right to tell a defendant to get his hair cut or go away and put on a coat or tie, the Chief Justice (Dr J J Bray) said yesterday.' John was making the point that the role of the courts was not to 'enforce morality as such, extraneous to the offence'. His comments provoked a fierce

---

13   Don Dunstan, already cited, p. 116.

reaction from Justice Travers, and throughout the week the local papers were bombarded with letters to their editors.

Justice Travers was quoted the following day in *The Advertiser*, 4 July 1967:

> In my opinion the whole foundation of our legal system is morality and
> I use the word in its broadest sense as including both sexual morality
> and morality in the sense of fair and honest dealing.

He warned that 'any people with hair down to their knees and dressed according to their fancy who wish to attend court other than in custody would, I think, do well to choose their court. If they select mine their stay is apt to be brief and somewhat unpleasant.'

The same day in *The Advertiser* Premier Don Dunstan backed John Bray: 'I do not consider it as disrespect for the courts that people may choose to dress in a manner which is not the same as members of the Bench.'

John himself declined to respond to Justice Travers, saying: 'It is improper for judges to enter into public controversy.' The next day both daily papers in Adelaide carried editorials on the subject. *The Advertiser* headed theirs 'Crime and Prejudice':

> Before the interesting argument between Dr Bray and Mr Justice
> Travers becomes a free-for-all on the subject of long hair versus short
> back and sides it is worth recalling the main point that the Chief Justice
> made in his speech to JP's on punishments awarded by courts of law.
> He was calling attention to the danger of making a punishment fit not
> so much the crime as the prejudice of those imposing it.[14]

Justice Travers revealed his prejudice in completely bypassing John's core argument and only noticing the incidental example of hair length.

The News, the afternoon tabloid owned by Rupert Murdoch which decades later would close but reappear as the current *Advertiser*, headed its editorial 'Long hair argument', also drew attention to the point that John was making,

---

14   *The Advertiser*, 5 July 1967, Editorial.

'that an offender should be judged on what he has done and not on what his attire may or may not represent'.

There were many letters to the editor and the whole week's local news was overwhelmed by the topic. That year 1967 was the beginning of the western countries' youth revolution, and John accidentally revealed the tensions festering in his own city over the widening gulf between old and young. Justice Chamberlain also entered the debate, when he was summing up to the jury in a case before him that week. His view of the role of the courts was in fact not far from John's: 'The court does not sit to enforce conventions, either outworn Victorian conventions or what you might think sensible Elizabethan conventions'.[15]

Letters to the Editor varied in view on long hair in court, but one perhaps was pertinent. 'Modern Mum' wrote to the *News*:

> I agree with remarks made by the Chief Justice, Dr Bray, over freedom
> of dress and hair length. How can other judges knock long hair anyway?
> They've been wearing long wigs for years.[16]

The former editor of *News*, Rohan Rivett, noticed the controversy in Adelaide over John's remarks and wrote to John privately:

> It has not occurred to the 40+ age group that anyone who had appeared
> with short hair in the last 1000 years before Queen Victoria would have
> been laughed to ridicule.[17]

The following week the Adelaide media moved on and John returned to the challenges of judicial life.

---

15   *The Advertiser*, 6 July 1967.
16   *News*, 6 July 1967.
17   SLSA Bray Papers, PRG 1098/1/7.

Chapter 15

THE DRAMATIC DUNSTAN DECADE

And the West is lost in a maze and has ceased to believe in an exit,
And its most prestigious products seem metamorphosed to synthetics.
So democracy dwindles down to a duel of ventriloquists' dummies,
Competing for charisma.

John Bray, from 'The Bay of Salamis: July 1978'

Bray was Chief Justice of South Australia for just a little over eleven years. During that period Bray's judgments began to attract increasing attention for his ability to draw on the common law and Roman law to articulate difficult legal principles in clear and elegant language. In one of the cases we will discuss shortly, he was cited by all five Lords in a Privy Council decision to allow an appeal from Northern Ireland involving an Irish Republican Army killing. One of the Law Lords commented on Bray's elegant reasoning, and with that it was finally accepted that a great Common Law mind did not have to reside in London.

Over the same eleven years, despite an enduring preference for a predictable pattern to life, Bray's personal life changed more than it had in decades. He revealed a few surprises even to his close circle of friends, especially the unforeseen revelation in 1976 that he had a 40-year-old son. But the elephant in the room during Bray's entire period in office would be those police patrol files. Peter Ward was incensed at their existence and built up political pressure systematically on Don Dunstan until in 1977 he finally had them investigated. The end result was not just their incineration but also the sacking of Police Commissioner Harold Salisbury in January 1978, and a Royal Commission into the sacking in February 1978. Bray found it all too close to his preference for a quiet life. He would not risk his health, nor the office of Chief Justice, and he resigned and went to Europe while the Royal Commission was being held.

This meant effectively that although Don Dunstan was never a close friend of Bray's, he was both the vehicle for Bray being appointed Chief Justice, and for leaving it. Don had represented the actors in Bray's *Papinian* all the way back in 1955 and since then they had known each other through their mutual literary connections.

In April 1968, Don Dunstan and Peter Ward unwittingly put Bray in a delicate legal position, and it was only later that Peter realised that could have been a disaster. The election that year coincided with the end of Sir Edric Bastyan's term as Governor. Don Dunstan wanted to appoint an Australian for the first time rather than a retired British military officer, which had been the custom.[1] His choice was Sir Mark Oliphant, but the appointment process lingered past the election, which was too close to call for the next couple of weeks. The leader of the opposition, Steele Hall, did not wish to appoint Sir Mark Oliphant if he got into office.

Governor Sir Edric Bastyan asked Bray's advice on the constitutional issues involved. For a governor to accept advice from the government it had to control the House, and it did not. Coming up to Easter in mid-April 1968, the votes were finally counted, and Labor and the Liberal Country League each held 19 seats. The balance of power was in the independent Tom Stott's hands.[2]

Don Dunstan arrived at Peter Ward and Dimitri Theodoratos's home at 75 Kingston Terrace suddenly:

---

1   Don Dunstan, *Felicia*, pp. 152–153.
2   Dean Jaensch, 'Parliament and Government'. In Dean Jaensch (ed.) *Flinders History of South Australia – Political History*, Adelaide: Wakefield Press, 1986, p. 378.

This was a strange occurrence. While I knew the man and his family, as described, and had helped his campaign in Norwood in 1965 and 1968, I was not a close friend and he had never visited me before, unannounced or otherwise.[3]

Peter invited Don on a weekend away for Easter with himself, Dimitri, John, Colin Ballantyne, Neil Tippett and Stuart Luke. They would stay at a house in Robe called Lakeside Manor, later turned into a resort hotel by Johnnie Mayer. Don accepted as he was scheduled to speak at Millicent on Easter Sunday, 14 April:

The weekend proceeded more or less much like a Labor Day long weekend holiday, though more constrainedly because of the presence of Dunstan and his driver Bronte. Dunstan, who found non-political and discursive conversations not involving himself hard going, took over the kitchen and did the cooking.

Peter later realised that it was a political risk for Bray to have been in the private company of the leader of the government about to fall, when he had given advice to the governor on a matter relating to that critical situation. As it turned out, Don Dunstan on Tuesday 16 April 1968 lost government on the floor of the house when Tom Stott decided to join the Liberal and Country League.[4] Steele Hall would lead the Liberal and Country League government until Don Dunstan won the 1970 election and that time managed to stay in power for almost nine years.

If unwise in hindsight, this weekend-long proximity of the head of the judicial arm of government with the head of the legislative arm during a Constitutional crisis was ultimately harmless. It was rather the long-term proximity to Don Dunstan that would lead to real drama.

---

3   Letter from Peter Ward to John Emerson, September 2009, p. 10.
4   Andrew Parkin, 'Transition, Innovation, Consolidation, Readjustment: the Political History of South Australia since 1965.' In Dean Jaensch (ed.) *Flinders History of South Australia – Political History*, Adelaide, Wakefield Press, p. 298.

Peter Ward knew Don Dunstan from the weekly Labor party broadcasts at 5KA, but in 1969, Peter left 5KA and became the South Australian correspondent for the *Bulletin*, then edited by Donald Horne. Don Dunstan's chief political advisor, Jerry Crease, was found dead in his bath later that year and Peter offered Don his help. Don offered Peter the job, much to Peter's surprise, and he would work closely with Don Dunstan for the next seven years.[5] This meant Peter got to see the very deepest and occasionally darkest, workings of Dunstan's politics and personal life.

In 1972 Peter and his partner Dimitri, and John became neighbours in Hurtle Square. Bray would never have left Bray House if he had had the choice, but he knew he would have to leave long before Gertrude died after a long illness on 25 November 1970. The house was left in equal thirds to John, Rowena and Bill. Bill would have been happy to keep his share in the house but Rowena, now 53, wanted the cash. The house was valued at around $130,000 – roughly 26 times an average salary. John could have paid Rowena as he had a balance of about $100,000 in his cheque account, but he had considered the folly of living alone in an 18-room house on an acre of land with ever-increasing rates and cost of upkeep.

After a few failed negotiations, he bought a house from his friend Horst Salomon, who owned the restaurant opposite the Sturt Arcade Hotel in Grenfell Street. Horst was also a property renovator and he was renovating a double-storey terrace block of four homes in Hurtle Square. Bray bought number 39 on the Halifax Street corner, and he lent the money to Peter and Dimitri to buy number 37 next door. The three of them formed a single household for the purposes of shopping and cooking and household chores, while maintaining their independence in each of the properties:

> In our arrangements there was no Arrangement but there were many abiding domestic and friendship assumptions, commitments and responsibilities to he honoured, and they were. The back courtyard with its high wall was a shared ground as were all the yearly domestic cycles.

---

5   Letter from Peter Ward to John Emerson, September 2009, p. 11.

John outside 39 Hurtle Square.
Private Collection.

One Sunday afternoon in 1972.
The Advertiser, with permission.

We were a tightly committed and affectionate domestic unit, which to John's irritation sometimes gave rise to many completely erroneous assumptions by the mean-minded and scurrilous.[6]

The jurisdiction of South Australia's Supreme Court went through several changes while Bray was Chief Justice. Until 1970 the three tiers of Police Courts, Local Courts and the Supreme Court took all matters, directed to one or other court according to importance or complexity. The Supreme Court always was the sole court for murder trials, but it also was handling divorce and child custody matters, civil matters involving Commonwealth parties such as the Tax Office, and was also the first level appeal court sitting as a full bench. The workload was too much for the seven judges who could no longer keep up.

The *Local and District Criminal Courts Act 1969* allowed the establishment in 1970 of the court system that is now known as the District Court of South Australia. The new court immediately took many of the criminal and civil matters and released the Supreme Court to concentrate on the most serious ones and the appeals. Later, in 1976 the Commonwealth government established the Family Courts with a completely new system of filing for divorce, and the Federal Courts to take over the increasing load of civil matters involving Commonwealth agencies. District and County Courts around Australia would become the principal trial courts, and the State Supreme Courts could concentrate on murders, major civil cases and appeals.

The Chief Justice's chambers during Bray's tenure were on the first floor on the Gouger and King William Street corner of the original Supreme Court building. Bray produced around 600 reported judgments, and many became established authorities, in the High Court of Australia and cited as far away as the United Kingdom in the notable case concerning the IRA bombers.

---

6   Letter from Peter Ward to John Emerson, 27 November 2002.

Bray's judgment cited by the Law Lords in *Director of Public Prosecutions for Northern Ireland v Lynch*[7] was in dissent in a Full Court Appeal for a tragic but otherwise unremarkable murder. Two men, Brown and Morley, were convicted of killing Mrs Leggett. Both were sentenced to death by hanging. Morley appealed on the defence of insanity, and he indeed had a history of psychiatric care. Brown appealed on the defence that Morley had threatened him, his wife and his parents, and that the trial judge had misdirected the jury on the law allowing duress as a defence.[8]

The Full Court of Criminal Appeal comprised Bray, and Justices Roma Mitchell and Charles Bright. They delivered a joint judgment, in which Justices Mitchell and Bright did not accept Brown's defence of duress. Bray did not agree and added his own judgment. This in itself led the way to Full Court judgments during Bray's tenure as Chief Justice increasingly being delivered by the individual judges rather than as a single joint decision.

In Bray's separate judgment, he modestly wrote: 'I have the misfortune to differ from my brethren on the question of the legal effect of duress as a defence to a charge of minor participation in murder and it is, in the opinion of the Court, convenient that I should pronounce a separate judgment on that topic.'[9] Modest though he began, he was not shy in challenging Justices Mitchell and Bright's acceptance of the trial judge's directions to the jury. Bray continued:

> In my view, the learned trial Judge told the jury that if the appellant Brown had taken an active part in the killing as for example, by coughing to disguise Morley's approach to Mrs Leggett's bedroom, threats would not excuse him and also in effect that if under threats he agreed to "go along" with Morley in the scheme to kill Mrs Leggett or made a show of so agreeing, that would not afford a defence unless he subsequently withdrew from it and communicated his withdrawal

---

7 [1975] AC at 653, (House of Lords).

8 [1968] SASR *R v Brown and Morley* 467 at 468.

9 Already cited, at 491, and for the following citation.

and did nothing thereafter to assist in the affair. With all respect to those who hold the contrary opinion, in my view these directions are erroneous or at least incomplete statements of law.

Bray then attacked the trial Judge himself for looking further, the key word being 'apparent':

> It has often been said that whatever effect duress may have it can never be a defence to some crimes, and particularly to murder. His Honour could have found ample apparent authority for adopting that proposition in its naked form.[10]

Bray summarised the authorities covering duress in the previous three centuries, showing that there was a clear sign of progress towards its acceptance. He turned to the two Privy Council decisions that Justices Mitchell and Bright relied upon to show that duress could never excuse any participation in a murder:

> With unfeigned respect to them in my view the first of these cases is an authority for the converse proposition that some types of duress may excuse some types of complicity in murder. That is *Sephakela v The Queen*.[11]

Quoting from the transcript published in *The Times*, Bray argued that the sentence: 'In their Lordships' opinion the evidence fell far short of what was necessary in law to establish such a defence', as 'being capable of only one interpretation, namely, that there could be evidence which would amount to what was necessary to establish the defence of compulsion to the charge under consideration, i.e. murder.'[12] Roma Mitchell and Charles Bright had not overlooked the implications of that statement, but in their joint decision

---

10   Already cited, pp. 491–492.

11   As above at p. 495. *Sephakela v The Queen* is reported briefly in *Criminal Law Review*, September 1954 and John also sourced *The Times*, 14 July 1954.

12   At p. 496. See pp. 485–487 for Justices Bright and Mitchell's interpretation of *Sephakela*.

considering duress as an excuse, they claimed that Sephakela 'does not, in the view of the majority of us, support this contention.'[13]

Bray also found that the second Privy Council case that Justices Mitchell and Bright cited could not support their decision either:

> There their Lordships apparently gave no reasons at all. But, according to the statement of the facts, the appellant there had admitted firing three or four bullets at the victim under threat of death though it was uncertain whether any of the bullets actually caused the death. It seems to me that that case can be no authority for the proposition that duress can be no defence to lesser acts of participation in murder not including any actual killing or attempted killing of the victim.[14]

Seven years later, in *Director of Public Prosecutions for Northern Ireland v Lynch*[15] Bray's dissenting judgment was cited by each of the five of the Law Lords, three of whom agreed with his discussion of the extent to which duress can excuse a charge of murder. Lord Morris of Borth-y-Gest was convinced:

> In a closely reasoned judgment the persuasive power of which appeals to me he held that it was wrong to say that no type of duress can ever afford a defence to any type of complicity in murder though he drew a line of limitation when he said, at p. 499: "I repeat also that as at present advised I do not think duress could constitute a defence to one who actually kills or attempts to kill the victim."

Lord Wilberforce cites Bray even more at length:

> Outside the United Kingdom there is the important authority of *Reg. v Brown and Morley* [1968] SASR 467, a case of aiding and abetting murder. A majority of the Supreme Court of South Australia held the defence of duress not admissible, in effect on grounds of public policy.

---

13   At p. 485.

14   As above, at pp. 496–497.

15   *Director of Public Prosecutions for Northern Ireland v Lynch* [1975] AC at 653 (House of Lords).

But there is an impressive judgment of Bray CJ in dissent. He fully examines the authorities, from Hale onwards, and concludes that they do not establish that duress is no defence in any circumstances.[16]

He then cites Bray's challenge to William Blackstone's words on duress on page 494 of the 1968 SASR, 'he ought rather to die himself, than escape by the murder of an innocent'. Bray agrees in general but questions the absolute nature of this view: 'It would seem hard, for example, if an innocent passer-by seized in the street by a gang of criminals visibly engaged in robbery and murder in a shop and compelled at the point of a gun to issue misleading comments to the public, or *an innocent driver compelled at the point of a gun to convey the murderer to the victim*, were to have no defence.' Lord Wilberforce then comments on Bray's re-interpretation of the two Privy Council decisions, *Sephakela v The Queen* and *Rossides v The Queen*: 'Events have shown that the learned judge's hypothetical examples were not fanciful.'[17]

Lord Simon of Glaisdale and Lord Kilbrandon were the two judges who found themselves in the minority in the *Lynch* appeal. Lord Simon, in particular, was not prepared to defy authorities such as Hale, Blackstone, Russell, Kenny and Lord Denman for a 'dissenting judgment of Bray CJ'.[18] Fortunately for Mr Lynch, who claimed the IRA forced him at gunpoint to drive their getaway car for them, Lord Edmund-Davies weighted the appeal in his favour and thus allowed a retrial. Lord Edmund-Davies cited four passages in succession of Bray's dissenting judgment, which he called 'an illuminating review of the relevant material, judicial and otherwise'.[19]

Bray's *Brown and Morley* judgment is a good example of his general approach to judicial reasoning. He would seek out authorities relevant to a case across centuries, analyse them specifically in relation to that case, and if he judged it necessary, add his own contribution to the development of the principles involved. On many occasions he would find himself in the

---

16   As above at p. 682.
17   As above at p. 683.
18   As above at p. 695.
19   As above at p. 714.

minority of Full Court decisions, like *Brown and Morley*, but in the years to come these dissenting judgments would attract wide attention. He would also be frank about any frustration or concerns he felt when he found himself tied by a line of authorities that led to unsatisfactory results. No more was this obvious than when Bray dealt with cases involving censorship matters.

Richard G Fox in his chapter of the January 1980 *Adelaide Law Review* volume dedicated to Bray's judicial impact, analysed his role in the evolution of censorship over the 1970s. He noted Bray's appointment by chance coincided with a revolution in the control of obscenity publications.[20] As we discussed in chapter 13, Bray had already made public his personal views on censorship in a talk given to the Adelaide Writers' Week in 1964, published the same year as 'Censorship' in *Australian Library Journal*.[21] Later as Chief Justice, Bray also published his Third Wilfrid Fullagar Memorial Lecture at Monash in the *Australian Law Journal*.[22]

Richard Fox warned against giving Bray credit for the legislative changes that finally introduced a formal system of classification of publications, but he does note that:

> For more than a decade, in his judgments and particularly in his extra-judicial writings, His Honour maintained a biting criticism of the deficiencies of the law which, if it did not directly shape, at least gave rational direction to the revamping which took place.[23]

Bray's judgements on obscenity and censorship are also the ones with the most wit. Using wit in judgments could easily go very wrong and offend at least one of the parties involved if not ending up in the tabloid media. Bray succeeded due to the fact that wit was something he used continually in his day-to-day conversations, and along with his poems these judgments have

---

20   Richard G Fox. 'Depravity, Corruption and Community Standards', in *Adelaide Law Review*, Vol. 7:1, January 1980, p. 66.

21   John Bray, 'Censorship'. *Australian Library Journal*. Vol. 13, pp. 60–70.

22   John Bray, 'The Juristic Basis of the Law Relating to Offences Against Public Morality and Decency', (1972) 46 ALJ 100.

23   Richard G Fox, as above, p. 66.

preserved it. It allows us an insight into his tolerant if bemused patience for his slightly less able fellow human beings.

The best single example of Bray's wit woven with historical perspective and legal principles is in his 1971 dissenting judgment in an appeal from Justice Hogarth's granting of an injunction to have a musical revue banned from performance. The musical was *Oh! Calcutta!* and had been touring Australia and had been performed in London, Paris, New York and Los Angeles. The element that was worrying the city's moral guardians was that the performers were nude throughout the performance. The element that concerned Bray was that they were asking for the law to intervene before the revue had even been performed:

> In the strict sense I do not think it can be said that the Court has no jurisdiction to grant an interlocutory injunction in a case like this, or in any action at all properly commenced in the Court, if it appears just and convenient to do so. But it does not follow at all that the Court ought now for the first time in the long history of the Anglo-Saxon legal system, apart from the decision of Little J in Victoria in *Attorney-General of Victoria v Lido Savoy Pty ltd and Others* delivered 23rd February, 1970 when the performance of "Oh! Calcutta!" in Victoria was restrained. To grant an interlocutory injunction to restrain the commission of an offence against decency or morality when no civil right of anyone, and interest remotely resembling a civil right of any individual, is involved and no interference with the material health, comfort, convenience or pocket of any particular person or persons or of the public at large is alleged. In my opinion it ought not to do so. It is not convenient to do so. And in cases like this it is not, in my view, just to do so either.[24]

Bray's historical and legal reasoning subtly reveals that he found the only exception to his reasoning, the equivalent and recent case against *Oh! Calcutta!* in Victoria, to be unjust. A little later in his 22-page judgment he

---

24   *Attorney-General v Huber* (1957) 142 SASR 161.

emphasizes his warning about courts attempting to restrain offences when they have not been committed:

> I regret again that I am at variance with my brethren, the force of whose learned and thorough research and careful reasoning I acknowledge. In one sense I agree we stand at the parting of the ways and either choice is open. The tides of the last century have carried the remedy of injunction far into the ocean of public law; but there is still time to anchor at the entrance to this unknown sea.[25]

The line of judgments in which Bray began to express his strongly reasoned views on censorship began in 1968 with *Simmons v Samuels*,[26] where Bray reluctantly had to follow the existing authorities, as the sole judge sitting on that appeal from the Magistrate's Court:

> The legislature then, albeit in a form slightly altered in some respects and expanded in others, has adopted the famous dictum of Cockburn CJ in *R v Hicklin*, that the test of obscenity (or in the context of s.33 of the *Police Offences Act*, indecency) is whether the tendency of the matters in question is to "deprave and corrupt those whose minds are open to such immoral influences, and into whose hands a publication of this sort may fall". I am bound by this piece of nineteenth century philosophy and it is my duty to accept its implications loyally, whether or not in a non-judicial capacity I might think its sociology based on unproved *a priori* assumptions and its reasoning circular. Cf. Crowe v Graham, per Windeyer J at pp. 409–410. I am bound, that is, to assume that there are classes of persons and age groups who are liable to be depraved or corrupted by literature, films, paintings and the like, though presumably those classes do not include the customs officers, police officers, court officials, barristers, solicitors, clerks and members

---

25   As above, at 166.
26   (1968) SASR 397.

of the magistracy and judiciary whose unhappy duty it may be to peruse the perilous material.[27]

In the next few years he also took a stronger stance not only against the weak reasoning of the judicial authorities, but also against the Police and the Magistrates who together were occasionally guilty of convicting people on charges which they had never laid. The shoddy Hicklin test, together with the shoddy process in the Magistrates' Courts, showed to what degree at least in South Australia if not also in many other Commonwealth jurisdictions the moralism dating back to the Victorian age was running rough-shod over the Common Law's principle of justice. Bray was now in a position to challenge this, having witnessed it over the entire course of his career at the bar.

The biggest single demonstration of moralism in South Australia attempting to manipulate the law were the charges tried in *R v Rivett and The News*. Each of those was dropped as Bray demonstrated that there was no case to answer on any of them; they should not have been made at all. Never far in his mind as well was the existence of those police surveillance files that had no legal justification.

In *Romeyko v Samuels* in 1972, Bray had the chance to deal a singular and final blow to moralism in South Australia. George Romeyko had originally sent a letter to a list of judges, magistrates, politicians and lawyers complaining about his treatment in a divorce action in New South Wales and demanding reform in South Australia. Among his recipients was Supervising Special Magistrate Mr D F Wilson, who took offence at Mr Romeyko's colourful adjectives, ones often heard in front bar conversations of those days but less readily used in public communications. Mr Wilson complained to the Police who assigned a Sergeant as the formal complainant, and Mr Romeyko was charged with breaching certain regulations of the *Post and Telegraph Act* 1901–1970 (Cth.). This led to the curious situation of Mr Wilson in his supervising role having to assign the magistrate who would hear the case, and subsequently being called as a witness. Magistrate Joe Nelligan QC

---

27   Simmons v Samuels (1971) 1 SASR 397, 399–400.

dutifully convicted George Romeyko of the offence of knowingly sending material by post that was 'indecent, obscene, blasphemous, libellous or [of] grossly offensive character' under s 107 of the *Post and Telegraph Act* 1901–1970 (Cth).[28] Mr Nelligan gave no reasons with his decision. He fined Mr Romeyko $200 and also ordered psychiatric treatment.[29]

Mr Romeyko appealed his conviction and Justice Zelling heard it in the Supreme Court. He ordered that the conviction be quashed, in part because there was no power under the *Justices Act 1921–1969* to convict someone of a 'joinder of charges' for offences against the Commonwealth. Justice Zelling disagreed that any words Mr Romeyko used in his letter were clearly proved as offensive. He also noted that English was not Mr Romeyko's native language and that his intention was not to offend but to express 'strong feelings of injustice' against the matrimonial law.[30]

Then Justice Zelling expressed his own view of the aims of justice, and we see immediately that John Bray was not alone in his concerns that the law was being misused to impose moral views:

> To my mind it is of the utmost importance to see that justice is done to the man with whose views one disagrees, and the stronger the disagreement, the more important it is to see that the sanctions of the criminal law are not wrongly applied to stifle a person who may be out of step with generally accepted views.[31]

The Crown appealed against this decision and so the Full Court appeal came before the Chief Justice, sitting with Justices Bright and Sangster. The Crown Solicitor, Brian Cox QC, now appeared with Tony Bishop, who had been representing them alone, and Mr Romeyko appeared with no representation, probably no longer able to afford it. Bray did not mince words with his view of the complaint:

---

28   *Romeyko v Samuels* (1971) 2 SASR at 529, 530.
29   As above, at 532, also for 'joinder of charges'.
30   As above, at 542.
31   As above, at 542–543.

If the complaint was defective, I think the conviction was even more so. It fails to make it plain of what the defendant was convicted. In remarks on sentence the learned Special Magistrate [Joe Nelligan QC] said: "In an extemporaneous judgment on 16th July 1971, I found the complaint proved in that it has been established beyond reasonable doubt that you have been guilty of despatching a newsletter containing indecent, obscene or grossly offensive language." It is clear then that he had not found that the newsletter contained words of a blasphemous or libellous character. Yet these two words found their way into the conviction.[32]

Strong enough, but Bray continues:

But the defect goes deeper than that. The passage refers to "indecent, obscene or grossly offensive language", not "indecent, obscene and grossly offensive language". At the end I am left in doubt what he really meant to find.

Bray lashed the Special Magistrate's lack of reasons on the question of guilt or innocence and then lack of reasons as to by what standards he found Mr Romeyko's language indecent, obscene or grossly offensive:

I do not think that the learned Special Magistrate looked at the publications as a whole in order to decide whether the words and phrases in question were indecent, but rather that he looked at those words and phrases in isolation.[33]

Bray finally considered the Special Magistrate's acceptance in the sworn evidence from both his colleague Mr Wilson and a detective on their opinion on that:

In my view he ought not to have taken these opinions into consideration at all on the questions of indecency or obscenity.[34]

---

32   As above, at 555–556.
33   As above, at 561.
34   As above, at 562.

Finally Bray recommended with characteristic wit that 'since Mr Wilson's attitude has been so clearly defined, the defendant would be well advised to leave him off his mailing list in the future or a subsequent charge of sending a postal article of a grossly offensive character might have some prospects of success.'[35]

Romeyko v Samuels is perhaps the case where we see Bray most explicitly attack the entrenched acceptance in South Australian courts of the time to allow untested community standards to prevail over the law itself. Even Justice Howard Zelling, a strict Baptist in his private life, in this case warned:

> The judiciary is of necessity cut off to a certain extent from unrestricted intercourse with other members of the community, little as they desire this to happen, and in any case their standards do not take in the standards of the young who comprise over 50% of the community. I do not find the proposition anywhere in the law books that community standards are those commonly held by persons over the age of fifty years.[36]

Andrew Ligertwood commented that this case was:

> a perfect example of how the common-law judge is able to decide the law in a way that achieves the judge's sense of justice on the facts of the particular case. And given Bray's attitude to prudish, self-righteous Adelaide, one might regard his decision as inevitable.[37]

Richard G Fox analysed a number of Bray's judgments on indecency and obscenity in the early seventies, before the Dunstan Labor government's introduction of legislation classifying material officially. Richard Fox did wonder how successful Bray felt about any influence he may have had on legislative changes:

---

35 As above, at 567.

36 As above at 543. See also Richard Fox, 'Depravity, Corruption and Community Standards', in *Adelaide Law Review*, vol. 7, January 1980, no. 1, pp. 73–74.

37 Andrew Ligertwood, 'Bray the Jurist'. In Wilfrid Prest, *Portrait of John Bray*, Adelaide: Wakefield Press, 1997, p. 87.

When John Bray assumed judicial office, literary and scholarly works were still under threat from the law of obscenity. He had hoped that reform would come when increasingly civilised values and standards brought greater maturity of taste. But his hopes were unrealised. It is true when he left the Bench, literature had been freed from the clumsy oppression of the State, but it had simply been by-passed in the popular lust for the more effective (but more gross) pictorial erotica which reached Australia in the late 1960s.[38]

He saw Bray as more aligned philosophically 'with Mill and Hart rather than with Stephen and Devlin.'

Bray gave judgments on several other notable censorship cases that relied on the Hicklin test, each time placing the onus back on the prosecution to prove the exact meaning of the terms 'indecency' and 'obscenity'.[39] Adelaide citizens of the time did not have to purvey salacious theatrical productions or send passionately worded newsletters to judicial officers to risk punishments that relied more on untested moral assumptions than the law.

One law at ongoing risk of being misused to this day across the common law world is the offence of 'fail to cease loitering'. The law allows police officers the discretion to create an offence on the spot in order to arrest someone they could not have otherwise arrested. It is used when police believe that a person is remaining in one area without any obvious motive other than committing a crime, or alerting other people who are committing a crime. Being in any given location is not in itself an offence, but if police order a person to 'cease loitering' and they fail to move on, they then become guilty of the offence 'fail to cease loitering', and can be arrested.

Discretionary laws are indispensable in maintaining law and order, particularly the more mysterious 'order', but Bray noticed occasional examples of this law being used to infringe basic civil rights. In *Stokes v Samuels* he

---

38   Richard G Fox, as above, p. 77.
39   These include *Simmons v Samuels* (1971) 1 SASR 397; *Lafitte v Samuels* (1972) 3 SASR 1; *Prowse v Bartlett* (1972) 3 SASR 473; *Dalton v Bartlett* (1972) 3 SASR 549; *Popow v Samuels* (1973) 4 SASR 594; and *Trelford v Samuels* (1974) 7 SASR 587.

was alarmed this law was used to arrest a girl who was participating in a demonstration against the Vietnam War in May 1972.[40] She was found guilty of failing to cease loitering by a magistrate and appealed to the Supreme Court. Justice Sangster referred the matter to the Full Bench, hoping perhaps that Bray would have the opportunity to hear it.

Bray wrote some 17 pages or around 8,000 words. Once again he found fault with the Magistrate. The Dunstan government had just introduced the *Public Assemblies Act* 1972, which has been assented to by Parliament in April 1972 to allow people in street demonstrations protection against arrest just for being present. The Magistrate chose not to take account of the *Public Assemblies Act*, on the grounds that it had not been proclaimed.[41] This is where Bray totally crushed the Magistrate's decision. He pointed out that the *Acts Interpretation Act* 1915–1957 confirmed that every Act passed since 1 January 1873 'shall be deemed a public Act'. They did not need proclaiming in the *Gazette* to have effect:

> I need not stress the consequences of holding that no court can take judicial notice of an Act to come into force when proclaimed unless the proclamation is strictly proved. Many of the most important statutes of the State are in this category. It is enough to say that if the learned Special Magistrate was right, he should not have given any judgment at all and, indeed, every order he has ever made was probably without power, for the *Justices Act* of 1921 itself, from which he derives his jurisdiction, is an Act which by s. 2 is to come into force on a date to be fixed by proclamation, and certainly the relevant *Gazette* was not tendered in this case, or, I should think, in any other case which he has heard.[42]

Having pointed out the seriousness of treating one Act differently from another Bray turned to the actual loitering conviction itself:

---

40   *Stokes v Samuels* (1973) 5 SASR 18.
41   As above, p. 25, also for the following quote.
42   As above, at p. 26.

Could loitering be regarded by an intelligent and educated layman as an apt description of the appellant's activities when Wyatt [the police officer] spoke to her? She had been marching in the demonstration; she was carrying a flag; the procession halted; and she halted too. She was standing in the street for about five or ten minutes; so were other marchers. Though it is not suggested that she could not have got away if she had pressed through the crowd, there is no doubt that she was embedded in the crowd. She was not engaged in any private or detached form of slothfulness. Would a driver of a car which was held up stationary in a stream of traffic be regarded as loitering? [...] I do not think loitering would be regarded by an intelligent layman as an apt description of what she was doing when Wyatt addressed her.[43]

Bray then turned to the word 'loiter' itself:

The word "loiter" is said to come from a Middle Dutch word meaning to "wag about like a loose tooth". Its use in English goes back at least to the fifteenth century. One typical dictionary definition is "to linger idly about a place."

He compared a number of loitering convictions over the previous 70 years and concluded that the prosecution has to prove aimlessness beyond all else.[44] He did not believe they had and allowed Ms Stokes's appeal. Justice Mitchell agreed, and Justice Wells was a little more reserved, but did not disagree.[45]

The Crown appealed to the High Court, in itself an extraordinary effort to go to for such a petty charge, where Bray was over-ruled. Justice McTiernan did not consider the demonstration that Ms Stokes was participating in to have any relevance:

---

43   As above, at p. 29.
44   As above, at pp. 29–30.
45   As above, at p. 67.

She did not cease loitering and leave the intersection and its vicinity, despite five requests directed personally to her by Constables Wyatt and Paxon, but remained until she was arrested. She waved a flag and defied them.[46]

The High Court judge did not agree either with Bray's application of the *Public Assemblies Act* 1972, finding that it provided Ms Stokes with no defence from the charge of loitering. Justice Menzies agreed and asserted that there was no defence for loitering, even for a lawful purpose if a police officer has asked a person to move on:

> Moreover, it does not seem to me oppressive, and therefore unlikely, that authority should be given to a member of the police force to ask a person lingering in a public place why he is doing so, or to authorize a member of the police force to request a person so lingering to stop doing so in any of the circumstances stated in s. 18 (2) (a), (b), (c) and (d) [of the *Police Offences Act*, 1972, SA].[47]

Chief Justice Barwick and Justice Gibbs agreed and the South Australian Crown won its appeal. Barwick CJ and Gibbs J more than the other two judges appeared more concerned that police authority not be challenged, regardless of circumstances. This was of course 20 years before the Mason court, and Michael Kirby.

The High Court in Australia before 1986 did not necessarily have the final word. Nevertheless, Ms Stokes's counsel did not risk the potential cost of an appeal to the Privy Council. But by chance, Bray had the opportunity to return to the High Court's interpretation of his *Stokes* decision on another loitering case and consolidate his own line of authority in the new decision. This was in *Power v Huffa* in 1976, where an Aboriginal demonstrator was arrested for failing to cease loitering, and claimed she had a lawful reason to remain where she was. In this case it would turn out that she was mistaken

---

46   *Samuels v Stokes* (1973) 130 CLR 490.
47   As above at p. 499.

in her belief, but Bray again turned to the challenges presented by the word 'loiter', in referring to the appeal from his own earlier decision:

> The word "loiter" in this connection was construed by the High Court in *Samuels v Stokes*. In that case this Court had held by a majority that loitering within the meaning of s 18(2) and (3) meant to linger or remain in the area in question either without apparent reason or for an unlawful reason. The prosecution we held, following earlier authorities in this Court, had to prove either apparent aimlessness or unlawful purpose. The High Court held that such an interpretation unduly restricted the meaning of the word, and the debate before us turns on whether the effect of the decision is that any remaining or tarrying in a public place amounts to loitering within the meaning of s 18(2) and (3), as was claimed by Mr Gray for the respondent, or whether there can still be some such lingering or tarrying which would not constitute loitering, as was argued by Mr Johnston QC for the appellant.[48]

The slight differences among the rulings in *Stokes* from each of the four High Court judges allowed Elliott Johnston to use those of Justices Gibbs and McTiernan to help his defence argument, and Malcolm Gray for the Crown to draw from those of Chief Justice Barwick and Justice Gibbs in his prosecution.

Bray now had the final word, and he found all four High Court decisions wanting:

> It is plain enough, then, that the mere existence of an apparent and lawful purpose for being or remaining in the public place in question can no longer be regarded as enough to prevent loitering. But suppose that the alleged loiterer was so remaining, not only for a lawful purpose, but in pursuance of some duty or obligation, legal, contractual, moral or social, to be there? Would there then be a "real necessity", to use the words of McTiernan J., for his so staying there? Would he be one

---

48   *Power v Huffa* (1976) 14 SASR 337, at 341.

of that class referred to by Gibbs J. who may be standing still in the street without loitering? None of the learned Judges directed his mind to this situation, which was not canvassed in *Samuels v. Stokes*, and two of them, as I read their language, contemplated that a person could remain in a public place without being a loiterer. I do not, with great respect, regard the generality of the language used in Barwick C.J. and Menzies J. as rejecting by implication the possible existence of such a class. The matter was not before them.[49]

The courage to challenge the nation's highest court shows Bray's confidence in his ability to articulate legal principles and procedures, and that he did not yield automatically to the authority of a higher court.

Bray's decisions continue to be cited in the High Court of Australia, a sign of his influence beyond the borders of the generally ignored State of South Australia. Thomson-Reuters *Legal Online* cite 87 cases in which he was cited the time of the final writing of this book in 2013, the most recent in 2012. As often as not, it was a dissenting judgment being upheld, such as *Nominal Defendant v Bagot's Executor & Trustee Co. Ltd* cited jointly in *Sweedman v Transport Accident* before Chief Justice Gleeson and Justices Gummow, Kirby and Hayne in 2006. In *Sweedman* a second of Bray's decisions was also cited, *Hodge v Club Motor Insurance Agency Pty Ltd*. The Court also noted that 'Bray CJ's dissenting judgment in the first of these cases [*Bagot's*] was upheld by this Court: (1971) 125 CLR 179 at 183.'[50]

From 1968 to the present, Bray has been upheld in the High Court in cases involving negligence, criminal law, judicial bias, company law, property law, leases, administrative law, industrial law, costs, immunity of barristers, statutory interpretation, damages, judicial discretion, censorship and consumer affairs. The legal reader is urged to consult the entire January 1980 issue of *Adelaide Law Review*, which is dedicated to detailed legal analyses

---

49   As above, at p. 342.

50   The case references are: *Nominal Defendant v Bagot's Executor & Trustee Co. Ltd* [1971] SASR 346 at 365–366; *Hodge v Club Motor Insurance Agency Pty Ltd* (1974) 7 SASR 86 at 91; both cited in *Sweedman v Transport Accident* (2006) 226 CLR 362 at 401.

of a selection of Bray's cases and case types, including the conflict of laws, the *Amoco v Rocca* case, sentencing, community standards, precedent and evidence. Further legal discussion can be found in some chapters of *Portrait of John Bray*: Arthur Rogerson's 'John Bray and Roman Law'; Michael Abbott's 'Bray as Barrister'; Andrew Ligertwood's 'Bray the Jurist' and Michael Kirby's 'Bray's Impact on Australian Jurisprudence'.[51] Michael Kirby describes the particularly powerful contribution of a 1976 judgment of John's in the eventual decision in the landmark *Dietrich* case turning on the right to a fair trial.[52]

Michael Kirby considered that the hallmark of John Bray's judicial writings, or jurisprudence, was:

> [...] the diversity of legal fields in which Bray's insights were recognised by Australia's highest court. [...] The other hallmark of the jurisprudence of Bray CJ is that it illuminated the decisions of other Australian courts, under the High Court. I consider that this is so because Bray brought with him to his judicial reasoning a great depth of insight. He looked beyond legal rules to their historical origins and philosophical and social foundations.

Over all Bray's decisions, one notices a single, consistent aim: to negotiate the delicate boundary between the individual and society. He used the full potential of the common law to do so. Andrew Ligertwood in 'Bray the Jurist' argued that because the 'the common law does not exist in formalised rule or doctrine', it 'relies for its effectiveness wholly upon the capacity of its judges and practitioners to assemble and deal with the many arguments that may be presented in relation to the individual case'.[53] John Bray 'possessed the requisite attitude, intellectual capacity and humanity to deal so powerfully with the individual case that I would argue that he must surely be regarded as one of the great common-law jurists'.

---

51 *Portrait of John Bray*, edited by Wilfrid Prest, Adelaide: Wakefield Press, 1997.

52 Michael Kirby, in *Portrait of John Bray*, pp. 96–97; p. 100 for the block quote.

53 Andrew Ligertwood, in *Portrait of John Bray*, p. 72 and p. 73, and for the following statement on John's ability as a jurist.

Andrew Ligertwood also discusses the relationship between Bray's 'life-long fascination' with Roman Law, which on the surface is the model for modern civil law systems, where judges do the reverse of the common law, and attempt to fit the individual case to a coded law. What attracted Bray to the Roman Law was not its apparent codification, but the fact that, quoting Bray's own words, it 'discovered legal science, the process of isolating and examining legal concepts as opposed to making a mere collection of rules: the idea, for example, of sale as such, and the relations of buyer and seller as such in the abstract, as opposed to a set of market regulations.'[54]

Bray's personal life over his judicial years was framed by the daily, weekly and monthly routines that defined the structure of his adult life. The routines were undoubtedly a way of navigating the course of his life as calmly as possible. He avoided as much as possible any form of direct personal conflict. In contrast around him, two of his closest friends were enfolded in drama.

Firstly, Brian Medlin, appointed the Foundation Professor of Philosophy at Flinders University back in 1966, had become increasingly politically active. The anti-Vietnam war movement reached a peak with a massive street demonstration on 18 September 1970. Many thousands of people arrived at the North Terrace and King William Street intersection and blocked it. Brian was one of the many who refused to move at the request of police, and he was arrested.

It was the beginning of a bumpy relationship between Premier Don Dunstan and the South Australian Police. Dunstan had instructed Police Commissioner Brigadier John McKinna to reroute traffic around the demonstration.[55] The Commissioner had decided to apply the *Road Traffic Act*, and undoubtedly the loitering laws, to the letter. Dunstan claimed he was powerless to challenge the decision, as *The Police Regulation Act* allowed

---

54   As above, p. 74. The quote of John's is from a speech to the University of Adelaide's Classical Ass-ociation, 29 September 1967, 'The Twelve Tables'. A copy is available in his papers in the SLSA.

55   Don Dunstan, *Felicia*, p. 185.

the Commissioner such executive decisions. He was also committed to an invitation to the American Embassy in Canberra:

> I decided to go, and that was probably one of the worst errors of judgment I ever made. The ALP held its own meeting against the war, attended by a few hundreds in Port Adelaide, in the morning, and I then caught the plane to Canberra. By the time I reached there, the damage had been done in Adelaide. A very large crowd of some 10,000 or more, peacefully-minded citizens had gathered to take part in the march. The leaders of the march halted in the North Terrace intersection, disobeyed police instructions to move on, and were forcibly arrested in scenes of violence.[56]

Before leaving for Canberra, Dunstan resigned from the general committee of the Campaign for Peace in Vietnam. Bray appeared subsequently in the Magistrates Court as a witness to testify to Brian's good character. Among the 129 charged were Lynn Arnold, future Premier of South Australia. *The Advertiser* Editorial for Monday 21 September 1970 was strongly critical of Dunstan, bearing in mind its Right-leaning perspective then:

> Last week the Premier's capacity to sense public opinion seemed to crumble altogether. To bring into the open his quarrel with the Commissioner of Police on the eve of a potentially explosive situation was an astonishing indiscretion. To proclaim that control was out of his Government's hands and then to associate himself publicly with the allies of the Moratorium was a dangerous vocation. To fly out of the State at the height of the tension – and to cap it all by pronouncing judgment on the horrifying events of the day from 1,000 miles away and on the basis of incomplete reports – was a piece of irresponsibility of extraordinary proportions.[57]

---

56 *Felicia*, p. 185.
57 *The Advertiser*, Editorial, 21 September 1970.

Commissioner McKinna retired in 1972, and Don Dunstan chose to find his replacement in the United Kingdom. He appointed Harold Salisbury, Chief Constable of a region in Yorkshire. Dunstan's conflicts with Commissioner McKinna would pale in comparison to those he would encounter with Harold Salisbury. In 1978 he would sack the Commissioner Salisbury, and the backlash would contribute to his own ill health and consequent resignation as Premier the following year.

The sacking of Harold Salisbury was perhaps the final result of Peter Ward's long-running media campaign to publicly expose the existence of the secret Police files that had surfaced on the appointment of Bray to Chief Justice.

Ward worked for Don Dunstan as a media advisor from 1969 until 1976. He watched with increasing concern as Dunstan's marriage to Greta split up, and then a new personal life began to encroach on his leadership responsibilities. In 1979, Des Ryan and Mike McEwen published *It's Grossly Improper* recounting Dunstan's relationship with John Ceruto, the principal distraction.[58] Dunstan was also pursuing a plan to build a new satellite town outside of Adelaide, Monarto. He organised a tour of European cities in 1974, on the search for ideas. He took Peter Ward:

> It was not a happy tour. Dunstan was distracted by a new affair and his pursuit of this meant he missed attending some important official events. [...] When everyone returned to Australia in, I think, June, I stayed on, was joined by Bray in London where we began a long-planned holiday which took us to Scotland, France, Italy, Greece, the Netherlands, Denmark, Japan and Hong Kong. It was a good trip and gave me time to reflect. As ever, Bray was a good listener.[59]

---

58   Published by Wenan, Adelaide, 1979.
59   Peter Ward, 'background memoir', unpublished.

This trip included the momentous trip to Epidaurus, where the Greek colonels skulked out of the performance of *Prometheus Bound*, later from the country when the Turks arrived, and Bray and Ward had to flee by boat.

Peter Ward resigned from his job with Dunstan in March 1976, and joined *The Australian* later that year as Bureau Chief and Senior Writer. In 1977 he published a series of feature articles exposing the existence of the police surveillance files that surfaced back in February 1967 when John McKinna produced the record kept on Bray.

Dunstan had seemed unconcerned at their existence since then, but in 1974 the Whitlam government in Canberra appointed Justice Robert Hope, then a Court of Appeal judge in New South Wales, to conduct a Royal Commission into Intelligence and Security in Australia. Justice Hope interviewed Don Dunstan in 1975. Dunstan reported the subsequent events in a speech to the House of Assembly in January 1978, in his political memoirs, *Felicia*:

> From him I learned that on his information Special Branches had a much wider role than the limited one of which I had been informed in 1975. In consequence of Mr Justice Hope's inquiries, a minute from the Director of my department was sent to the Commissioner of Police in June, 1975, and on July 1, 1975, the Commissioner of Police sent a reply which was couched in vague and general terms.[60]

The next 12 pages of *Felicia* reproduce the speech. The reader learns that after those two inquiries sent from Dunstan's office in 1975, nothing else happened until mid-1977. In 1975 Peter Ward was still working for Dunstan; in 1977 he was the Adelaide bureau chief for *The Australian*.

The editors and bureau chiefs all conferred by a weekly teleconference. One week in mid-1977, they decided to all write to their respective State's Police Commissioners:

> As some of us expected, most commissioners ignored the request. Only one police force came up with a form of words and some fudging. In

---

60 *Felicia*, pp. 285–297.

South Australia, in the absence of any communication from Salisbury's office, I wrote a column reporting that the question had been put, that there had been no reply, but that in any case it was known that the surveillance of people not suspected of criminal behaviour had long existed and the practice of maintaining files on them clearly continued.[61]

Peter Ward published three more columns on the question of Special Branch files. He also sent some questions to Don Dunstan, who did not reply either. Dunstan told Ward's fellow journalist John Templeton that 'Peter knew how to frame questions properly and I wouldn't answer that sort of question.'[62] For Peter Ward, 'the matter seemed to die', until the column he published in December 1977. Dunstan was in Malaysia. Ward claimed that the Prices Commissioner, whose name was Baker, had a file kept by Special Branch, but his source had got the name confused with a low-ranking hospital employee of the same name being watched for pilfering large quantities of food:

> The error was catalytic. The public service reaction to the naming of a senior public servant could not be ignored. It prompted a probably rattled Corcoran [the Acting Premier] to commission from Acting Justice White a general investigative report into the issue of special branch files.

In *Felicia*, Dunstan wrote that Peter Ward's articles prompted Robin Millhouse, the member for Mitcham, to ask questions in the House of Assembly about the Special Branch activities:

> [...] Des [Acting Premier Des Corcoran] rang me to say Caucus was concerned and thought we ought to have a judicial investigation. I welcomed the idea, and it was agreed that Mr Acting Justice White would conduct and investigation of the Special Branch files.

---

61 Peter Ward, letter to John Emerson, already cited, p. 17, and for the following quote about the naming of a senior public servant.

62 *Felicia*, p. 285, and for the following quote.

Acting Justice Michael White received his Terms of Reference on 7 November 1977 and delivered his report to the Premier on 21 December 1977. Over 135 pages, Acting Justice White summarised the origins of Special Branch, its links to ASIO and the FBI, the categories of people it kept under surveillance, and the way in which it related its operations to the South Australian government.

Michael White found over 40,000 index cards referencing and cross-referencing about 28,500 individuals who were fully identified, and 11,500 referred to with just a first name or description.[63] Of these, he found:

> Material which I know to be inaccurate, and sometimes scandalously inaccurate, appears in some dossiers and on some cards. Some of this information appears to have been used in "vetting" procedures. Time did not permit me to do more than make random spot checks – even if time had been available, I could not know whether material on cards and files of persons unknown to me was accurate or inaccurate. There was, however, some internal evidence that information about persons unknown to me was probably inaccurate and therefore potentially damaging to them in the way it had been used.

He found that Special Branch maintained records on individuals and groups of 'genuine security value', but that 'such records form a relatively minor part of the total.' These included 'specific terrorist organisations and activities within ethnic groups, Nazi party, Ustachi, Mafia', 'local branches of overseas national Communist parties' and 'mentally disturbed persons with dangerous tendencies who might attack important visitors'.[64]

He also found a large number of categories that did not appear to be 'legitimately the subject matter of files': These included an 'armful of files' on socialist groups, trade unions, ACTU personalities, and notably:

---

63   J M White, *Initial Report*, Special Branch *Security Records*, 1977, p. 7; p. 4 for the following
        quote; and p. 7 again for the one on material being 'scandalously inaccurate'.
64   As above, p. 9 for the next two quotes about categories.

All ALP candidates and elected members "came under notice" as index cards were opened when cutting from newspapers, all references to their public utterances, writings and personal histories.

There are no corresponding files about Liberal Party or Country Party personalities.[65]

Acting Justice While also found files on university personalities, students and staff, who were involved in demonstrations, anyone involved in peace movements, members of the Council of Civil Liberties, homosexuals, anti-apartheid demonstrators, 'not to pro-apartheid sympathisers', women's liberation movement, divorce law reform and about half the Judges of the Supreme Court.[66]

Very revealing was that none of these categories was mentioned in any of the memos and letters from Special Branch about its operations to Commissioner McKinna in 1967, and from Commissioner Salisbury in 1975 and 1977:

In 1967, Sergeant Huie prepared a document purporting to describe Special Branch functions and files (Appendix 2). That document records accurately some of the history and functions of Special Branch, but it misrepresents, by silence about political, trade union and other files, the true state of the records. The omitted files represent, in total, a most significant and certainly the most sensitive section of the records. It was true, as he said, that records were held about various listed categories of extremists and possible troublemakers. But it was not true that his list was representative of Special Branch categories of files in 1967.[67]

Michael White compared this 1967 memo to the letters sent to Premier Don Dunstan in 1970 and 1975, and found that 'a marked similarity will be

---

65   As above, p. 10.
66   As above, pp. 12–14.
67   As above, pp. 18–19, for the quotes about the 1967 Special Branch report.

noticed between them.' He believed that the 1967 memo was used as a basis for these letters:

> There are additions and subtractions in the 1975 memo and a saving clause advising that the list of categories is not exhaustive. However, the savings clause does not, in my view, prevent the 1975 memo from being misleading by omission, as the listed categories purported to be substantially represented when they were not.

Dunstan had not inquired further after the replies he received in 1975, and only sent the 1977 memo to Police Commissioner Salisbury after having received a list of questions from Peter Ward who would have seen the 1975 memo, while still working for Don Dunstan. Noting the lack of follow-up two years later, now a senior journalist with *The Australian*, Peter sent a letter to Don Dunstan on 1 September 1977 with eight questions. He asked if the SA Police Force still maintained over 10,000 dossiers on people not convicted of any offence; if so, how many; if Special Branch maintained relationships with Federal security agencies; how many officers work there; if the Premier had asked them to cease keeping such files; and if not, why not.[68]

Don Dunstan passed on Peter Ward's questions to the Commissioner immediately, who replied the following day, 2 September 1977. The response declared some of Peter Ward's questions as 'improper, even impertinent, and that they should not be answered.' It referred the Premier back to the earlier responses in 1975. It did state one clear number, however, of interest in the light of which Acting Justice White would uncover three months later:

> It does not have 10,000 dossiers on unconvicted persons but does have to a much lesser degree information on organisations, groups and individuals who, by overt actions, have shown a tendency to commit or incite others to commit acts of damage or violence at gatherings and demonstrations.

---

68   As above, p. 110; p. 111 for the response of 2 September 1977 from the Police Commissioner.

Although Michael White delivered the report just before Christmas, Don Dunstan did not read it until he returned from a medical break in Queensland in January 1978. He took a copy of the report over to Police Commissioner Harold Salisbury to read and consider. They met again on Friday 13 January and Dunstan listened to the Commissioner's explanations for the concealment of the full extent of Special Branch's activities. He later wrote in *Felicia* that the discussion had included 'considerable diatribe concerning Mr Millhouse MP, and, to a lesser extent, Mr Peter Ward of *The Australian*'.[69]

Neither man would yield ground. Dunstan was outraged at being misled, and as a result, misleading the South Australian public. Commissioner Salisbury was furious at what he viewed as political interference in security matters. He was also unhappy at some of Michael White's terminology, notably the word 'scandalous', which we referred to earlier.[70] Over the days that followed, Cabinet reviewed Michael White's report, and decided it should be made public. Dunstan requested Commissioner Salisbury to resign and he refused:

> After communicating the matter to other Ministers, I attended on the Governor and apprised him of the position, and an Executive Council meeting was called for later that afternoon. At that Executive Council meeting the Governor in Council issued instructions in accordance with the recommendations of Mr Acting Justice White in respect of security information, and dismissed the Commissioner.[71]

Dunstan released a press release to *The Advertiser* with a midnight embargo. This meant that *The Australian* would not learn of the dismissal until it was too late for their edition the following morning.

Rupert Murdoch, whose company News Ltd did not then own *The Advertiser*, was in Sydney for a meeting with all his State bureau chiefs for *The Australian*. Peter Ward was in Sydney and learned of the dismissal only

---

69   *Felicia*, pp. 292–293.
70   As above, p. 295.
71   Aa above, p. 296.

at 6.00 am the following morning, when Mark Day, editor of the afternoon Sydney daily, the *Mirror*, rang him and asked for a 1000 words by eight o'clock. Later, Murdoch blasted him for missing the dismissal, a petty triumph for Dunstan, but of course the dismissal would not have happened without Ward publishing his articles in *The Australian* on the files in the first place.

The sacking of Police Commissioner Salisbury was the most controversial act Don Dunstan did as Premier of South Australia. It normally would have had no impact on John Bray in his role as Chief Justice, except that the entire drama was driven at its origin by Peter Ward's shock at learning of those patrol reports on John in 1967. Around three years later, when he learned while working for Dunstan of the existence of Special Branch files, he became increasingly concerned at Dunstan's apparent lack of concern about their existence:

> What Dunstan did or did not know, over time, about Special Branch or other police surveillance of people not convicted or suspected of committing indictable offences remained a front-page issue for a week or more and was complicated by my threatening to sue him for some of his less flattering comments about me. At one stage the disagreement between the journalist and the Premier became the story, leaving Dunstan appearing intemperately disabled during a fluid, volatile political situation. Eventually the legal threats were withdrawn and a joint statement by both of us was published in *The Australian*.[72]

Under pressure in the media and in parliament, and from a rally in Victoria Square, Dunstan announced a Royal Commission into the sacking of Harold Salisbury on 11 February 1978, with Justice Roma Mitchell presiding.[73]

On 20 January 1978, Peter Ward's lawyer and godson of John Bray, Michael Abbott, issued a writ against Don Dunstan for slandering Ward at a media conference on 19 of January. One of the examples listed in the

---

72 Peter Ward, letter to John Emerson, already cited, p. 19.
73 Stewart Cockburn, *The Salisbury Affair*, Melbourne: Sun Books, 1979, p. 200.

writ quotes Dunstan saying before the group of journalists, also Peter Ward's colleagues:

> It is very unfortunate Mr Ward is prepared with constant jaundice to write inaccurate and at times scurrilous reports about the South Australian government, about me, and of course that has affected the relationship between the government and our ability to release with confidence material to his newspaper.

Peter dropped the writ after a meeting with Dunstan and Neal Blewett, then a professor of politics at Flinders University, acting as 'circuit breaker'.[74]

The Royal Commission into the Dismissal of Harold Hubert Salisbury held its preliminary hearing on Friday, 17 February 1978. In the previous day's *The Advertiser*, an article on page 8 was the first and only one in which the Chief Justice was mentioned: 'Dr Bray won't comment' read the headline. The Senior Judge of the District Criminal Court, Neil Ligertwood, had written to the newspaper suggesting that the Premier might consider members of the judiciary to act as monitors of the Special Branch file. Peter Brebner, John's Associate, told the paper that the Chief Justice 'will not comment on the views of the Senior Judge':

> The Premier (Mr Dunstan) said later the Chief Justice had told him he believed such work should be limited, and that it was undesirable for judges' time to be taken up with non-judicial work to any marked extent.[75]

Justice Mitchell's Royal Commission took place over the next month and there was a lively exchange of letters to the editor on the topic of the Police Commissioner's dismissal featured almost every day in *The Advertiser*, plus articles, and an occasional editorial. These showed considerable difference in opinion, many readers disagreed strongly with Dunstan's decision. They were, of course, only informed through the media. They were not constitutional lawyers.

---

74   Peter Ward, letter to John Emerson, already cited, p. 19.
75   *The Advertiser*, 16 February 1978, p. 8.

Early 1978, turbulent times in South Australia.
The Advertiser, with permission.

Roma Mitchell took oral testimony from 23 witnesses, including Peter Ward, Don Dunstan and former Police Commissioner Brigadier McKinna. In her report, delivered on 30 May 1978, she was very critical of Peter, particularly of his erroneous allegation in the December 1977 article claiming that the Commissioner for Consumer Affairs, Mr Lance Baker, had a file on him in Special Branch.[76] At the same time she had to request the Premier to clarify his claims that he only knew about Special Branch from 1970, when an article in the Adelaide *News* on 9 October 1968 quoted him as saying that:

individual matters concerning individuals who have not committed crimes do appear in police files. I have been given certain information from these files by the Commissioner.[77]

Justice Mitchell then reported:

Mr Dunstan said that the statement as to "matters concerning individuals who have not committed crimes" related to an incident in 1967 when, the Government being about to make an appointment to a high office, the then Commissioner of Police, Brigadier McKinna, made available to it certain comments from a police file relating to the person about to be appointed to that office. Brigadier McKinna confirmed in his evidence that this was correct and said that the comments came from a patrol report and not from Special Branch.

For Peter Ward, the 'lighting of a slow burning fuse' ignited by Brigadier McKinna presenting police reports in 1967 to stop the appointment of John had certainly led to an explosion. Whether Peter got his names wrong, or whether the file on John was a patrol report and not a Special Branch report is entirely irrelevant. Equally irrelevant is that the South Australian Police kept files on a large number of people not convicted of any crime, as these sort of files, now called 'ancillary files', are indispensable for efficient policing.

---

76   *Royal Commission 1978: Report on the Dismissal of Harold Hubert Salisbury.* Adelaide, Government Printer, 1978, pp. 31–32.
77   *Royal Commission 1978 Report*, already cited, p. 29 (paragraph 96), for both block quotes.

But it indeed was a serious flaw for the Police Commissioners not to believe themselves accountable for those files to the elected government. Roma Mitchell found that Don Dunstan was completely justified in dismissing Harold Salisbury, but she also found that it 'was not the only course open to the Government'.[78]

Prominent *Advertiser* journalist and columnist Stewart Cockburn was so incensed by the dismissal and its subsequent official justification that he published *The Salisbury Affair*, condemning the whole affair as a 'political assassination'.[79] But in common with most of the people who disagreed with the dismissal, he was not fully aware of the serious breach of fundamental democratic principles that Harold Salisbury had allowed to perpetuate. Alex C Castles and Michael C Harris later assessed the dismissal of Harold Salisbury as:

> an important, indeed an essential, reaffirmation of a basic precept of responsible government in the case of an officer of government who was found by a Royal Commission to have acted with what seems to have been a lack of understanding of principles of government already in place and accepted not only in Britain but also in Australia before the end of the nineteenth century. It was most unfortunate that a person with a previously unblemished record of public service in Britain and Australia had to suffer the indignity of being dismissed. Governments of any political persuasion, however, would be failing in their fundamental duty to maintain the tenets of responsible government if they did not act in such circumstances. In Salisbury's case, this was particularly so, as the unit he sought to protect, special branch, was modelled on similar groups in Britain and elsewhere which had been created within police organisations and were normally subject to ordinary legal regulation and to scrutiny of superiors who in turn were responsible to the relevant minister of the crown.[80]

---

78   As above, p. 40, paragraph 157.

79   Stewart Cockburn. *The Salisbury Affair*, Melbourne: Sun Books, 1979, p. 289.

80   Alex C Castles and Michael C Harris, *Lawmakers and Wayward Whigs*, Adelaide: Wakefield Press, 1987, p. 294.

From as far back as the time of his appointment as Chief Justice, John had been experiencing what Peter Ward called 'vascular and respiratory disabilities'.[81] He was now 65 years old, and he received a medical report 'which turned the scales'.[82] He gave notice of his early retirement, and his term as Chief Justice would officially end on 27 October 1978. His last working week ended on 27 May and Justice David Hogarth became Acting Chief Justice until the appointment of Len King on 30 October. His last reported judgment was on an appeal for damages for personal injuries, delivered on 19 May.[83]

Roma Mitchell presented her report to the Governor on 30 May 1978. Just over a week later, she sent John a letter to wait for his return at the end of August. He and Peter and Dimitri were already in France.

Last day as Chief Justice, 27 October 1978.
The Advertiser, with permission.

81   Peter Ward, in *Portrait of John Bray*, p. 17.
82   Peter Ward, Background Memoir.
83   *Faraonio v Thompson*. 19 SASR 56.

Chapter 16

FOR BETTER OR FOR WORSE

This is my arm, my thought, my sense,
Not props in some illusionist pretence.
I am myself, for better or for worse.

John Bray, from 'The Stone Garden of Ryoan-Ji, Kyoto 1976'

Roma Mitchell had thought of sending her letter directly to John's poste restante address in Athens, but decided to let it wait for his return in early August:

> by then I hope that the whole wretched Salisbury Commission will have been allowed to die a natural death and I can forget it.[1]

Roma admitted to John her reason for accepting the Salisbury Royal Commission:

> I hoped I could avoid any adverse publicity for you which would have been monstrously unfair. And I was not confident that anyone who was not fully apprised of the disgraceful performance of the then Police Commissioner and others in 1967 could have done this.

Roma had in fact interrupted John McKinna during the Commission hearing. Counsel assisting, Ted Mullighan, asked him whether the information from 'an occasion in 1967' had come from Special Branch. The former Police

---

1   Letter from Roma Mitchell to John Bray, 9 June 1978. Private Collection, and for the following quote.

Commissioner was on the point of clarifying exactly which 'occasion' that was, but the Royal Commissioner bluntly stopped him: 'We do not want the details.'[2]

Susan Magarey and Kerrie Round also quoted parts of Roma's letter in *Roma the First*. They concluded:

> There is, of course, a great silence at the heart of these events, a silence that changing times can now render voluble.[3]

Roma Mitchell's biographers believed that Roma 'could only have been grieved at the damage done to such giants of those times by the longstanding prohibition on homosexual relations'. They were referring both to John Bray and Don Dunstan, who resigned from ill health the year following the Royal Commission, aged just 52.

The issue of sexuality raises as many questions as it does eyebrows. One of John's other correspondents on the Salisbury topic was a young Christopher Pearson, to whom John jointly dedicated *Satura*, published by Wakefield Press in 1988. He sent his letter to John's poste restante in Athens on 3 July 1978:

> You enquired about local reaction to the report of the Royal Commission. It has been more mixed that I expected. Stewart Cockburn nit-picked about the fact that Salisbury hadn't been given a copy until ten minutes before Dunstan released it. Your ex-brother Chamberlain got into the act again, pointing out that Big Sister had chosen to use the odd phrase "I am constrained by the evidence before me" and, like Tonkin (who looked more than usually foolish and full of sound and fury), asserted that the Crown had stodged the evidence by saving your now-no-longer-Acting brother White from cross-examination. [...] *The Advertiser* wasn't sure, but had the goodness to admit that Dunstan had been vindicated. There were hundreds of letters to the editor saying Oh no he hasn't, and that Roma's statement that she "was unable to understand Mr Salisbury's

---

2   *Roma the First*, p. 218.
3   As above, p. 219.

motives for lying to the Govt" revealed the need for a fresh Royal Commission headed by an interstate male judge and showed how foolish it was
to fly in the face of nature and appoint female judges.[4]

In that same letter, Christopher Pearson also asked John some very private
questions, which lead us in to this dimension of John's life, linked as it is to
the 'heart' of the events leading to patrol reports being kept on John, and
Peter Ward's decade-long determination to have them and any other secretly
held records on private citizens publicly exposed. Pearson controversially in
1996 claimed to be a lover of John's in the *The Sydney Morning Herald's Good
Weekend*.[5]

'I gather from the letter,' Christopher wrote, 'that things went off reasonably well with your Scottish admirer – better at least than you feared they
might.' But Christopher wondered if 'he must be a little crazy to be buying
you a disposable gold-plated cigarette lighter. Was he content, I wonder, to
visit the D.O.K. with you or did he monopolise your time in Amsterdam and
oblige you to go there by stealth?'[6]

Christopher Pearson was referring to a friendship John had maintained,
largely by correspondence, since 1974 with a man about 25 years younger
called Ian. They had met in Amsterdam during John's 1974 European holiday.
They met again in Europe a month before Christopher posted his letter to
Athens. We can get a brief glimpse into each man's reaction to this reunion.
In 19 June 1978 Ian wrote to John in Athens, beginning: 'Words fail me when
it comes to describing how happy I was being with you for those all too few
days.'[7]

But the day before, 18 June 1978, John wrote to Ian, his letter beginning:
'This is a very hard letter to write and I have been pondering it for the last
week.' He breaks the young man's hopes of a permanent relationship. He

---

4   Letter from Christopher Pearson to John Bray, 3 July 1978. Private Collection.
5   *Good Weekend*, 30 March 1996, pp. 40–47. Christopher Pearson by 1996 had become a well-
     known media columnist and speech-writer for Prime Minister John Howard.
6   As above.
7   Letter from Ian M. to John Bray, 19 June 1978. Private Collection.

also answers several questions for those of us who wish to understand him a little more:

> I enjoyed your company in and out of bed but I was never in love with you. Indeed I have never been in love with anyone in the exclusive monogamous romantic way though there are many people for whom I feel love in the sense of affection – notably Peter and Dimitri.

> I suppose I was to blame for allowing our correspondence to assume gradually a warmer tone. Dimitri thinks I should have been firmer about this and that I should have returned your chains. Perhaps I should have done that but I thought it would hurt your feelings unnecessarily. I did from time to time send warning notes. I told you that my nature demands a large allowance of privacy, that I have my interests, professional, literary and social, and that romantic sexual attachments are no part of my plan of life.[8]

What John reveals is his lack of interest in not just a relationship with a man, but in any monogamous relationship. It is not clear that he actually posted the letter, or at least this version, as the original in his handwriting remains in his papers. Regardless, the next letter from Ian is dated 14 December 1978, and he continued to write for several years after, in very friendly terms, but with no further suggestion of a relationship.

A few years earlier, John had received a letter from one of Australia's most distinguished law academics, who most likely met him at a conference. Professor Enid Campbell (1932–2010), who was 20 years younger than John, was appointed the first female professor of law in Australia in 1967. Like John, she would have felt the solitude that is the price of a rare intellect:

> My dear Chief Justice, what I am about to tell you and ask of you may come as a shock. I have hesitated to write, but have convinced myself that I stand to lose more by not writing at all than by writing as I do.

---

8   Letter from John Bray to Ian M., 18 Florence 1978, Florence. Private Collection.

John Bray, 1979.
The Advertiser, with permission.

I find to my consternation that since our brief meeting last week you have been much in my thoughts and that I have a hankering to know you better. Somehow, though clearly not by your design, you have made an impact on me and in so doing have breached defences which I had imagined to be impregnable.[9]

Enid Campbell's touching letter is a model of elegance, and the two corresponded in the following years. Another of John's female friends, Marlis Thiersch, wished she could marry John, and wrote him a letter that Peter Ward described as 'emotional and personal' just before her death.[10]

It is probably important not to confuse the term 'homosexual relations', with either the noun or adjective 'homosexual'. Don Dunstan, for example,

---

9   Letter from Enid Campbell to John Bray, 24 July, year not given. She was awarded an Order of the British Empire (OBE) in 1979 and later Companion of the Order of Australia (AC).

10   Letter from Peter Ward to Bill Bray, 23 September 1996. Private Collection.

had two long-term female partners, both of whom he married, and one long-term male partner. He had three children with his first wife, Gretel. He indeed had 'homosexual relations', but it would be incomplete to claim he was only homosexual, or more succinctly, mono-sexual. He appeared to need relationships at various times with both sexes. John did not need long-term relationships as did Dunstan. He expressed his view at being labelled as 'homosexual' very clearly to the writer of a letter sent to him care of Wakefield Press at the end of July 1991. It came from someone in Sydney unknown to John, Paul Knober:

> Dear John Bray, I am compiling an Index of Male Homosexual Poets and Poetry: poets who are or were homosexual and poets who wrote poems about male homosexuality.[11]

Paul Knober enclosed his proposed index entry for John, listing just two poetry collections John published, *Seventy-Seven* in 1990 and *Satura* in 1988, and drawing attention to John's own *Lines to Hadrian* and to his adaptation of *Love and Wine* by Rufinus.[12]

John's response was passionate and informative about his sexual identity and views on sexuality. In his papers is a copy of the letter he wrote to Paul Knober on 1 August:

> I find your letter disconcerting for several reasons. To begin with it makes assumptions about my sexual preferences and sexual behaviour, subjects which are too complex to be covered in a short letter and which I have no intention of submitting to the public gaze. My private life is not in the public domain and as far as possible I will stop it getting there. This is in no sense an admission of anything, only an assertion of my right to privacy which I expect to be respected.

---

11   Letter from Paul Knober to John Bray, 24 July 1991. Private Collection.

12   John Bray, *Satura*, Adelaide: Wakefield Press, 1988. 'Lines to Hadrian', pp. 106–107; 'Love and Wine' p. 118. Both poems had been originally published in John Bray, *Poems 1972–1979*, Canberra: ANU Press, 1979.

[...]

Hadrian was a great ruler. A commentary on his career could hardly omit mention of his love for and deification of Antinous. But it is not fair to single him out as "the gay Roman Emperor" as if he were the only one. To name four of his predecessors, Augustus Tiberius, Nero and Trajan were all at least occasional homosexuals. Apart from a general objection to the use of "gay" as a synonym for homosexual, which destroys the normal use of an expressive word, it is singularly inapt when applied to this morose and unhappy man.

In short my poems do not deal with expressly homosexual themes. I do not want to be identified with such themes and it might be better if the whole entry were omitted, though undoubtedly it includes some poets who were homosexual.[13]

John ended the letter reasserting his insistence on his private life not being made public. At the same time, he is very firmly distancing himself from being identified as homosexual.

The two poems that Paul Knober refers to are revealing, however. These lines from *Lines to Hadrian* may echo John's awareness of the potential frustration of marriage for social respectability:

And I thought how unhappy you were in your ceaseless peregrinations,
Clamped to a chattering wife while your heart was consumed in
 captivity
To a wholly unsuitable passion for a wholly desirable youth,
Whom the green Nile gulped at nineteen – was it accident, murder or
 suicide?[14]

In *Love and Wine*, John's adaptation of Rufinus's poem shows sympathy with the idea that he would not be interested in female intimacy unless he were

---

13   Letter from John Bray to Paul Knobel, dated 1 August 1991. Private Collection.
14   In *Satura*, p. 107; p. 118 for 'Love and Wine'.

John Bray, 1979 at the launch of *Poems, 1972–1979*.
The Advertiser, with permission.

drunk. But there is also the slightly vain assumption that a female might wish to instigate sexual activity in the first place:

> Fortified with reason's shield,
> Venus cannot make me yield.
> One to one, I can withstand
> All the cunnings of her hand.
> When Bacchus joins her I'm undone.
> How can I fight, two to one?

This adaptation echoes the circumstances of the conception of John's son Digby Thomas, who was born in 1936.[15] According to the family's understanding, John went home after a wedding with his two good friends, Mac

---

15   Digby Thomas died in 2014.

and Sue Thomas, who already had one child. Due to the presence of two men, John's paternity cannot ever be 100 per cent guaranteed without DNA confirmation, but Digby's name appears as a beneficiary in John's wills from 1941 on, and eventually in John's final will he left Digby a full 50 per cent of the residual estate.[16]

John kept the fact that he had a son hidden from most of his closest friends and family. Digby was 40 in 1976 when, having had enough of rumours within the Amateur Sports Club where he was a regular, he confronted John one night at the bar and asked him: 'Are you my fucking father?' According to Digby, John drily responded: 'You could put it like that'.[17] Over the years that followed, John got to know Digby's wife and two sons, effectively his grandsons. Peter Ward never was completely convinced that Digby was John's son, but acknowledged John's belief that he was.[18]

After returning from his European vacation in 3 August 1978, John finally had the opportunity at the age of 66 to live the life of a leisurely man of letters. In some ways little changed, suggesting that he had been reasonably content over the 40 years of his working life. He remained Chancellor of the University of Adelaide until 1983 when he resigned and Roma Mitchell was appointed. He remained on the Libraries Board of South Australia until 1988 – at total of 44 years. He never travelled overseas again, much preferring the routine of his modest perambulations almost entirely within the confines of the City of Adelaide.

At the time of his retirement, he had published two small collections of poems, *Poems* in 1962 and *Poems 1961–1971* in 1972. A year after his retirement as Chief Justice he published *Poems 1972–1979*. He was by no means prolific, the next collection, *Bay of Salamis and Other Poems* was published in 1986 and *Seventy Seven* in 1990. In between, The Wakefield Press published the 'best

---

16   Bray Papers, SLSA, PRG 1098/50/2.
17   Interview notes, 2005.
18   Letter from Peter Ward to Bill Bray, 2 February 1997. Private Collection.

John Bray and Peter Ward in 1980 at the launch of *Poems, 1972–1979*.
The Advertiser, with permission.

of John Bray's prose and poetry' in 1988 under the title of *Satura*. While most of the short works had already been published, it was the first publication for selections from John's life-time work in progress, his biography of Roman Emperor Gallienus.

John began trying to find a publisher from the late 1980s, but had no luck until he settled on a subsidy arrangement with The Wakefield Press. The scholarly manuscript was not an ostensible candidate for a commercially viable readership. It almost reached publication before John's death, and he left $30,000 to enable his literary executors and The Wakefield Press to publish it, as faithful as possible to his revisions, in 1997.

Gallienus lived over two hundred years after (ca. 218–268 AD) the famous names of the Julio–Claudian dynasty: Julius, Augustus, Tiberius, Caligula, Claudius and Nero. Gallienus may have attracted John partly for the same reason that he was drawn to Papinian, who died six years before Gallienus

John Bray, 1988.
The Advertiser, with permission.

was born. Both Roman men believed in a fairer and more tolerant society. Papinian was executed for his beliefs, and Gallienus was assassinated, but as much for his lifestyle than for those beliefs.

Gallienus led an exceptionally flamboyant personal life, even for a Roman emperor. For example, in the festivities to celebrate the tenth year of his reign in the year 262, the emperor organised a procession that included 'twelve hundred gladiators ostentatiously adorned in the gold-embroidered clothes of women'.[19]

The emperor was also accused of effeminacy because of behaviour such as colouring his hair yellow like his concubine's, and minting a series of gold coins with his own image on one side and a feminine version on the other.[20]

---

19   *Satura*, 1988, pp. 49–50.
20   *Satura*, pp. 53–55; p. 59 for the quote on minting coins.

John dismissed rumours from modern historians that Gallienus may have been homosexual, while acknowledging a complex personality:

> Undoubtedly, too, there were tensions in his nature, tensions in the recesses of his psyche between the encapsulated admonitions of his childhood and his mature attitudes, beliefs and inclinations, tensions on a more conscious level between the counsels of his prudence and policy on the one hand, and on the other the promptings of his impatient and exuberant exhibitionism.[21]

Gallienus introduced important administrative and military reforms, which allowed promotion through competency rather than through birth, and fixed terms in the senate. Rome was consequently stronger against continuing attacks from the Goths and the Persians for many more decades as a result. These reforms naturally offended many entrenched office holders, and eventually even his new military elite finally could not tolerate the public overlap of Gallienus's personal life:

> I do not think they would have gone so far as to arrange his assassination if they had not been bitterly offended and irrevocably alienated by the bizarre flamboyance of his life-style and his public acts.[22]

John added:

> There is here a cautionary tale for rulers. They must not offend at the same time all the politically influential sections of the community. ... Radical social change will of course offend the traditional ruling class, but that need not be fatal if an alternative power base is available.

John began his life-time study of Gallienus curious to gain insight into the motives driving this Roman born to the highest class and privileges, who sought to open the corridors of power rather than close them. In the end John

---

21   As above, pp. 61–62.
22   *Gallienus*, pp. 314–315; 316 for the following one on 'a cautionary tale'.

had to admit: 'Administrator, intellectual, poet, exhibitionist, his character retains its secrets.'[23]

Nicholas Rothwell in his review of *Gallienus: a study in sexual and reformist politics* in *The Australian's Review of Books* reflected on this observation, asking: 'Is this not John Bray, also, or one aspect of him?'[24] He suggested earlier in his review that the reader is 'surely justified in seeing, behind the emergent face of Gallienus as this volume progresses, Bray's veiled self-portrait, an exploration, often intuitive, of key aspects of his own nature.'[25]

But John above all is making the point in *Gallienus* that people are complex and inconsistent, difficult to box into a category. It is possible that he shared with Gallienus a repressive father. But then again, he never left home, while his brother Bill and sister Rowena left as soon as they came of age in order to escape Harry Bray's continual criticism. It is more certain that John, like Gallienus, was too ready to trust and too ready to forgive.[26] Brian Medlin's description of John as 'intolerably tolerant' is strong evidence of this. It is difficult to imagine John identifying so closely with women as did Gallienus, yet women certainly were attracted to him. From his response to Paul Knober, John would not have agreed with Nicholas Rothwell's description of him as 'a gay man'.[27]

John had looked forward to his retirement to finally have the time to read, reading extraordinary quantities of books and writing poems. He would become a regular contributor of poems to the *Adelaide Review*, founded by Christopher Pearson in 1984. He did not like getting old at all, and poems such as *Tobacco: A Valedictory, Meditation on a Lost Tooth, Mid-October, Early Morning Reflection* and *The Old Galah* reveal his ongoing resentment at the

---

23 As cited, p. 316.
24 As cited, p. 13.
25 *The Australian's Review of Books*, February 1998, p. 1; pp. 12–15.
26 *Gallienus*, p. 317.
27 *The Australian's Review of Books*, February 1998, p. 11.

John around 1992.
Photographer unknown. Private Collection.

inflictions of aging.[28] He did not think he would make 80 years old so he held a large party for his 77th birthday in 1989, but also another large one for his eightieth birthday, in 1992. Letters to his brother describe some of the awful ailments he endured in his final decade.

Until the end John maintained his weekly routine of trips to the University of Adelaide's Barr Smith Library and the State Library of South Australia, and lunch or drinks at one of the nearby hotels. By late 1994 he was finding it harder and harder to impose his cherished life-long routines on the increasingly disabling symptoms of emphysema. Brian Medlin recalled:

> In the very last stages – Mondays, we would go to lunch. I was by now
> retired. We would go to lunch at the Rob Roy. We would wheel him

---

28 John Bray, *Collected Poems 1962–1991*. St Lucia: University of Queensland Press, 2000, pp. 143, 149, 161 and 223.

Michael Kirby and John Bray in Adelaide around 1993.
Courtesy the Hon. Michael Kirby.

down, chair – Wardy, Dimitri, Neil Lovett, myself and maybe some other people but I can't remember who ... at times, I can't remember, but I can remember those. Bray would always pay. He'd pay for the dinner, we'd pay for the drinks, round fashion. And there was a waitress there, a young woman of about twenty-two, chubby, cheerful – always.

"And how are you today, Judge Bray?" Always, "Not very well if you must know," and always me, "For Christ's sake, Bray, why can't you be pleasant to the girl? It wouldn't cost you much." Oh, so silly. He got grumpier and grumpier. One day Lovett and I turned up, as we didn't always do, and it turned out Dimitri was just back from Greece, Wardy was busy, and Bray had expected that he wouldn't be going out to lunch that day, and we turned up and we had lunch with him, and it was the most hilarious lunch we had. [...]

Anyhow, on this occasion, after having been admonished repeatedly by me to be cheerful to the girl, to be polite, she comes up to him and says "And how are you today, Judge Bray?"

"Oh, much the same."

"Oh, that's nice", and he and I looked at each other and we laughed, and he saw the funny side of it. Eighteen hours later he was dead."[29]

That Monday lunch was 26 June 1995. The next morning, Peter discovered John near the stairs in his house. He had died during the night. Brian, at the time of that interview in 2002, was himself in his final months, suffering in turn from cancer. He ended the interview: 'Anyhow, that's that, and grief is forever.'

---

29   Interview with Brian Medlin, 19 October 2002.

Appendix

JOHN BRAY'S RESPONSE TO THE POLICE SURVEILLANCE FILES

Pages 261–265: John Bray's handwritten response to the police surveillance files that Don Dunstan showed him in February 1967. Private Collection.

An account of the events immediately preceding my
appointment as Chief Justice of South Australia.

In about August 1965 the Attorney-General (D A Dunstan)
sent for me. He told me he was making some recent appointments to
the Bench. He explained that he was not issuing any
invitation to me but he desired to appoint me as
Chief Justice after the retirement of Sir Mellis Napier which
he expected to take place in April 1966. I pointed out
that my Bohemian & unconventional temperament & manner of life
made me perhaps a dubious choice for the post. He demurred.
He said that he saw no reason why I should not
continue to indulge in such activities as drinking in
hotels swimming in the beach or associating with my
present circle of friends. I said that a Chief Justice
should not drink in the licensed bar by drinking
after 6 o'clock at night. He agreed. I said that
I would not at that stage give him any definite
acceptance.

In April 1966 he informed me that the Chief Justice
was postponing his retirement until December 1966.
In December 1966 he told me that the Chief Justice
was going to retire as from 1st March 1967.

On the Monday the _____ February 1967 he rang me in the
afternoon. I said that there would be an announcement with the
retirement of Sir Mellis's retirement as from 1st March.
He said that I was to be sworn in on Thursday
2nd March.

On Tuesday the 7th February I called on him.
I asked him if he was sure he wanted me for the post.
I reiterated my refusal to know whether his
or his entourage the Minister of justice. He said so
far as I could I need not trouble. He received
his lack of concern. Indeed he seemed to welcome
the announcement. I then indicated my definite
acceptance. This was the result of two days
of thought on the matter since it was first broached.

3

Comment This might well have happened on several
occasions. The [illegible] man would have been J R Bray
who is blind, [illegible] in [illegible] & [illegible] [illegible] at his [illegible].
On many occasions he used to come with me for drinks to 56 Hutt
St after the Amateur Sports Club closed. On many such occasions
I have refused to take the risk of endeavouring to help him
up the front steps of the premises. If he had fallen and I
might not [illegible] have been able to save him. On
such occasions in the summer we would sit on the verandah
steps & have a chat. While seated we would [illegible] some
[illegible] have been hidden from view from the street by the
fence. The verandah is composed of stone. On [illegible]
[illegible] me naturally [illegible] clothes. When he was
ready to go I would [illegible] [illegible]. On occasions I
would give him an arm so that he could walk to
up to the fence, which in parts was [illegible] & [illegible] to a
lesser extent supplemented by a hedge, & where [illegible].
I was not told the precise date of this alleged episode
either but again I gained the impression that it
was supposed to have happened many years ago:

(3) It was said that on at least one occasion
during the years 1959–1960 the ~~po~~ vice squad was
[illegible] to certain premises at 56 Hutt St ~~[illegible]~~
where a [illegible] lesbians & homosexuals including
transvestites were observed. It was not alleged
that I was present on any such occasion

Comment This might well have happened. At
about this time my [illegible] was prevailed upon
out of sympathy evoked by a story of emergency &
homelessness to let the flat at the rear of the
premises to three girls. [illegible] [illegible] [illegible] believe that
at least one of them was a lesbian & their
visitors were many & often bizarre in appearance.
The occupants of the flat changed [illegible] [illegible].
They failed to pay the rent & were eventually evicted

be thought that the police would have had me watched & my activities noted on their own initiative. Equally I find it almost impossible to believe that the Commissioner of Police would have approached the Chief Secretary spontaneously. I believe that he was prompted to do this. Various suggestions have been made to me & I have engaged in speculation of my own as to the identity of the prompters. I have decided however to pursue the matter no further unless & until subsequent events should make it necessary. Feb 20. I have thought it wise however to record the matter because of the fallibility of human memory & in order that it should, if I still think fit, be preserved for history after the present generation is dead as a reminder of the baseness, the meanness & the malignity of men & that the price of liberty is eternal vigilance.

I must not omit to record here also the courage, the affection & the comradeship of my friends whom I thought to take into my confidence at a time when I thought that my present associates were aimed at me which served as a more than sufficient counterbalance to the qualities referred to in the last sentence of the last paragraph.

[redacted]

Dated this 15th day of March 1967

This account stands as I wrote it in 1967 except that I have erased the last paragraph. That paragraph contains comments which faithfully reflect my attitudes in 1967 but I no longer hold the same attitudes & the paragraph has become inappropriate. 27 January 1980

BIBLIOGRAPHY

List of Books Published by John Bray

Bray, John. *Poems*. Melbourne: Cheshire Press, 1962.

——. *Poems, 1961–1971*. Milton, Qld: Jacaranda, 1972.

——. *Poems, 1972–1979*. Canberra: Australian National University Press, 1979.

——. *The Bay of Salamis and other poems*. Unley: Friendly Street Poets, 1986.

——. *Satura: selected poetry and prose*. Adelaide: Wakefield Press, 1988.

——. *Seventy Seven*. Kent Town: Wakefield Press, 1990.

——. *Tobacco: a valedictory, and other poems*. Canberra: National Library of Australia, 1990.

——. *Gallienus: a study in reformist and sexual politics*. Kent Town: Wakefield Press, 1997, c. 1995.

——. *Collected Poems, 1962-1991*. St Lucia: University of Queensland Press, 2000.

——. *Three Verse Plays*. Adelaide : Literary Executors of the late Dr. J.J. Bray, 2001. (Limited edition of 40 copies).

——. *The Emperor's Doorkeeper: occasional addresses*. Wall, Barbara and Muecke, Douglas (eds), Adelaide: University of Adelaide Foundation, 1988.

Published Works Cited

Adelaide Law Review.

Australian Book Review. National Book Council (Australia).

Australian Dictionary of Biography. Online version adb.anu.edu.au.

Australian Library Journal. Library Association of Australia.

The Australian's Review of Books.

Alan Brissenden, 'Max Harris: A Life and its Legacy', in *The Age*, 4 February 1995, Books, page 8.

Castles, Alex C and Harris, Michael C. *Lawmakers and Wayward Whigs*, Adelaide: Wakefield Press, 1987.

Cockburn, Stewart. *The Salisbury Affair*, Melbourne: Sun Books, 1979.

Cockburn, Stewart. *Playford: benevolent despot*. Published by Axiom: Kent Town, 1991.

Dunstan, Don. *Felicia*. Melbourne: Macmillan, 1981.

Emerson, John. *First Among Equals: Chief Justices of South Australia*. Adelaide: University of Adelaide Barr Smith Press, 2006.

Emerson, John. *History of the Independent Bar of South Australia*. Adelaide: University of Adelaide Barr Smith Press, 2006.

Friendly Street Poetry Reader, 1980. Adelaide: Adelaide University Union Press.

Elliott, Jack. *Memoirs of a Barrister*. Kent Town: Wakefield Press, 2000.

Good Weekend.

Inglis, Stuart. *The Stuart Case*. Melbourne: Melbourne University Press, 1961, 2002.

Jaensch, Dean (ed.) *Flinders History of South Australia – Political History*, Adelaide: Wakefield Press, 1986.

McCusker, Peter, 'Bray and Davey', *The Adelaide Review*, September 1995, page 34.

Magarey, Susan and Round, Kerrie. *Roma the First*. Adelaide: Wakefield Press, 2007.

Mary's Own Paper, September 1955.

O'Brien, Bob. *Young Blood: the story of the family murders*. Pymble, NSW: HarperCollins, 2002.

Parkin, Andrew, 'Transition, Innovation, Consolidation, Readjustment', in *Flinders History of South Australia (Political)*, 292–338. Adelaide: Wakefield Press, 1986.

Pike, Douglas. *Paradise of Dissent : South Australia 1829–1857*. Melbourne: Melbourne University Press, 1967.

Prest, Wilfrid, ed. *Portrait of John Bray* Adelaide: Wakefield Press, 1997.

Ryan Des and McEwen, Mike. *It's Grossly Improper*. Adelaide: Wenan, 1979.

Saul, John Ralston. *Voltaire's Bastards*. New York: Vintage, 1993.

WEA Bookroom Bulletin. Published by Workers Educational Association of South Australia, around 1961–1968.

Archival Material

Bray J J Papers. State Library of South Australia (SLSA). Private Record Group (PRG) 1098. 8 metres, over 100 sub-records.

Summary (from the SLSA catalogue): Papers and personal effects of Dr J.J. Bray comprising illuminated addresses, Letters Patent, certificates, regulations, caricatures, letters, legal opinions (with index), subject files, scrapbooks of newspaper cuttings, typescript of legal dissertation, transcripts of proceedings, ceremonial dress and metal containers, photographs, papers relating to organisations and clubs, writings, reviews, research paper, correspondence, typescript and manuscript poems, and papers relating to poetry and biographical work on Gallienus. Also included are papers and personal effects of his grandparents Sir John and Lady Bray, his parents Harry Midwinter and Gertrude Bray and his siblings. Speeches and papers relating to the launch in 2000 of 'John Bray Collected Poems 1962–1991' have been added to the group.

Bray J J Papers, Privately Held by John Bray's Literary Executors and loaned to the author.

Bright, Sir Charles. Legal Notes. State Library of South Australia, D 6452(L).

Emerson, John. Interview with Brian Medlin, 19 October 2002 (privately held).

Horner index to departures by passenger ship from South Australia directly for overseas taken from the *Register* newspaper 1836–1887. [microform]State Library of South Australia.

Index to reported judgements of John Bray. PRG 1098/62.

Josephi, Beatrice. Interview with John Bray [sound recording], 1985. OH 651/3.

Jury C R Papers. State Library of South Australia (SLSA). Private Record Group (PRG) 20.

Royal Commission 1978: Report on the Dismissal of Harold Hubert Salisbury. Adelaide, Government Printer, 1978.

St Peter's College Archives.

Ward, Peter. A background memoir, 2009 and other documents. Held privately.

White, J M. *Initial Report, Special Branch Security Records*, 1977.

Law Reports

AC (House of Lords).

Commonwealth Law Reports [CLR].

Queen's Bench.

South Australian State Reports [SASR].

INDEX OF
SELECTED PROPER NAMES
AND SPECIFIC TERMS